Instructor's Manual with Test Bank

 W9-BXP-639

Constitutional Law and the Criminal Justice System

FIFTH EDITION

Kären Matison Hess, PhD
Normandale Community College

Christine Hess Orthmann, MS
Orthmann Writing and Research, Inc.

With contributions by

Sgt. Jonathon Kingsbury, JD
Minneapolis, Minnesota, Police Department

Prepared by

Susan V. Pons
Guilford Technical Community College

WADSWORTH
CENGAGE Learning™

Australia • Brazil • Japan • Korea • Mexico • Singapore • Spain • United Kingdom • United States

ISBN-13: 978-1-111-35700-9
ISBN-10: 1-111-35700-5

Wadsworth
20 Davis Drive
Belmont, CA 94002-3098
USA

Cengage Learning is a leading provider of customized learning solutions with office locations around the globe, including Singapore, the United Kingdom, Australia, Mexico, Brazil, and Japan. Locate your local office at: **www.cengage.com/global**

Cengage Learning products are represented in Canada by Nelson Education, Ltd.

To learn more about Wadsworth visit **www.cengage.com/wadsworth**

Purchase any of our products at your local college store or at our preferred online store **www.cengagebrain.com**

For product information and technology assistance, contact us at **Cengage Learning Customer & Sales Support, 1-800-354-9706**

For permission to use material from this text or product, submit all requests online at **www.cengage.com/permissions**
Further permissions questions can be emailed to **permissionrequest@cengage.com**

READ IMPORTANT LICENSE INFORMATION

Printed in the United States of America
1 2 3 4 5 6 7 15 14 13 12 11

TABLE OF CONTENTS

Chapter 1
An Historical Overview

LEARNING OBJECTIVES

Upon completing this chapter, the student will know:

1. What law is.
2. What pluralism contributes to our society.
3. Why colonists resisted increased taxes.
4. What the Boston Tea Party symbolized.
5. What resulted from the First and Second Continental Congresses.
6. What the Declaration of Independence is.
7. What the Articles of Confederation were.
8. What the Magna Carta is.
9. What important role the Magna Carta played in framing the U.S. Constitution.
10. What the primary purpose of the Constitution is and how it is achieved.
11. What the first three articles of the Constitution accomplished.
12. How the balance of power was established.
13. What the supremacy clause established.
14. When and where the Constitution was signed.
15. Who the Federalists and Anti-Federalists were.
16. Why some states were reluctant to accept the Constitution.
17. What the Bill of Rights is and how it was included with the Constitution.
18. What serious omission occurred in the Bill of Rights.
19. Where the Constitution and the Bill of Rights are housed.

KEY TERMS

- **amendments**—Changes to a constitution or bylaws. [p. 21]

- **Anti-Federalists**—Colonists who opposed a strong federal government. [p. 21]

- **constitution**—A system of basic laws and principles that establish the nature, functions and limits of a government or other institution. [p. 5]

- **constitutionalism**—A belief in a government in which power is distributed and limited by a system of laws that must be obeyed by those who rule. [p. 15]

- **Federalists**—Colonists who favored a strong federal government. [p. 21]

- **Great Compromise**—The agreement reached in drafting the Constitution giving each state an equal vote in the Senate and a proportionate vote in the House. [p. 16]

- **law**—A body of rules promulgated (established) to support the norms of a society, enforced through legal means, that is, punishment. [p. 5]

- **Loyalist**—A colonist who did not support the boycott of British goods in the colonies and who still paid allegiance to the British monarchy. [p. 9]

- **minutemen**—Colonial soldiers. [p. 9]

- **Patriot**—A colonist who supported the boycott of British goods in the colonies and who owed allegiance to America rather than to the British monarchy. [p. 9]

- **pluralism**—A society in which numerous distinct ethnic, religious or cultural groups coexist within one nation, each contributing to the society as a whole. [p. 5]

- **ratify**—Approve a constitutional amendment. [p. 21]

- **supremacy clause**—Constitutional doctrine that federal law will reign when there is conflicting state law (U.S. Const. Art. VI, Paragraph. 2). [p. 20]

LECTURE OUTLINE

I.   Introduction

II. Where It All Began
     A. Constitution and Laws

III. Contributions from the Past
     A. Pluralism—diversity in American colonies
     B. "Melting pot"—assimilation among colonists
     C. Organization and development of the colonies
     D. Liberty and limited government

IV. Development of the United States of America
     A. Expansion plans of world powers

V.   Colonial Dissension Grows
     A. British defeat of France
     B. Great Britain's continuing problems
        1. Westward settlement by colonists
        2. Debts incurred to expand British Empire
     C. The Stamp Act
     D. The Quartering Act
     E. The Boston Massacre
     F. The Boston Tea Party

2

VI.   The First Continental Congress
    A. Agreement between colonies to stand against Britain
        1. Loyalists v. Patriots

VII. The Tension Mounts
    A. Preparing for confrontation—minutemen
    B. Patrick Henry—"Give me liberty or give me death" speech

VIII. The Revolution Begins
    A. Lexington and Concord

IX.   The Second Continental Congress
    A. Established Continental Army, named George Washington Commander
    B. Colonies form own governments, assume powers of independent states

X.   The Declaration of Independence
    A. July 4, 1776—formally severed ties with Great Britain
    B. Sections of Declaration
        1. Break political ties with Great Britain
        2. Right to rule based on consent of governed
        3. List of rights violated by the king's government
        4. Attempts to obtain justice and lack of response
        5. Proclamation of independence
    C. What It Cost the Signers

XI.   The Articles of Confederation
    A. States proclaim "firm league of friendship" and a "perpetual union"
    B. "Shay's Rebellion" and the need for a constitution

XII. The Influence of the Magna Carta
    A. Established supremacy of law over the ruler; ensured individual rights and "due process"
    B. Precedent for democratic government and individual rights

XIII. The 1787 Convention of Delegates—A Move Toward the Constitution
    A. Purpose: establish central government, incorporate checks and balances to limit government power

XIV. The Constitution Takes Shape
    A. Issues
        1. Structure and powers of Congress
        2. Executive branch
        3. Judicial system
    B. Constitutionalism
    C. Rule of secrecy during convention
    D. The Virginia resolution

CHAPTER SUMMARY

From the very beginning, the colonists sought structure and collaboration. Law is a body of rules promulgated (established) to support the norms of that society, enforced through legal means, that is, punishment. The U.S. Constitution was written to serve the needs of a pluralistic society. *Pluralism* refers to a society in which numerous distinct ethnic, religious or cultural groups coexist within one nation, each contributing to the society as a whole.

The history of the Constitution is rooted in the colonists' desire for freedom from foreign rule. The colonists resisted increased taxes because they felt it was taxation without representation. The Boston Tea Party, in which colonists boarded British ships and threw their cargos of tea in the harbor, represented the colonists' unwillingness to pay taxes without representation.

As tension between the British and the colonists increased, the First Continental Congress was called and resulted in the first written agreement among the colonies to stand together in resistance to Great Britain. The British retaliated by sending more troops to quell the "rebels." In 1775, the Second Continental Congress established the Continental Army and named George Washington as its commander. On July 4, 1776, the president of the Congress signed the American Declaration of Independence, which formally severed ties with Great Britain.

The Congress also drafted the Articles of Confederation, which formally pledged the states to "a firm league of friendship," and "a perpetual union" created for "their common defense, the security of their liberties" and their "mutual and general welfare." This loose governmental structure proved unsatisfactory and resulted in the colonists seeking a stronger central government—one established by the Constitution.

The U.S. Constitution was greatly influenced by the Magna Carta, which established the supremacy of the law over the ruler and guaranteed English feudal barons individual rights and "due process of law," including trial by jury. Americans continued to believe in the principles contained in the Magna Carta, which was a precedent for democratic government and individual rights and the foundation for requiring rulers to uphold the law. The Magna Carta greatly influenced the writers of the U.S. Constitution.

The purpose of the Constitution was to establish a central government authorized to deal directly with individuals rather than states and to incorporate a system of checks and balances that would preserve the fundamental concepts contained in the Magna Carta, that is, to limit the power of the government. The first three articles of the Constitution establish the legislative, executive and judicial branches of government and the country's system of checks and balances. The balance of power was established vertically through the separation of power between the federal government and the states and laterally through the three branches of government with its system of checks and balances. In the supremacy clause, the Constitution declared itself the supreme law of the land.

The U.S. Constitution was signed in Philadelphia on September 17, 1787. The next step was for the individual states to ratify it. The Federalists favored a strong central government. They were greatly challenged by the Anti-Federalists, who favored a weaker central government. Some states opposed the Constitution because it did not contain a bill of rights. In an important compromise, 10 amendments, known as the Bill of Rights, were added to the Constitution in 1791 to ensure the individual rights of American citizens. The Constitution and Bill of Rights had one serious shortcoming: They failed to abolish slavery. The Declaration of Independence, the U.S. Constitution and the Bill of Rights are housed in the Rotunda for the Charters of Freedom at the National Archives in Washington, DC.

SUGGESTED ANSWERS TO THE DISCUSSION QUESTIONS

1. Few people could live together and not have laws. Why?

   A more realistic statement is that people must have laws, or rules, that make it possible to live together *peaceably*. While more of a philosophical question, history has shown that when people gather, rules are necessary to formalize norms, expectations and consequences.

2. Does pluralism have any negative aspects? Why have some fought so hard against the concept in the United States?

   Arguments against pluralism seem to be based on belief structures. Those who do not believe that different people should co-mingle generally cite religious or other personal beliefs to explain why "different" is not good. Like other belief systems, some are strongly supported. Violence, racism, sexism and various other means of treating "different" people differently has occurred throughout history, and continues even today.

3. Do demonstrations such as the Boston Tea Party have any effect? Are they positive or negative?

   Public demonstrations to make political or personal points are as American as apple pie. Events like the Boston Tea Party drew worldwide attention, as have other demonstrations, including protests against various military actions, political leaders, and social issues (e.g., abortion, gun control, and racial issues). Drawing attention to an issue causes people to consider it; whether the effects are positive or negative is a matter of perspective. However, when demonstrations are large and/or frequent, as was the case during the Vietnam War, it causes others to stand up and take note that other beliefs and perspectives are present. Americans and people throughout the world should recognize these permissible public demonstrations as wonderful examples of our precious First Amendment rights, regardless of what one believes about the issue at hand.

4. What factors make it amazing that any organization among the colonies was successful?

   Imagine organizing people spread throughout such a large area without the benefit of organized communication of any kind, including mail, radio, newspaper, television or telephone. To bring together so many across such a broad geographical area and to develop a common government is, indeed, truly amazing.

5. Were the Articles of Confederation a wasted effort or were they needed?

   The Articles of Confederation, like other documents drafted throughout the development of America, can hardly be considered a waste of effort. In fact, the Articles were needed, as they helped serve as the bricks and mortar of the structure that was to become American law as we know it. Keep in mind that American society and its laws have never stopped changing, and none of the changes can be considered a waste because they form the history of what and who we are as a society.

6. What do you think about the Constitutional Convention being closed to the public? Was this necessary?

Many might be surprised that the Constitutional Convention was closed to the public because Americans presumed everything should be public when it deals with our government. But this is not always the case. Even today certain events, such as grand juries, have remained closed, even secret. Whether a matter of security or keeping the process on track by limiting the number involved, there are arguments in favor of limiting attendance. Was it necessary then? Perhaps all we can say is that it was successful.

7. Why is the Constitution called a living document? Give examples.

American constitutional law does seem to have a life of its own. It has expanded, retreated and changed as the needs of those it serves have changed. In a manner of speaking, it lives out society's ideals. Whether the issue has been slavery, consumable alcohol, voting age or the role of women in society, many changes to the Constitution show that it is alive and well.

8. What do you think the Anti-Federalists were really afraid of?

The Anti-Federalists, favoring a weaker central government, wanted even *less* governmental power and, therefore, control. Perhaps the desire of the majority to develop a centralized federal government shows, more than anything, the desire of the colonists to develop a strong *form* of government that would serve an entire country and its peoples as they continued to develop over centuries.

9. Why shouldn't the Bill of Rights have been left up to each state to develop on its own?

While the Bill of Rights was, arguably, an afterthought to the general formation of the new American government, the rights contained within were considered so important that *all Americans* should have them guaranteed. While each state was permitted to develop its own general organization and ideals, these had to be based on the conceptual framework set forth by the U.S. Constitution. Anything less would not have achieved the ideals sought by the framers of the Constitution.

10. If the U.S. Constitution works so well, why don't all countries adopt it?

People and their countries are different. Different forms of government under different controls have, and do, work well elsewhere. Even if the reason they work, at least for a period of time, is that there is a basis of force making sure it works, what works for, and is tolerated by, a people under that governmental format is what works *then*. History, tradition, expectations and desires all play a part in why different societies, cultures, peoples and countries live the way they do. There is no one system that works for everyone, everywhere.

STUDENT ACTIVITIES/ASSIGNMENTS

- History.com at http://www.history.com/topics/american-revolution has a section on the American Revolution containing a series of short video clips on "People and Groups", "Themes", "Events", and "Related Topics", the majority of which illustrate topics covered in this chapter.

- Listen to Patrick Henry's "Give me liberty or give me death!" speech on the Colonial Williamsburg website at http://www.history.org/almanack/people/bios/biohen.cfm.

- Ask the class to identify three issues about which they believe a Constitutional amendment should be considered. Have them debate the factors that favor and disfavor an amendment relating to each issue.

- Go to the National Archives Web site as http://www.archives.gov and navigate to find information about America's Founding Fathers. Select one of the 39 delegates and read his biography.

- Use http://www.findlaw.com to find *Kinsella v. Singleton* (re: necessary and proper clause). Outline the key points.

- Go to the World Book Online Web site at http://www.worldbookonline.com and find what it says about the Mayflower Compact.

- Explore the Magna Carta and listen to the "Virtual Curator" at the British Library's website: http://www.bl.uk/treasures/magnacarta/basics/basics.html#Clip3_transcript.

INTERNET CONNECTIONS

- The **Library of Congress** web site offers an integrated collection of the official proceedings of the Federal Convention of 1787, including Madison's and other delegates' notes, at http://memory.loc.gov/ammem/amlaw/lwfr.html.

- For more **Library of Congress** goodies, access *The Journals of the Continental Congress* and browse the records of both the 1st and 2nd Continental Congresses (1774–1789) at http://memory.loc.gov/ammem/amlaw/lwjc.html.

- Links to the various **state constitution** web sites are available at http://www.constitution.org/cons/usstcons.htm.

CHAPTER 1 TEST BANK

Multiple Choice

1.1   Formal ties between Great Britain and the United States were severed:
   a. when the American Declaration of Independence was signed.
   b. when the colonists boarded British ships and threw tea overboard.
   c. through the drafting of the Magna Carta.
   d. at the meeting of the First Continental Congress.
   ANS: A
   REF: 11
   LO: 6

1.2   The Magna Carta was created:
   a. to ensure that states maintained power apart from the national government.
   b. to outline colonists' complaints against the British crown.
   c. in England to guarantee that the king could not put himself above the law.
   d. by British Parliament in protest of the U.S. Declaration of Independence.
   ANS: C
   REF: 13
   LO: 8

1.3   The second paragraph of the Declaration of Independence stated that a government's right to rule is based upon:
   a. the obligation of the wealthy to provide for those less fortunate.
   b. permission from the people who are governed.
   c. the need for a strong centralized government on American soil.
   d. the Magna Carta's guarantee that rulers shall not place themselves above the law.
   ANS: B
   REF: 11
   LO: 6

1.4   The primary reason some states were reluctant to accept the Constitution was:
   a. It failed to establish a balance of power.
   b. It failed to abolish slavery.
   c. It did not contain a bill of rights.
   d. It did not allow smaller states adequate representation in the national government.
   ANS: C
   REF: 21
   LO: 16

9

1.5 The Second Continental Congress resulted in all of the following, <u>except</u>:
a. the naming of George Washington as Commander of the Continental Army.
b. the battles at Lexington and Concord.
c. instructing each colony to assume the powers of independent states.
d. the signing of the Declaration of Independence.
ANS: B
REF: 10
LO: 5

1.6 The Magna Carta was an important prelude to the U.S. Constitution because it. :
a. guaranteed due process and limited government power.
b. provided the inspiration for the Great Compromise.
c. was based upon the separation of powers between branches of government.
d. ensured that there would be no monarchy in the United States.
ANS: A
REF: 13-14
LO: 9

1.7 The first written agreement among the colonies to stand together in resistance to Great Britain was:
a. a result of the First Continental Congress.
b. a result of the Second Continental Congress.
c. known as The Federalist Papers.
d. the Mayflower Compact.
ANS: A
REF: 9
LO: 5

1.8 American law is:
a. entirely original, having no roots in any previous legal system.
b. designed to resist changes.
c. influenced by the laws of the societies that helped found America.
d. based solely on the Napoleonic Code.
ANS: C
REF: 5
LO: 1

1.9 Balancing the rights of the states and individual citizens against the power of the central government was the purpose of the:
a. Bill of Rights
b. Articles of Confederation
c. first three Articles of the Constitution
d. Great Charter
ANS: A
REF: 22
LO: 17

1.10   The Constitution and Bill of Rights are housed at:
        a.   the Smithsonian museum.
        b.   the National Archives.
        c.   the White House.
        d.   the Supreme Court Building.
        ANS: B
        REF: 27
        LO: 19

1.11   What serious omission occurred in the Bill of Rights?
        a. it failed to provide recourse for violations by the federal government.
        b. it failed to ensure state sovereignty.
        c. it failed to abolish slavery.
        d. it failed to provide the right to privacy.
        ANS: C
        REF: 27
        LO: 18

1.12   The branch of government is authorized to declare war is the:
        a.   executive branch
        b.   legislative branch
        c.   judicial branch
        d.   military branch
        ANS: B
        REF: 17
        LO: 11

1.13   The Articles of Confederation formally pledged the states to:
        a.   a unified tax structure.
        b.   a perpetual union.
        c.   the formation of the Confederate Army.
        d.   maintain a centralized government.
        ANS: B
        REF: 12
        LO: 7

1.14   The necessary and proper clause, establishing the authority of the federal government to
        address national issues, was addressed by the Supreme Court in:
        a. Marbury v. Madison
        b. McCulloch v. Maryland
        c. Gibbons v. Ogden
        d. Adams v. Hamilton
        ANS: B
        REF: 18
        LO: 11

1.15   The famous supremacy clause, declaring the "Supreme Law of the Land," is contained in:
a. the Declaration of Independence.
b. the First Amendment to the Bill of Rights.
c. Article 6 of the Constitution itself.
d. the Great Compromise.
ANS: C
REF: 20
LO: 13

1.16   According to the text, pluralism challenged the colonists to:
a. strive to maintain their original culture.
b. exercise tolerance and respect for the opinions, customs, traditions and lifestyles of others.
c. band together in self-defense.
d. combine English and Roman common law with Native American customary law.
ANS: B
REF: 6
LO: 2

1.17   Membership in which of the following is based on state populations?
a. Senate
b. House of Representatives
c. State Judiciary
d. Constitutional Convention
ANS: B
REF: 16
LO: 11

1.18   The following are true of the Legislative Branch of the United States government, except:
a. it passes laws but has no power to enforce them.
b. it is comprised of the House and Senate.
c. it can enter into treaties with other nations.
d. it regulates interstate and international commerce.
ANS: C
REF: 17
LO: 11

1.19 In 1774, the First Continental Congress accomplished all of the following, <u>except</u>:
   a. defining the rights of the colonists and outlining violations of these rights by the British government.
   b. addressing American grievances to King George and calling for restoration of rights.
   c. calling for a boycott of British goods until demands were met.
   d. formally severing ties with Great Britain.
   ANS: D
   REF: 9
   LO: 5

1.20 The Great Compromise was:
   a. another term for the Constitution.
   b. the foundation of the Bill of Rights.
   c. the agreement that gave each state an equal vote in the Senate and a proportionate vote in the House.
   d. the purchasing agreement made for most of the Indian land west of the Mississippi River.
   ANS: C
   REF: 16
   LO: 12

1.21 Pluralism refers to:
   a. a society in which numerous distinct ethnic, religious or cultural groups coexist within one nation, each contributing to the society as a whole.
   b. the combination of constitutional, statutory and common law.
   c. a single act being classified as both a crime and a tort.
   d. a society in which numerous distinct ethnic, religious or cultural groups maintain their individual beliefs and form of government.
   ANS: A
   REF: 5
   LO: 2

1.22 When the Articles of Confederation were drafted, the number of independent states in the Union was:
   a. 7
   b. 9
   c. 11
   d. 13
   ANS: D
   REF: 12
   LO: 7

1.23 The Boston Tea Party was <u>not</u>:
 a. a demonstration of the unwillingness of the colonists to pay taxes to Great Britain without representation.
 b. an act of protest against British rule over the colonies.
 c. the culmination of growing resentment towards Parliament for passage of laws such as the Stamp and Quartering Acts.
 d. a formal meeting between British and colonial officials to establish a trade agreement.
 ANS: D
 REF: 8-9
 LO: 4

1.24 Who said, "Forbid it, Almighty God—I know not what course others may take, but as for me, give me liberty, or give me death!"
 a. Samuel Adams.
 b. Paul Revere.
 c. Patrick Henry.
 d. George Washington.
 ANS: C
 REF: 9
 LO: 5

1.25 The Amendment which describes the requirements for a fair trial, including the right of the accused to a speedy and public trial, an impartial jury, to be advised of the charges against them, to confront witnesses against them and to be represented by a lawyer is the.
 a. Fifth Amendment
 b. Eighth Amendment
 c. Sixth Amendment
 d. Fourth Amendment
 ANS: C
 REF: 25
 LO: 17

1.26 The Amendment which requires a grand jury indictment in felony cases, prohibits double jeopardy and provides the right against self-incrimination is the:
 a. Fifth Amendment
 b. Eighth Amendment
 c. Sixth Amendment
 d. Fourth Amendment
 ANS: A
 REF: 25
 LO: 17

1.27   Of the following, the one that permits the U. S. Supreme Court to become the ultimate
       decision maker in whether laws and actions of government circumvent the Constitution
       and invalidate them if they do so, is/are the:
       a.   Bill of Rights
       b.   Articles of Confederation
       c.   Supremacy Clause
       d.   Quartering Act
       ANS: C
       REF: 20
       LO: 13

1.28   The Amendment that guarantees the right against unreasonable searches and seizures is
       the:
       a.   Fifth Amendment
       b.   Sixth Amendment
       c.   Fourth Amendment
       d.   Eighth Amendment
       ANS: C
       REF: 25
       LO: 17

1.29   The Amendment that contains the famous due process clause, "nor shall any person be
       deprived of life, liberty, or property without due process of law," is the:
       a.   Fifth Amendment
       b.   Sixth Amendment
       c.   Fourth Amendment
       d.   Eighth Amendment
       ANS: A
       REF: 25
       LO: 17

1.30   Opponents of the death penalty most frequently cite which Amendment's prohibition
       against cruel and unusual punishment?
       a.   Fifth Amendment
       b.   Sixth Amendment
       c.   Fourth Amendment
       d.   Eighth Amendment
       ANS: D
       REF: 26
       LO: 17

1.31   The Federalists, who favored a strong central government, were challenged by the Anti-Federalists, who advocated against the creation of any type of central government.
ANS: F
REF: 21
LO: 15

1.32   Laws of the United States may only originate in the House of Representatives
ANS: F
REF: 17
LO: 11

1.33   Laws are enforced through punishment.
ANS: T
REF: 5
LO: 1

1.34   Constitutionalism is one of the most original, distinctive contributions of the American system of government.
ANS: T
REF: 15
LO: 10

1.35   The Constitution did not abolish slavery, an error that was rectified in the Bill of Rights.
ANS: F
REF: 27
LO: 18

1.36   As a result of the Boston Tea Party, British Parliament restricted town meetings in American colonies to one a year and required British troops to be housed in private homes.
ANS: T
REF: 9
LO: 4

1.37   The Articles of Confederation established a Congress to conduct the necessary tasks of a central government.
ANS: T
REF: 12
LO: 7

1.38   The Constitution was signed in Philadelphia on July 4, 1776.
ANS: F
REF: 20
LO: 14

1.39   Cultural and ethnic diversity has always been an attribute of America.
        ANS: T
        REF: 5-6
        LO: 2

1.40   The balance of power was established by creating three separate branches of government,
        all of which work completely independently of each other.
        ANS: F
        REF: 19
        LO: 12

Fill-In

1.41   The right of the people to "keep and bear arms" is contained in the _____
        Amendment.
        ANS: Second
        REF: 24
        LO: 17

1.42   The _____ was established vertically through the separation of power
        between the federal government and the states, and laterally through the three branches of
        government.
        ANS: balance of power
        REF: 19
        LO: 12

1.43   Freedom of religion, speech and the press is contained in the _____
        Amendment.
        ANS: First
        REF: 24
        LO: 17

1.44   The _____ Amendment states: *"The enumeration in the Constitution of
        certain rights shall not be construed to deny or disparage others retained by the people,"*
        thus answering the objections of those who thought that naming some rights but not all
        might result in the government's claiming more power than was intended.
        ANS: Ninth
        REF: 26
        LO: 17

1.45   In the supremacy clause, the_____ declared itself to be the supreme law of
        the land.
        ANS: Constitution
        REF: 20
        LO: 13

17

1.46   England's historic _____, a precedent for democratic government and individual
        rights, played an important role in the framing of the United States Constitution.
        ANS: Magna Carta
        REF: 13
        LO: 8

1.47   The _____ Amendment prohibits excessive bail, excessive fines and cruel
        and unusual punishment.
        ANS: Eighth
        REF: 26
        LO: 17

1.48   The _____ Amendment prohibits the government from housing soldiers
        in private homes in peacetime without the owner's consent.
        ANS: Third
        REF: 24-25
        LO: 17

1.49   The _____ Amendment concerns the right to privacy and security and
        forbids the government or its agents from searching individuals, their homes or their
        personal possessions or from seizing them unless the government has "probable cause" to
        believe that a crime has been committed.
        ANS: Fourth
        REF: 25
        LO: 17

1.50   The term _____ refers to the interaction and assimilation that occurred over time
        among the colonists.
        ANS: melting pot
        REF: 6
        LO: 2

Essay

1.51   Explain the primary purpose of the Constitution and how it is achieved.

        ANS: The purpose of the Constitution was to establish a central government with limited
        powers delegated to it by the people. The balance of power is achieved through vertical
        separation of powers between the federal and state governments, and lateral separation of
        powers between the legislative, executive and judicial branches.
        REF: 14-19
        LO: 10

1.52 Discuss some states' reluctance to accept the Constitution and how it was remedied.

ANS: Federalists and Anti-Federalists disputed how weak or strong a central government should be and how to balance government power against the rights of the states and individuals. Resolution came via adoption of the Bill of Rights to ensure the individual rights of all citizens.
REF: 21-23
LO: 15, 16

1.53 Describe the purposes and accomplishments of the two Continental Congresses.

ANS: The First Continental Congress (September 5–October 26, 1774) met to discuss mounting complaints against and potential responses to England's Intolerable Acts. The Second Continental Congress (May 10, 1775–March 1, 1781) established the Continental Army, declared independence from British rule, fought the Revolutionary War, and governed the new country until the adoption of the Articles of Confederation.
REF: 9-10
LO: 5

1.54 Explain the role of the Magna Carta in framing the U.S. Constitution.

ANS: The Magna Carta established the supremacy of law over total rule by any single individual, guaranteed both individual rights and due process of law, and was a precedent for democratic government.
REF: 13-14
LO: 9

1.55 Explain the problem of dual sovereignty of the federal and state governments and how it was resolved.

ANS: Potential existed for conflicts to arise from future laws established by either the federal government or the various state governments. In the supremacy clause, the Constitution declared itself the supreme law of the land. Thus, in all matters over which the Constitution grants the federal government authority, the states must concede.
REF: 19-20
LO: 13

Chapter 2
An Overview of the U.S. Legal System

LEARNING OBJECTIVES

Upon completing this chapter, the student will know:

1. The two prominent theories about the underlying purpose of law.
2. The basic purpose of the American legal system.
3. What the scales of justice symbolize in law.
4. When common law began, what it is based on, and what it is synonymous with.
5. What *stare decisis* requires.
6. How the Constitution ensures individual liberty.
7. Why American law is said to be a living law.
8. Where statutory law originates.
9. The difference between a crime and a tort.
10. The two main functions served by courts.
11. The two levels on which the judicial system operates.
12. Who officers of the court are.
13. What doctrines govern whether a case will be heard in court.
14. The three components of both the criminal and juvenile justice systems.

KEY TERMS

- **adversarial judicial system**—A legal system such as that used in the United States, which places one party against another to resolve a legal issue, stipulating that only in an actual conflict will a judicial body hear the case; also called adversary system. [p. 45]

- **amicus briefs**—A "friend of the court" brief submitted by a person not a party to the action, but interested in the outcome. [p. 46]

- **appellate jurisdiction**—Describes a court authorized to review cases and to either affirm or reverse the actions of a lower court. [p. 40]

- **case law**—Common-law approach, so named because it is based on previous cases. Law that is set in prior cases brought before the courts and that provides a legal precedent that future cases may rely upon in making decisions on similar facts. Case law may make new law or serve to define or clarify legal questions. As a term in American law, it is synonymous with common law. [p. 35]

- **codified law**—Law specifically set forth in organized, structured codes such as the U.S. criminal code, state statutes or local ordinances. Also called statutory law. [p. 38]

- **common law**—Early English judge-made law based on custom and tradition; a legal system that, as in the United States, decides present cases on past decisions. It also refers to judge-made or case law, as differentiated from statutory or constitutional law. As a term in American law, it is synonymous with case law. [p. 35]

- **comparative law**—Comparing and contrasting laws to expand understanding of law and legal theory. [p. 49]

- **concurrent jurisdiction**—Two or more courts authorized to hear a specific type of case. [p. 40]

- **conflict theory**—Holds that laws are established to keep the dominant class in power, in contrast to the consensus theory. [p. 33]

- **consensus theory**—Holds that individuals in a society agree on basic values, on what is inherently right and wrong, and that laws express these values, in contrast to conflict theory. [p. 33]

- **crimes**—Acts defined by federal or state statute or local ordinance that are punishable; wrongs against the government and the people it serves. While an individual has been victimized, the real victim is considered to be society itself, in contrast to a tort, which is a wrong against an individual. An act could be both a crime and a tort. [p. 39]

- **exclusive jurisdiction**—The only courts that can hear specific cases. [p. 40]

- **general jurisdiction**—Courts having the ability to hear a wide range of cases. [p. 40]

- **jurisdiction**—The authority of a legislative body to establish a law, the authority of a particular court to hear certain types of cases, or the authority a law has over a specific group of people. Three levels of jurisdiction are federal, state and local. [p. 38]

- **limited jurisdiction**—Restriction of the types of cases a particular court might hear. [p. 40]

- **mootness**—Exists when the issues that gave rise to a case have either been resolved or have otherwise disappeared. [p. 47]

- **ordinances**—Laws or codes established at the local level, that is, the municipal or county level. [p. 38]

- **original jurisdiction**—Courts authorized to hear cases first, try them and render decisions. Often called trial courts. May also apply to the U.S. Supreme Court. [p. 40]

- **penal codes**—Criminal codes or laws. [p. 39]

- **petition for certiorari**—Request that the Supreme Court review the decision of a lower court. [p. 43]

- **procedural law**—How the law is to be enforced, for example, how and when police can stop people. [p. 38]

- **promulgate**—Publish or announce officially a law or rule; to make law through a legal process. [p. 35]

- **ripeness doctrine**—Invoked when a case comes to court too soon, preventing the court from getting prematurely involved in a case that may eventually resolve through other means. [p. 47]

- **social contract**—A philosophy proposed by the French historian-philosopher Montesquieu, whereby free, independent individuals agree to form a society and to give up a portion of their individual freedom to benefit the security of the group. Durkheim described this social solidarity as a society's "collective conscience." [p. 33]

- **standing**—The right to object to the unreasonableness of a search or seizure because of a reasonable expectation of privacy and to claim a violation of other constitutional rights. In constitutional law, it must involve a case or controversy and an actual interest in the matter of dispute to bring a case or to argue a legal issue in court. [p. 46]

- *stare decisis*—Latin for "to stand by decided matters." A legal principle that requires that precedents set in one case be followed in cases having similar circumstances, thus assuring consistency in the law. [p. 36]

- **status offenses**—Offenses deemed to be illegal when committed by juveniles because of their age, which are not unlawful for adults, such as smoking, drinking and curfew. [p. 48]

- **statutory law**—Law set forth by legislatures or governing bodies having jurisdiction to make such law. Also called codified law. [p. 38]

- **substantive law**—Establishes rules and regulations, as in traffic law. [p. 38]

- **torts**—Civil wrongs by one individual against another, with the remedy most often being either an order by the court for particular action or compensation, in contrast to crimes, which are wrongs against society. [p. 39]

- **venue**—The geographical area in which a specific case may come to trial, and the area from which the jury is selected. [p. 40]

LECTURE OUTLINE

I. Introduction

II. Theories About and the Purpose of the Legal System
  A. Consensus Theory
  B. Conflict Theory

III. The Law Defined

IV. Development of the Law
  A. Early Roman Law
  B. English Common Law
  C. *Stare Decisis*
    1. *Moore v. City of Albany* (1885)

V. The Continuing Need for Law

VI. American Law Lives
  A. Constitutional Amendments
  B. American Law is living law

VII. Categorizing Law
  A. Who? (Jurisdiction)
    1. Who makes the law? Who does the law affect?
    2. Statutory law
  B. How? (Procedural)
    1. Substantive Law
    2. Procedural Law
  C. What? (Criminal or Civil)
    1. Public wrong or private wrong?
    2. Torts and crimes
    3. Burdens of proof

VIII. The Components of the US Legal System
  A. Original jurisdiction
  B. Appellate jurisdiction

IX. The Court System
  A. The State Court System
    1. Lower Courts
    2. Intermediate Appellate Courts
    3. State Supreme Courts
  B. The Federal Court System
    1. Special US Courts
    2. US District Courts

      3. US Courts of Appeal
      4. The US Supreme Court

X.   Officers of the Court
      A. Judges, lawyers, clerks of court, sheriffs, marshals, bailiffs

XI.   An Adversarial Judicial System
      A. Accuser v. accused
      B. Doctrines Governing What Cases Will Be Heard
         1. Standing
         2. Mootness
         3. Ripeness

XII.   The Constitution and Criminal Justice in the United States
      A. The Juvenile Justice System
      B. The Criminal Justice and Juvenile Justice Systems Compared
         1. Law Enforcement
         2. Courts
         3. Corrections

XIII.   The Changing Face of American Criminal Justice and Constitutional Law

XIV.   American Criminal Justice Beyond our Borders
      A. Exportation of American law enforcement
      B. INTERPOL / U.S. National Central Bureau

XV.   Summary

CHAPTER SUMMARY

In the United States, two prominent theories about the underlying purpose of law are consensus theory and conflict theory. The basic purpose of the U.S. legal system is to ensure fairness in balancing individual and societal rights and needs, while preventing excessive government power. This balance between individual and societal rights and needs is represented by the scales of justice.

Our legal system has its roots in the common law of England, the early English judge-made law based on custom and tradition and followed throughout the country. In American law, common law is synonymous with case law. *Stare decisis* is a common law doctrine requiring that precedent set in one case shall be followed in all cases having the same or similar circumstances, thus ensuring consistency in the law. The Constitution ensures individual rights by limiting government power. And although the law, in fairness, must be consistent, it is also flexible. American law is considered a living law because it can change along with society.

In addition to common law, the legal system also relies upon statutory (codified) law, which is promulgated by legislatures or governing bodies. The U.S. legal system categorizes offenses into two specific areas: civil and criminal. Civil laws deal with personal matters and wrongs against individuals—called *torts*. Criminal laws deal with wrongs against society—called *crimes*. An act may be both a tort and a crime. When civil or criminal laws are broken, the courts' two main functions are to settle controversies between parties and to decide the rules of law that apply in specific cases.

The U.S. judicial system is two-tiered, consisting of state and federal court systems. Each tier includes specific levels of courts. The officers of the court are judges, lawyers, clerks of court, sheriffs, marshals and bailiffs. Three important doctrines govern whether a case will be heard by the court: standing, mootness and ripeness.

The juvenile justice system has the same three components as the criminal justice system: law enforcement, courts and corrections.

SUGGESTED ANSWERS TO THE DISCUSSION QUESTIONS

1. Could a country such as the United States function without a federal constitution? Would it be possible for each state to merely abide by its own constitution?

    A country like the U.S. requires a federal constitution to serve as a common "backbone" to the body politic. Its existence makes us truly the *United* States by preventing the 50 state jurisdictions from wandering off in 50 unguided directions.

2. Why shouldn't the Constitution include an overall criminal code specifying crimes and punishments that could apply throughout the United States?

    Only the basic format of government is controlled by the U.S. Constitution. This is intentional, as it prevents the central government from amassing excessive power. Thus, the citizens of the various states are free to exercise their own jurisdictional imperatives, including, for example, the establishment of their own criminal codes.

3. Why is society considered the victim of a crime rather than the individual victimized?

    The law considers society the victim of crimes because the expectations of society have been disrupted. We collectively suffer when our way of life is violated, even when that violation is directed at but one of us.

4. Why must the legal system provide an appeal procedure?

   Because mistakes do occur, and a just society must provide a mechanism for pursuing and obtaining relief from the unjust effects of such mistakes.

5. Can you develop an argument against *stare decisis*?

   Because no two cases are exactly alike, no single case should be strictly compared to other cases that are merely "similar."

6. Why shouldn't courts be permitted to argue "what if" questions?

   "What if" questions are appropriate in philosophical discussions. Courts must function on "what is." The relevant questions are "What is the charge?;" "What is the evidence?;" "What is the finding of the jury after consideration of the evidence?". A "what if" approach poses the hypothetical; findings of guilt and innocence must, by law, be based on the factual.

7. Which underlying theory about the purpose of law do you feel makes most sense—consensus or conflict theory?

   Students' responses will vary. This is an excellent debate topic.

8. If the basic purpose of the U.S. legal system is to ensure fairness in balancing individual and societal rights and needs, is that end best served by an adversarial system in which the person with the best lawyer often comes out on top? Does this system of justice provide equal access to people of different socioeconomic classes?

   The opposing sides that function within the adversarial system operate under the intense scrutiny of their counterpart. It is this scrutiny that serves to bring truth to the fore. Although all socioeconomic segments of society are theoretically able to secure equally qualified" representation, there is no denying the fact that the wealthier among us have a greater ability to acquire investigative resources, research assistance, and other forms defense that those at the lower end of the economic scale simply cannot access.

9. Discuss whether you consider U.S. law a "living law."

   While many describe the ability of American law to change and adapt as evidence of its "life," the argument can be made that it lacks the capacity to change *enough*, either substantively or in terms of timeliness.

10. Should people have a right to a defense attorney?

   In cases involving the possibility of serious consequences (i.e., extended loss of liberty), trained counsel must be provided. To offer defense counsel for every minor infraction, however, would severely overburden the system.

STUDENT ACTIVITIES/ASSIGNMENTS

- Have students prepare a chart or table reflecting all courts, both original jurisdiction and appellate, within your state's court system.

- Research and outline information on one of the following terms (be sure the material relates to chapter content): *amicus briefs, case law, common law, conflict theory, consensus theory, legal standing, mootness, petition for certiorari, procedural law, ripeness doctrine, social contract, stare decisis, status offenses, statutory law, substantive law, torts.*

- Go to the Bill of Rights Institute for information on *Youngstown Sheet and Tube Company v. Sawyer* (1952), "a case that turned on the constitutional principle of separation of powers and rights in times of crisis: During the Korean War, did President Harry Truman have the power to take over steel mills to ensure their continued operation during a strike?" http://www.billofrightsinstitute.org/page.aspx?pid=544.

- Poll the class to see if any students have participated in a court proceeding. Of those who have, ask if any would be willing to relate their experience to the class, including their impressions of the court's procedures and the performance of court personnel.

INTERNET CONNECTIONS

- An excellent outline of America's legal system, created by the U.S. State Department's International Information Programs (12/2004) can be downloaded in a pdf file for free at http://www.america.gov/publications/books/outline-of-u.s.-legal-system.

- The **U.S. Courts** web site offers a comprehensive explanation of the federal court system at http://www.uscourts.gov/FederalCourts.aspx.

- Examine a typical state court system at the New York State Court's **New York State Unified Court System** web site at http://www.courts.state.ny.us/home.htm.

CHAPTER 2 TEST BANK

Multiple Choice

2.1   A basic purpose of the American legal system is to:
a. remove power from the government.
b. develop a living law.
c. ensure fairness in balancing individual and societal rights and needs.
d. create a system that, while not perfect, is the best in the world.
ANS: C
REF: 34
LO: 2

2.2   The concept that courts will continue to rely on prior cases to ensure consistency in the law is called:
a. original jurisprudence.
b. *lex talionis*
c. *stare decisis.*
d. venue.
ANS: C
REF: 36
LO: 5

2.3   The place where a specific case may come to trial and the area from which the jury is selected is known as:
a. voir dire
b. jurisdiction
c. district
d. venue
ANS: D
REF: 40
LO: 10

2.4   Those who are not party to a legal action but who still have an interest in the case may:
a. subpoena the judge to have their testimony heard.
b. file a writ of certiorari with the court and enter themselves as a "hostile" witness.
c. submit an amicus brief arguing their perspective, although such briefs are considered only at the pleasure of the court.
d. not do anything--only those who are directly party to the legal action may address the court.s
ANS: C
REF: 46-47
LO: 13

2.5   States' penal codes contain:

a. Civil laws
b. Criminal laws
c. Codified laws
d. common law
ANS: B
REF: 39
LO: 8

2.6   The standard of proof required in a civil case is:
a. more stringent than that required in a criminal case.
b. the same as that required in a criminal case.
c. a preponderance of the evidence.
d. proof beyond a reasonable doubt.
ANS: C
REF: 39
LO: 9

2.7   Marx regarded punishment as a way to:
a. provide social solidarity.
b. control the lower class.
c. limit the power and influence of the upper class.
d. exact revenge.
ANS: B
REF: 33
LO: 1

2.8   Law does all of the following, except that it does not:
a. respond to the perceived needs of the society it serves.
b. define unacceptable behavior.
c. establish consequences for unlawful behavior.
d. provide justice for all.
ANS: D
REF: 33-35
LO: 2

2.9   Common law was:
a. that which applied to the common people, not to those in the upper echelon of society.
b. set forth in well-documented codes.
c. established by early English and Roman rulers.
d. based on customs and traditions followed throughout England.
ANS: D
REF: 35
LO: 4

2.10   American law is considered a living law because:
       a. it can change as society changes.
       b. it can never be rescinded or cancelled.
       c. once a law is passed, it stands forever.
       d. there are no constraints on its application or interpretation.
       ANS: A
       REF: 37
       LO: 7

2.11   The number of U.S. Courts of Appeals in the federal court system is:
       a. 4
       b. 12
       c. 52
       d. 94
       ANS: B
       REF: 43
       LO: 11

2.12   The Constitution ensures individual liberty by:
       a. limiting government power.
       b. giving the government enough power to protect the innocent.
       c. giving individuals the freedom to decide.
       d. restricting the authority of state governments to enforce the law.
       ANS: A
       REF: 37
       LO: 6

2.13   Statutory law can also be referred to as:
       a. case law
       b. codified law
       c. common law
       d. canonized law
       ANS: B
       REF: 38
       LO: 8

2.14   Which of the following is <u>not</u> an officer of the court?
       a. Sheriff
       b. Judge
       c. Lawyers
       d. Plaintiff
       ANS: D
       REF: 45
       LO: 12

2.15   Since the ratification of the Bill of Rights more than 7,000 amendments have been
        proposed in Congress. Of those, the number that have been successfully ratified is:
        a. 53
        b. 115
        c. 700
        d. 17
        ANS: D
        REF: 37
        LO: 7

2.16   The following statements are true about both torts and crimes, except:
        a. Both could result from the same single act.
        b. Both differ by who is considered the victim.
        c. Both must be heard separately by the court(s).
        d. Both are subject to the same standard of proof in court.
        ANS: D
        REF: 39-40
        LO: 9

2.17   To bring a case or to argue a legal issue in court, one must have an actual interest in the
        matter of dispute, which is called:
        a. standing
        b. ripeness
        c. mootness
        d. jurisdiction
        ANS: A
        REF: 46
        LO: 13

2.18   The two main functions of the courts are to:
        a. determine guilt or innocence and interpret laws
        b. settle controversies and review cases for legal improprieties.
        c. settle controversies and decide the rules of law that apply in the case.
        d. determine guilt or innocence and apply appropriate sanctions.
        ANS: C
        REF: 40
        LO: 10

2.19   The scales of justice represent:
        a. keeping individual and societal needs in balance.
        b. the struggle for power between good and evil.
        c. the two sides of prosecution and defense.
        d. the weighing the evidence of guilt or innocence.
        ANS: A
        REF: 34
        LO: 3

2.20   Conduct prohibited by law simply because the person engaging in the behavior is a minor is considered a/an:
a. Delinquent act
b. Status offense
c. Infraction
d. Youthful offense
ANS: B
REF: 48
LO: 14

2.21   When a court decision would have no practical effect, a case is apt to be dismissed for:
a. standing
b. ripeness
c. mootness
d. jurisdiction
ANS: C
REF: 47
LO: 13

2.22   Which of the following is not one of the three levels of court function in both state and federal courts?
a. trial courts
b. appellate courts
c. circuit courts
d. courts of last resort
ANS: C
REF: 41
LO: 11

2.23   Which of the following is not true of the adversarial judicial system?
a. only actual conflicts will be heard by a court.
b. "what if" questions will not be heard.
c. sides are drawn-accuser vs. accused-with one side challenged by the other.
d. the accused has the burden of proof.
ANS: D
REF: 45
LO: 10

2.24 For an amendment to the U.S. Constitution to be ratified, the number of state legislatures or special conventions which must agree is:

a. one-fourth
b. one-half
c. two-thirds
d. three-fourths
ANS: D
REF: 37
LO: 7

2.25 The juvenile justice system is comprised of the following components:
a. intervention, courts, and rehabilitation
b. law enforcement, courts, and corrections
c. intervention, adjudication, and punishment
d. law enforcement, counseling, and rehabilitation
ANS: B
REF: 48-49
LO: 14

2.26 The vast majority of cases heard in U.S. District Courts are:.
a. criminal cases
b. civil cases
c. drug cases
d. homeland security cases
ANS: B
REF: 43
LO: 11

2.27 A case with the caption *United States* v. *Smith* is most likely a:
a. criminal case
b. civil case
c. class action suit
d. federal appeal
ANS: A
REF: 39
LO: 9

2.28 In a civil case, the party bringing suit is represented by:
a. the prosecutor
b. a plaintiff's lawyer
c. a defense attorney
d. the public defender's office
ANS: B
REF: 45
LO: 12

2.29   The philosophy which is based on free, independent individuals agreeing to form a
        society and to give up a portion of their individual freedom to benefit the security of the
        group is generally known as:
        a. a social contract
        b. communal well-being
        c. the federalist philosophy
        d. natural law
        ANS: A
        REF: 33
        LO: 1

2.30   Simply put, a law is:
        a. that which those in power deem to be right and just.
        b. a rule with the power of government behind it.
        c. a matter of interpretation, being different things to different people.
        d. the way a society is defined.
        ANS: B
        REF: 35
        LO: 1

True/False

2.31   The U.S. Supreme Court's chief function is as an appellate court.
        ANS: T
        REF: 44
        LO: 10

2.32   The doctrine of *stare decisis* firmly prevents the law from changing or reconsidering
        itself in matters in which undesirable law resulted.
        ANS: F
        REF: 36
        LO: 5

2.33   Each state has its own federal circuit court of appeals.
        ANS: F
        REF: 43
        LO: 11

2.34   State supreme courts derive their power from the United States Constitution.
        ANS: F
        REF: 43
        LO: 11

2.35   Case law is promulgated by legislatures or governing bodies.

      ANS: F
      REF: 35
      LO: 8

2.36   A significant influence on the development of the American legal system was the system
      of common law that evolved in England during the Middle Ages.
      ANS: T
      REF: 35
      LO: 4

2.37   The Durkheimian perspective saw punishment as revenge and a means to restore and
      solidify the social order.
      ANS: T
      REF: 33
      LO: 1

2.38   Regardless of the level of jurisdiction, a statutory law may not violate the Constitution.
      ANS: T
      REF: 38
      LO: 6, 8

2.39   An act must be distinguished as either a crime or a tort; it cannot be both.
      ANS: F
      REF: 39
      LO: 9

2.40   Clerks of court are responsible for keeping the courtroom proceedings orderly and
      dignified.
      ANS: F
      REF: 45
      LO: 12

Fill-In

2.41   Overrepresentation of racial and ethnic minorities in arrest, prosecution, imprisonment
      and capital punishment as both the product of inequality and an expression of prejudice
      against minorities may be explained by _____ theory.
      ANS: conflict
      REF: 34
      LO: 1

2.42.   As a term in American law, common law is synonymous with _____ law.

ANS: case
REF: 35
LO: 4

2.43   Stare decisis is a common law doctrine requiring that _____ set in one case shall be followed in all cases having the same or similar circumstances.
ANS: precedent
REF: 36
LO: 5

2.44   Local jurisdictions, such as at the county or municipal level, may enact their own specific codes, often referred to as _____.
ANS: ordinances
REF: 38
LO: 8

2.45   Courts with general jurisdiction may hear a wide range of cases, whereas those of _____ jurisdiction hear a much narrower range of cases.
ANS: limited
REF: 40
LO: 11

2.46   Those who _____ law create it.
ANS: promulgate
REF: 35
LO: 8

2.47   _____ describes the authority of a court to hear cases first, try them and render decisions.
ANS: Original jurisdiction
REF: 40
LO: 10

2.48   The _____ doctrine prevents the court from getting prematurely involved in a case that may eventually be resolved through other means.
ANS: ripeness
REF: 47
LO: 14

2.49   _____ describes the authority of a court to review cases and to either affirm or reverse the actions of a lower court.
ANS: Appellate jurisdiction
REF: 40
LO: 10

2.50   The court of last resort in most federal cases is the _____.
        ANS: U.S. Court of Appeals
        REF: 44
        LO: 11

Essay

2.51   Discuss in detail the similarities and differences between the consensus theory and
        conflict theory.

        ANS: Similar in that both see laws as necessary to an orderly society; different in how
        they view the *purpose* of punishment. Consensus theory is more humanitarian, seeing
        punishment as revenge and a way to restore social order. Conflict theory views
        punishment as a way to control the lower class and preserve the power of the upper class.
        REF: 33-34
        LO: 1

2.52   Explain the difference between a crime and a tort.

        ANS: A crime is public wrong, codified in law, prosecuted by the state, must be proven
        beyond a reasonable doubt, and consequences can range from fines or imprisonment to
        the death penalty. A tort is a civil wrong against an individual and it is up to the
        individual to bring legal action. Torts only require a showing of a preponderance of the
        evidence and the consequences are not considered to be as severe, usually limited to
        injunctions or financial awards to compensate the victim. An act can be both a tort and a
        crime, and failure to prove guilt in a criminal case does not preclude a victory in civil
        court.
        REF: 39-40
        LO: 9

2.53   Explain the basic purpose of the American legal system and why American law is said to
        be a living law.

        ANS: The legal system's basic purpose is to ensure fairness in balancing individual and
        societal rights and needs, while preventing excessive government power. It is said to be a
        "living law" because it can grow and change along with society.
        REF: 34-37
        LO: 2, 7

2.54   Discuss how the Constitution ensures individual liberty.

        ANS: The law and the Constitution set forth how and when the government can and
        cannot interfere with citizens' lives. No state or federal law may violate the basic
        protections outlined in the Constitution. The Constitution cannot be amended at the
        whim of a powerful few—it is extremely difficult to amend the Constitution and when an
        amendment is accomplished, it reflects true societal changes.
        REF: 37-38
        LO: 6

2.55   Contrast the criminal and juvenile justice systems.

        ANS: Similar in that they are made up of the same three components, and the same
        Constitutional rights apply. Different in: a. that the focus of criminal justice is punitive,
        whereas the juvenile justice goal is rehabilitative; b. terminology; c. adversarial nature;
        and d. types of offenses (status offenses apply only to juveniles).
        REF: 47-49
        LO: 14

Chapter 3
The U.S. Supreme Court: The Final Word

LEARNING OBJECTIVES

Upon completing this chapter, the student will know:

1. The authority under which the Supreme Court operates.
2. The jurisdiction of the Supreme Court.
3. How the Supreme Court has effectively created most of its own power and authority.
4. The precedent case that determined whether the Supreme Court can review acts of Congress.
5. The precedent case that determined whether the Supreme Court can review cases that are pending in or that have been decided in state courts.
6. Why appointments of justices to the Supreme Court are lifetime.
7. Whether the current Supreme Court is liberal or conservative.

KEY TERMS

- *certiorari*—Latin for "to be informed." The Court uses this term to state which cases it will hear. Legal shorthand might simply state "cert granted." [p. 60]

- **concurring opinion**—Agreeing with the majority. [p. 68]

- **conservative**—Decisions that favor the government's interest in prosecuting and punishing offenders over recognition or expansion of rights for individuals. [p.62]

- **dissenting opinion**—A justice's opinion that disagrees with the majority decision of the court. [p. 68]

- **judicial review**—The power of a court to analyze decisions of other government entities and lower courts. [p. 58]

- **liberal**—Decisions that are pro-person accused or convicted of a crime, pro-civil liberties or civil rights claimants, pro-indigents, pro-Native Americans and anti-government. [p. 62]

- **opinion**—A written statement by a judge that provides a description of the facts; a statement of the legal issues presented for decision, the relevant rules of law, the holding and the policies and reasons that support the holding. [68]

- **recesses**—Periods when the Supreme Court does not hear cases, but rather considers administrative matters and writes opinions. Also, breaks taken during the course of the trial. [p. 67]

- **sittings**—Periods during which the Supreme Court hears cases. [p. 67]

- **strict construction**—A rigid interpretation of a law not likely to expand the specifically set forth law of the particular statute, particularly in expanding the intent of that law. [p. 68]

LECTURE OUTLINE

I.   Introduction

II. Authority for the Supreme Court
     A. Article 3 U.S. Constitution
     B. Federal Judiciary Act of 1789

III. Jurisdiction of the Supreme Court
     A. Section 2, Article 3
        1. Appeals
        2. Original jurisdiction
     B. *Ex parte McCardle* (1868)
        1. Congressional limits on jurisdiction

III. Judicial Review
     A. *Marbury v. Madison* (1803)
        1. Authority to nullify and void acts of Congress that violate Constitution.
     B. *Martin v. Hunter's Lessee* (1816)
        1. Authority to review state court decisions involving federal legal issues
     C. Controversy over Judicial Review
        1. Judicial review v. legislative supremacy
     D. Alternatives to Judicial Review

IV. *Certiorari*: Deciding Which Cases to Hear
     A. Writ of certiorari
        1. Discuss list
        2. Four justices must vote in favor of granting certiorari
     B. When certiorari is denied

V.   The Supreme Court Justices
     A. One chief justice, eight associate justices
        1. Lifetime appointment
        2. Nominated by President, confirmed by Senate
     B. Definitions of "liberal" and "conservative"

CHAPTER SUMMARY

The Constitution ordained in Article 3 that there shall be a Supreme Court. The Supreme Court has original jurisdiction in cases dealing with foreign dignitaries and legal disputes between states. All other cases are considered only on appeal.

The Supreme Court has created most of its own power and authority through the process of judicial review. Two precedent cases confirmed this power. *Marbury v. Madison* (1803) established that the Supreme Court has the authority to nullify and void an act of Congress that violates the Constitution. *Martin v. Hunter's Lessee* (1816) held that the Supreme Court can review and reverse state court decisions and can review pending state cases.

Because justices decide matters vital to national interest, a Supreme Court appointment is a lifetime appointment so a justice may not be unduly influenced. The current Supreme Court is considered by many to be a conservative "law and order" court.

SUGGESTED ANSWERS TO THE DISCUSSION QUESTIONS

1. Should any one court be given the final say? Why or why not?

   Ultimately, a final decision must be determined. To fail to do so would prohibit people from getting on with life.

2. Is there a negative side to appointment for life on the Court? Does this and the inability to lessen a justice's salary really prevent influencing a Supreme Court justice?

   This is a question based largely on philosophy that has been argued for many years. The decision to appoint justices for life has sought to ensure the basic fairness that our system demands. One of the strongest arguments *against* lifetime appointment is that at some point the aging process indeed affects one's abilities. But whether anyone's perspective can, in any way, be guaranteed not to be influenced is probably unlikely. Here a way of doing things was determined to lessen this likelihood.

3. Do you think the Supreme Court is a *de facto* lawmaker? Why or why not?

   Certainly the U.S. Supreme Court is a de facto lawmaker. By deciding which laws are constitutional and which are not, and therefore which laws are valid and which are not, the Court is determining law. While some would argue that the Supreme Court is merely overseeing the legality of legislation that is produced elsewhere, to overlook the obvious here would be less than realistic.

4. Is it possible for the justices to provide a fair review of a case when they hear about it so briefly from the lawyers arguing it before them?

   Remember that almost every case presented to the U.S. Supreme Court is there on appeal and, therefore, presented with written arguments based on the previous record. The real role of the attorneys presenting the case before the Supreme Court is to present the basic arguments. Hopefully the decision reached by the Court will be made on the information contained in the record presented to them.

5. Should the Supreme Court accept so few cases? Does the fact the justices decide this totally in private concern you?

   Again, the "buck" has to stop somewhere, and with legal issues, it is at the doorstep of the U.S. Supreme Court. It makes no sense to have the Supreme Court review every case presented to it if the issue is not significant or controversial enough. Furthermore, time and resources would not permit such review. The fact that the Court decides privately which cases it will accept does seem contrary to the way most other legal matters are handled in America. However, this is one of the very significant powers that the Supreme Court has retained over its history.

6. Do you think the current Supreme Court is carrying out the desires of the founders of our Constitution?

This question is very philosophical and personal. Most constitutional scholars, however, concur that the role established for the Supreme Court is being carried out by those appointed to it.

7. Explain where you see the real power of the Supreme Court. What makes the justices so powerful as individuals and as a group?

Judicial review of legislation is where most of the Court's power lies. It is in having the power to determine which laws are valid that the Court is considered a de facto lawmaker. And, of course, having the "final say" assures tremendous power.

8. Do you believe the Supreme Court acted properly in the 2000 presidential election in *Bush v. Gore* (2000)?

Students' answers may vary. This might make an excellent class debate topic.

9. If you were sitting on the Supreme Court, what sorts of cases would you look for to review?

This question was written to encourage students to consider why members of the Supreme Court select the cases they do to review.

10. Do you favor strict construction (rigid reading and interpretation) of the law or a more liberal approach?

Again, the student is being encouraged to put themselves "in the shoes" of the bench.

STUDENT ACTIVITIES/ASSIGNMENTS

- Have each student research the 17 Chief Justices who have guided the Court, and select his or her "Top 3" Chief Justices. Compile the votes, then let the class discuss the rankings.

- February 24, 2003 marked the 200th anniversary of the Marbury v. Madison decision. Have students read and discuss Joel B. Grossman's article *"The 200th Anniversary of Marbury v. Madison: The Reasons We Should Still Care About the Decision, and The Lingering Questions It Left Behind"* on Findlaw at http://writ.news.findlaw.com/commentary/20030224_grossman.html.

- For interesting information on selection, procedures, and traditions of the U.S. Supreme Court, go to "Frequently Asked Questions" on the Supreme Court's website at http://www.supremecourt.gov/faq.aspx.

INTERNET CONNECTIONS

- Access the **U.S. Supreme Court's** homepage at http://www.supremecourtus.gov/.

- Visit the fascinating **OYEZ Project**, a self-described "multimedia archive devoted to the Supreme Court of the United States and its work," at http://www.oyez.org/.

- The University of Pittsburgh School of Law's **Jurist Legal News & Research** web site, accessible at http://jurist.law.pitt.edu/currentawareness/ussupremes.php, contains scholarly articles and news pertaining to the U.S. Supreme Court, and a wealth of links to various other Supreme Court sites.

CHAPTER 3 TEST BANK

Multiple Choice

3.1 The framework for the federal judiciary is:
a. based on common law.
b. found in the Declaration of Independence.
c. outlined in The Federalist Papers, issue V
d. found in Article 3 of the U.S. Constitution.
ANS: D
REF: 55
LO: 1

3.2 The first Supreme Court was established by the:
a. Bill of Rights
b. Federalist Papers
c. Federal Judiciary Act of 1789
d. First Amendment
ANS: C
REF: 55
LO: 1

3.3 The U.S. Supreme Court has original jurisdiction:
a. in cases dealing with foreign dignitaries and in legal disputes between states.
b. in cases brought before it on appeal.
c. when citizens claim violations of their rights under the Constitution.
d. in cases dealing with treaties and those involving federal officials.
ANS: A
REF: 56
LO: 2

3.4 Judicial review refers to:
a. a quarterly review of the Supreme Court by Congress.
b. the rating system that allows American citizens to express their level of satisfaction regarding Supreme Court rulings.
c. the methodology used by a president in selecting a justice for appointment to the Supreme Court.
d. the power of the Supreme Court to analyze the constitutionality of decisions of other government entities and lower courts.
ANS: D
REF: 58
LO: 3

3.5   The case of *Marbury v. Madison* established:
        a. lifetime appointment for justices.
        b. that the Supreme Court has the authority to review acts of Congress.
        c. that police must notify suspects of their rights prior to questioning.
        d. that the Supreme Court must function only as an appellate court.
        ANS: B
        REF: 59
        LO: 4

3.6   The laws that emanate from the Supreme Court:
        a. are the law of the land.
        b. may be appealed to another court having similar jurisdiction.
        c. constitute statutory law.
        d. may hold only until the end of the presiding chief justice's term.
        ANS: A
        REF: 55
        LO: 1

3.7   When the Court grants certiorari, it will:
        a. officially end that term.
        b. hear and decide that case.
        c. consider hearing that case.
        d. allow the ruling of the lower court to stand.
        ANS: B
        REF: 60
        LO: 2

3.8   Of the cases put before the Court, it accepts for review about:
        a. 1%
        b. 10%
        c. 50%
        d. 85%
        ANS: A
        REF: 61
        LO: 2

3.9   The reason a Supreme Court appointment is lifetime is:
        a. so a justice may not be unduly influenced.
        b. because it is very time consuming to select and train a justice.
        c. because it would be age discrimination to require them to retire.
        d. to continue the political legacy of the appointing President.
        ANS: A
        REF: 61
        LO: 6

3.10   How many justices sit on the Supreme Court?
        a. five
        b. seven
        c. eight
        d. nine
        ANS: D
        REF: 55, 61
        LO: 1

3.11   In *Ex parte McCardle* (1868), Congress reserved the right to:
        a. overrule Supreme Court decisions with a two-thirds vote of the Senate.
        b. limit the jurisdiction of federal courts, including the Supreme Court.
        c. limit the jurisdiction of federal courts, but not the Supreme Court.
        d. override the Constitution by promulgating unconstitutional law.
        ANS: B
        REF: 56
        LO: 2

3.12   Supreme Court decisions that are pro-person accused or convicted of a crime, pro-civil
        liberties or civil rights claimants, pro-indigents, pro-Native Americans and anti-
        government are considered to be:
        a. Liberal decisions
        b. Conservative decisions
        c. Libertarian decisions
        d. Independent decisions
        ANS: A
        REF: 62
        LO: 7

3.13   The ability of a president to select a Supreme Court justice is a powerful political
        opportunity because:
        a. the justice selected will treat that president with favoritism, should they ever be
           involved in a legal dispute.
        b. the justice selected must rule the way the president wishes.
        c. it might be possible to select a candidate with similar political views.
        d. most judicial candidates are powerful people themselves.
        ANS: C
        REF: 62, 64
        LO: 6

47

3.14 Strict construction refers to:
      a. a justice expressing hostility or anger in an opinion.
      b. a rigid reading and interpretation of a law.
      c. the manner in which our legal system was designed and developed.
      d. a lenient means of interpreting the law.
      ANS: B
      REF: 68
      LO: 7

3.15 The current Chief Justice is:
      a. Sandra Day O'Connor.
      b. William Rehnquist
      c. Clarence Thomas
      d. John G. Roberts, Jr.
      ANS: D
      REF: 63
      LO: 7

3.16 The only other court or legislative body that can overrule a Supreme Court decision is:
      a. another federal court having original jurisdiction.
      b. the lower court to which the case was remanded.
      c. Congress, with a three-fourths vote in the House and a two-thirds vote in the Senate.
      d. no other body may overrule the U.S. Supreme Court.
      ANS: D
      REF: 55
      LO: 1

3.17 Which of the following is not within the power of the Supreme Court?
      a. It can override the will of the majority expressed in an act of Congress.
      b. It can require redistribution of political power in every state.
      c. It can issue proactive opinions to address and avoid future controversies.
      d. It has original jurisdiction in all cases involving ambassadors, other public ministers
          and consuls.
      ANS: C
      REF: 55-56
      LO: 3

3.18 *Martin v. Hunter's Lessee* held that the Supreme Court could:
      a. reverse state court decisions that involved federal legal issues.
      b. declare acts of Congress unconstitutional.
      c. be the final arbiter in disputes between states.
      d. have original jurisdiction in cases involving Constitutional issues.
      ANS: A
      REF: 59
      LO: 5

3.19 It is the Supreme Court's responsibility to monitor government infringement on civil rights according to the doctrine of:
a. strict construction
b. judicial restraint
c. judicial review
d. natural law
ANS: C
REF: 60
LO: 3

3.20 The minimum number of justices required to vote in favor or granting certiorari to review a case is:
a. 2
b. 4
c. 3
d. 1
ANS: B
REF: 60
LO: 2

3.21 The percentage of cases submitted to the Supreme Court which are summarily denied, having no justices expressing an interest in them is approximately:
a. 30%
b. 50%
c. 70%
d. 90%
ANS: C
REF: 60
LO: 2

3.22 Federal judges (including Supreme Court justices) can be removed from their office "on impeachment for and conviction of" all of the following, except:
a. high crimes and misdemeanors
b. treason
c. dereliction of duty
d. bribery
ANS: C
REF: 62
LO: 6

3.23   The Court has jurisdiction over two general types of cases, cases that reach it on appeal
        and cases over which the Court has:
        a. original jurisdiction.
        b. appellate jurisdiction.
        c. the power of judicial review
        d. subject-matter jurisdiction
        ANS: A
        REF: 56
        LO: 2

3.24   The case which authorized the Court to maintain a position of the ultimate de facto
        lawmaker by deciding what legislation is and is not constitutional is:
        a. Martin vs. Hunter's Lessees
        b. Ex parte McCardle
        c. Plessy v. Ferguson
        d. Marbury v. Madison
        ANS: D
        REF: 59
        LO: 4

3.25   The number of women who have served on the Supreme Court through 2010 is:
        a. zero
        b. one
        c. three
        d. four
        ANS:D
        REF: 63
        LO: 7

3.26   The current Supreme Court:
        a. overwhelmingly supports judicial review.
        b. is impartial on the issue of judicial review.
        c. supports the expansion of rights for offenders within the criminal justice system.
        d. is perceived to be a "law and order" court that supports expanded discretionary
            authority for criminal justice professionals.
        ANS: D
        REF: 65
        LO: 7

3.27   When the Supreme Court denies certiorari, it means the Court:
     a. is upholding the lower court ruling.
     b. believes the case lacks merit.
     c. finds the issue moot.
     d. takes no official position on the case.
     ANS: D
     REF: 61
     LO: 7

3.28   Since the origin of the Supreme Court, _____ justices have served.
     a. nearly 40
     b. between 60 and 65
     c. more than 100
     d. nearly 210
     ANS: C
     REF: 63
     LO: 6

3.29   Of the following statements about dissenting opinions, all are accurate except:
     a. They carry no legal authority.
     b. They date to the King's Bench of Great Britain in 1792.
     c. They are often used in hope of influencing future decisions.
     d. They carry the same legal authority as the majority opinion.
     ANS: D
     REF: 68
     LO: 2

3.30   The Supreme Court established its authority as the final interpreter of the Constitution in the case of:
     a. Martin vs. Hunter's Lessees
     b. Ex parte McCardle
     c. Plessy v. Ferguson
     d. Marbury v. Madison
     ANS: D
     REF: 58
     LO: 3, 4

True/False

3.31   Decisions made by the Supreme Court affect the everyday lives of Americans.
     ANS: T
     REF: 54
     LO: 2, 3, 7

3.32   In determining which cases to hear, the justices are often looking for cases involving matters that directly influence the law and the nation.
ANS: T
REF: 61
LO: 2

3.33   The Supreme Court, powerful as it is, cannot override the will of the majority expressed in acts of Congress.
ANS: F
REF: 59
LO: 4

3.34   Due to its strict conformance to stare decisis, the Supreme Court cannot overrule itself.
ANS:F
REF: 55
LO: 3

3.35   The framers of the Constitution were very specific as to how the Supreme Court was to be organized.
ANS: F
REF: 55
LO: 1

3.36   The Supreme Court has tremendous power through the process of judicial review.
ANS: T
REF: 58
LO: 3

3.37   A petition is a written statement from the Court.
ANS: F
REF: 68
LO: 2

3.38   The Supreme Court has original jurisdiction in any criminal case where controversies over the death penalty are involved.
ANS: F
REF: 56
LO: 2

3.39   In the case of Martin v. Hunter's Lessee, the final determination was that the Supreme Court had the authority to review cases involving federal law, even though the case is pending in a state court.
ANS: T
REF: 59
LO: 5

3.40   In *Ex parte McCardle* (1868), Congress reserved the right to limit the jurisdiction of
        federal courts, including the Supreme Court.
        ANS: T
        REF: 56
        LO: 2

Fill-In

3.41   _____ is a Latin term that means "to be informed."
        ANS: Certiorari
        REF: 60
        LO: 2

3.42   Decisions that favor the government's interest in prosecuting and punishing offenders
        over recognition or expansion of individual rights tend to be classified as _____
        decisions.
        ANS: Conservative
        REF: 62
        LO: 7

3.43   The current Supreme Court is considered by many to be _____.
        ANS: conservative
        REF: 65
        LO: 7

3.44   An opinion that agrees with the majority is called a _____ opinion.
        ANS: concurring
        REF: 68
        LO: 2

3.45   After the President nominates a judge for appointment to the Supreme Court, the
        _____ must confirm the nomination.
        ANS: Senate
        REF: 62
        LO: 6

3.46   The Supreme Court has effectively created most of its own power and authority through
        the process of _____.
        ANS: judicial review
        REF: 58
        LO: 3

3.47   All questions are allowed, and politics become readily apparent, during a Supreme Court
        nominee's _____ process.
        ANS: confirmation
        REF: 64
        LO: 6

3.48   During _____, the justices consider administrative matters and write opinions, but
        do not hear cases.
        ANS: recesses
        REF: 67
        LO: 2

3.49   The justices not only render decisions, they also _____ the Constitution.
        ANS: interpret
        REF: 58
        LO: 3

3.50   It can be interpreted from *The Federalist Papers* that the Supreme Court was assigned the
        awesome task of practically overseeing the _____.
        ANS: Bill of Rights
        REF: 69
        LO: 3

Essay

3.51   Describe the ideological makeup of the current Supreme Court. In your opinion, do
        labels such as "liberal" or "conservative" provide an accurate portrayal of the current
        Court? Explain.
        ANS: See Table 3.1. Students answers on the second part of the question will vary, but
        should be justified by information from the text.
        REF: 63-64
        LO: 7

3.52   Describe the authority the Supreme Court has and how it has come by this authority.

ANS: Has appellate jurisdiction over lower state and federal courts on issues that involve either interpretation of federal law or the applicability of the Constitution to the subject at hand, and over cases dealing with treaties the U.S. has entered into, admiralty and maritime cases, or those involving certain public officials and political entities. Has original jurisdiction in cases dealing with foreign dignitaries or cases involving legal disputes between states. Its authority is established in Article 3 of the U.S. Constitution. Additionally, the Court has the power of judicial review, as set forth in its decision of *Marbury v. Madison*, and the power to review state court cases, as established in *Martin v. Hunter's Lessee*.
REF: 55-59
LO: 3

3.53   Explain the process used in deciding which cases will be heard by the Supreme Court.

ANS: Figure 3.1 illustrates the path a case travels to reach the Supreme Court.
REF: 57
LO: 2

3.54   Explain the types of opinions that may be written by Supreme Court justices, who may write them, and the purpose of each.

ANS: The chief justice or most senior justice voting with the majority assigns the writing of the majority opinion. Any other justice may write a concurring or dissenting opinion. Concurring opinions give justices who did not author the opinion the opportunity to address why they agree with the outcome but not with the reasoning. Dissenting opinions provide the bigger picture and other perspectives on the issue at hand, and are often written in hopes of influencing future decisions on the issue.
REF: 68
LO: 2

3.55   Describe the influence of the Supreme Court on the justice system.
ANS: As interpreters of the Constitution and overseers of the Bill of Rights, the Supreme Court has a profound influence on the justice system. Some courts, such as the Warren Court in the 1960s, focus on the rights of the accused and expand procedural safeguards, thereby limiting the power of law enforcement. Other courts, such as the current Roberts Court, focus on "law and order" and tend to side with law enforcement, expanding their powers and limiting the rights of defendants. As the court of last resort which has the final say in matters that come before it, Supreme Court decisions become "the law of the land" and both federal and state justice systems must obey them.
REF: 61-63
LO: 2, 7

Chapter 4
Researching the Law

LEARNING OBJECTIVES

Upon completing this chapter, the student will know:

1. The levels at which information about law may be written.
2. What primary and secondary sources are.
3. What secondary sources are available.
4. What a legal citation is and what it includes.
5. What the National Reporter System is.
6. What the components of a legal opinion are.
7. What skills are needed to read case law.
8. What six sections are usually included in a case brief.
9. How to determine whether a case has been overturned or expanded upon.
10. How to distinguish between reliable and questionable information on the Internet.

KEY TERMS

- **affirm**—A court agreeing with a lower court's decision. [p. 80]

- **brief**—A summary presented to the court that describes the manner in which each side in a legal contest thinks the laws should apply to the facts of the case. To brief a case is to outline its pertinent facts. [p. 80]

- **caption**—The title of a case setting forth the parties involved (e.g., *Smith v. Jones*). [p. 79]

- **concurring opinion**—one written by a Justice who agrees with the holding, but who gives additional or different reasons for voting with the majority. [p. 80]

- **dicta**—Statements by a court that do not deal with the main issue in the case, or additional discussions by the court. [p. 81]

- **dissenting opinion**—written by a Justice who disagrees with the holding and voted against the majority. [p. 80]

- **holding**—The rule of law applied to the particular facts of the case and the actual decision. [p. 80]

- **information literacy**—Online research skills that include identifying issue, narrowing topic, locating data, discerning fact from fiction and presenting material in an academic and/or professional manner. [p. 84]

- **legal citation**—A standardized way of referring to a specific element in the law, with three basic parts: a volume number, an abbreviation for the title and a page or section number. [p. 78]

- **National Reporter System**—A private publisher's compilation of case law throughout the United States, organized by regional court systems. [p. 79]

- **popular literature**—Publications written for the layperson (e.g., *Time* or *Newsweek*). [p. 75]

- **primary information sources**—Raw data or the original information. [p. 76]

- **professional literature**—Publications written for the practitioner in the field (e.g., *The Police Chief, Police* or *Corrections Today*). [p. 75]

- **remand**—Return a case to the lower court for further action. [p. 80]

- **reverse**—Overturn the decision of a lower court. [p. 80]

- **scholarly literature**—Publications written for those interested in theory, research and statistical analysis (e.g., *Justice Quarterly*). [p. 76]

- **secondary information sources**—Information based on the raw data or the original information, such as periodicals, treatises/texts, encyclopedias and dictionaries. [p. 76]

- **Shepardizing**—Using the resource *Shepard's Citations*, published for each set of official volumes of cases, indicating whether a case's status has changed. [p. 82]

- **string cites**—Additional legal citations showing where a case may be found in commercial digests. [p. 78]

- **treatise**—A definitive source of material written about a specific topic or area of study. [p. 76]

- **vacate**—set aside or annul a case. [p. 80]

LECTURE OUTLINE

I.   Introduction

II. The Importance of Knowing How to Research the Law

III. Popular, Scholarly and Professional Sources
     A. Popular literature
     B. Professional literature
     C. Scholarly literature

IV. Primary and Secondary Sources
     A. Primary Information Sources
     B. Secondary Information Sources
        1. Legal Periodicals
        2. Treatises/Texts
        3. Legal Encyclopedias
        4. Legal Dictionaries
        5. Other sources

V.   Reading Legal Citations
     A. Legal citations
     B. String cites

VI. Case Law
     A. National Reporter System
     B. Reading Case Law
        1. Caption
        2. Opinions
           a. holding
           b. affirm
           c. reverse
           d. remand
           e. vacate
        3. Concurring and dissenting opinions
     C. Skills Required to Read a Case
     D. Briefing a Case
     E. Brief of *Marbury v. Madison*
     F. Brief of *Miranda v. Arizona*

VII. Shepardizing

VIII. Computerized Legal Research
      A. The Law on the Web
      B. Information Literacy
      C. What's Next?

IX.   Researching a Law of Interest

X.   Summary

CHAPTER SUMMARY

Information may be written at a popular level for the layperson, at a professional level for the practitioner or at a scholarly level for the researcher. Information may be classified as primary or secondary. Primary information is raw data or the original information. Secondary information is based on the raw data or original information. Among the important secondary information sources for legal research are periodicals, treatises/texts, encyclopedias and dictionaries. Many legal citations are found within these information sources. A legal citation is a standardized way of referring to a specific legal source. It has three basic parts: a volume number, an abbreviation for the title and a page or section number. The National Reporter System publishes seven regional sets of volumes, as well as individual sets for specific states.

A legal opinion usually contains (1) a description of the facts, (2) a statement of the legal issues presented for decision, (3) the relevant rules of law, (4) the holding and (5) the policies and reasons that support the holding. The skills and process needed to read case law are (1) thinking in reverse, (2) untangling the interplay of the basic components and (3) drawing inferences.

Most case briefs contain the case name and citation, a summary of key facts, the legal issues involved, the court's decision, the reasons for that decision and any separate opinions or dissents. Shepardizing a case involves using *Shepard's Citations,* a reference that tracks cases so legal researchers can easily determine whether the original holding has been changed through any appeals. An invaluable tool in researching the law is the Internet. To evaluate the reliability of information found on the Internet, consider the credibility of the source and the currency of the information.

SUGGESTED ANSWERS TO THE DISCUSSION QUESTIONS

1. Why is it necessary to know how to research the law?

    As complex as law is, you will inevitably have questions of your own or that others ask you about, for personal or professional reasons. The simple way out (asking someone else) is not always satisfactory. They may not know the correct answer, or in researching the answer additional questions or issues may arise. A requirement of being a professional in any field is knowing how to research your subject matter. Those involved in any area of law, including criminal justice professionals, need to know how to find answers to their questions.

2. What is the danger of relying on only texts to learn about the law?

While textbooks are valuable tools, particularly when learning about a topic in a broad manner, they should not be the only source relied upon. The biggest problem is that texts may be dated. It is not unusual for a textbook to be used in a class a number of years after it is published, and if that book is relied upon as part of one's library after taking the class, it might well provide outdated material. Legal changes occur so frequently that knowing how to locate current information is a professional necessity.

3. What information can be obtained from reading a legal opinion?

Incredible information can be gleaned from reading a legal opinion. Besides learning the parties involved by name, you will come to know the facts, the legal issues, the rule(s) of law, the legal holding and the reasons the judge(s) used in making the decision. Furthermore, valuable insight can be obtained from the manner in which the opinion was written. "Dicta," which does not constitute law per se but more of a legal discussion by the judge writing the opinion, can provide insight into what the court considered in drawing their conclusion and perhaps how other decisions might be decided. Other judges considering the case might provide concurring or dissenting opinions with their own reasons for viewing the case as they did. And rather than just finding out what the law is, an opinion explains *why* this particular law was decided upon.

4. Why can legal research become frustrating?

Probably because it can be never-ending! There is seldom just one answer; rather, it is a little bit like "surfing the Internet"—one concept or idea leads to another, which leads to another, etc. Because no two cases are exactly alike, what lawyers do is consider similar cases and apply the facts and determinations made in them and then argue why their particular case should be decided similarly or differently. As one becomes more proficient in reading and researching the law, answers do come more easily, especially once you learn where to look. To walk into any library, particularly a well-stocked legal library, and just start looking around is a sure way to become frustrated. Legal research is absolutely one of those areas where "practice makes perfect."

5. What are the benefits of actually reading and briefing a case relevant to your specific legal question?

The obvious benefit is that you actually work with the case rather than just scanning it. When dissecting the facts and rules of the case, you develop an intimate and working knowledge of the case, making it much easier to fully understand and appreciate it.

6. Why is a newspaper a legitimate source of legal information?

Perhaps "legitimate" is not the best word here. Certainly a newspaper provides nothing beyond a brief accounting of a case that someone, somewhere has determined newsworthy. While there are writers who have legal backgrounds, and some who have even attended law school in order to apply their academic knowledge to their journalism, this should never be relied upon. About the best a person can count on newspapers for regarding legal issues is identifying a case that that newspaper has decided to include. With that said, it's not really such a bad way to maintain an awareness of what is happening in at least a small corner of the legal world. And to expect very many people to subscribe to many legal digests and periodicals is simply too much to expect. After all, newspapers are the layperson's link with the world "out there."

7. What shortcoming do you think a newspaper might have in providing legal information?

Limited information, written in a nonscholarly format and with only those cases being reported on that someone has determined newsworthy.

8. What problems could arise for any professional not keeping up with the law?

The biggest problem would be in making errors because that pertinent information within that profession has changed. And in the law, particularly in the area of criminal justice, not being updated on changes can result in drastic consequences.

9. How has the Internet changed legal research?

Basically, the Internet has made legal research accessible to anyone. Rather than having to physically go to a law library and learn to use a rather unwieldy system for the layperson, now anyone can find step-by-step instructions to navigate any number of online resources. These include official reporters as well as sources with more generic and introductory information.

10. How would you rate your level of information literacy? What could you do to raise it?

Answers will vary regarding individual levels of information literacy. The best way to improve one's level of information literacy is, like anything else, to practice. The ability to be information-literate does not necessary come naturally or automatically. It takes effort to frame issues in a specific and workable format~ to know where to look and to write well. Like any other skill, the more one does it, the more confident and proficient they become.

STUDENT ACTIVITIES/ASSIGNMENTS

- Students can go to Duke Law's legal research site and download a free PDF version of their site "Legal Research on the Web," a comprehensive listing of the best, and mostly free, legal research sites on the Internet at http://www.law.duke.edu/lib/researchguides/intresearch.

- Assign students to research statutes and case law related to vehicular manslaughter involving alcohol for your county and your state and report their findings to the class.

- Assign students to research national statistics pertaining to the race and ethnicity of perpetrators and victims in capital murder cases (or other topic—see the alphabetical listing on the site) using the Bureau of Justice Statistics website at http://bjs.ojp.usdoj.gov/.

INTERNET CONNECTIONS

- **The Virtual Chase** web site, an informative resource for legal research, is provided by Ballard, Spahr, Andrews & Ingersoll, LLP, at http://www.virtualchase.com/.

- Access the American Bar Association's **Legal Technology Resource Center** web site http://www.abanet.org/tech/ltrc/lawlink/home.html.

- The **Fedlaw** web site, providing references of use to people doing federal legal research, is available at http://www.thecre.com/fedlaw/default.htm.

CHAPTER 4 TEST BANK

Multiple Choice

4.1   When a court sets aside or annuls a decision, it has:
a. reversed the decision.
b. remanded the decision.
c. vacated the decision.
d. overturned the decision.
ANS: C
REF: 80
LO: 6

4.2   When an appeals court reviews a case, it passes judgment on the actions of:
a. the prosecutor.
b. a lower court.
c. a defendant.
d. the police.
ANS: B
REF: 80
LO: 7

4.3   When reading case law, it is helpful to think in reverse because:
a. the opinion usually starts with the holding, which is the end result of the deliberations, and then provides an explanation.
b. the opinion begins with the policies and reasons that support the holding.
c. the reader must research earlier decisions for the rule of law.
d. all cases preceding the ruling are summarized first in the opinion.
ANS: A
REF: 80
LO: 7

4.4   Which of the following is <u>not</u> a primary information source?
a. raw data or the original information.
b. the U.S. Constitution.
c. U.S. Reports.
d. treatises and legal texts.
ANS: D
REF: 76
LO: 2

4.5 Which of the following is an example of a legal citation?
a. 42 USC 1983.
b. *Reader's Digest,* page 25.
c. *Law Week,* Issue 17, page A4.
d. "Reversed and remanded."
ANS: A
REF: 78
LO: 4

4.6 Case law is recorded as:
a. an opinion.
b. a statute.
c. an article.
d. an ordinance.
ANS: A
REF: 79-80
LO: 7

4.7 Traditionally, law has been taught through:
a. the Socratic method.
b. studying case law.
c. reading general statutes.
d. analyzing scenario-based case studies.
ANS: B
REF: 80
LO: 7, 8

4.8 When an appeals court's holding returns the case to the lower court for further action, it is said to have:
a. reversed the decision.
b. remanded the case.
c. concurred with the outcome.
d. affirmed the lower court's ruling.
ANS: B
REF: 80
LO: 7

4.9 *Miranda v. Arizona,* 384 U.S. 436, 86 S.Ct. 1602, 16 L.Ed.2d 694 (1966) is an example of a:
a. secondary source.
b. scholarly literature review.
c. string cite.
d. case brief.
ANS: C
REF: 78
LO: 4

4.10   Publications which examine current case law and which record and critique the activities of legislators and judges, and which discuss legal developments are generally known as:
a. Treatises.
b. Legal periodicals
c. Legal encyclopedias.
d. Legal opinions.
ANS: B
REF: 76
LO: 2, 3

4.11   Professional literature is written for the:
a. layperson.
b. practitioner in a given field.
c. research analyst.
d. undergraduate level student.
ANS: B
REF: 75
LO: 1

4.12   On what page number does this case begin: *Miranda v. Arizona,* 384 U.S. 436 (1966)?
a. 384
b. 436
c. 1,966
d. Not enough information is provided.
ANS: B
REF: 78
LO: 4

4.13   Literature is written for people interested in theory, research, statistical analysis and the like is called:
a. Popular literature
b. Professional literature
c. Technical literature
d. Scholarly literature
ANS: D
REF: 76
LO: 1

4.14   Which of the following statements about the National Reporter System is *not* true?
a. It is the official reporting system for the U.S. Supreme Court.
b. It publishes seven regional sets of volumes.
c. It publishes individual sets of volumes for specific states.
d. It contains court decisions of cases decided from about 1887 to present.
ANS: A
REF: 79
LO: 5

4.15   Primary information sources:
        a. are easier for nonlawyers to understand and work with.
        b. are merely analysis and synthesis of information.
        c. include legal encyclopedias.
        d. include appellate court decisions at the state and federal level.
        ANS: D
        REF: 76
        LO: 2

4.16   The caption of a case tells:
        a. in what other digests the case may be found.
        b. the parties that are involved in a case.
        c. when the case was first filed with the court.
        d. who won the case.
        ANS: B
        REF: 79
        LO: 4, 6

4.17   A legal citation is:
        a. a brief summary of the ruling in a case.
        b. a standardized way of indicating the location of a specific legal document, opinion, or
           publication.
        c. the constitutional definition of a legal term or concept.
        d. an element of common law.
        ANS: B
        REF: 78
        LO: 4

4.18   The ability to effectively identify an issue, narrow that issue, access appropriate online
        sites, separate fact from fiction and present the findings professionally is known as:
        a. dicta
        b. briefing cases
        c. shepardizing
        d. information literacy
        ANS: D
        REF: 84
        LO: 10

4.19   "Briefing" a case means to:
        a. outline the pertinent aspects of the case..
        b. refer it to a lower court.
        c. read about it in the popular literature.
        d. write an opinion about the case.
        ANS: A
        REF: 80
        LO: 8

4.20 A comprehensive text on a legal subject that goes into a specific subject in depth is known as a:
a. legal periodical
b. treatise
c. legal dictionary
d. legal encyclopedia
ANS: B
REF: 76
LO: 3

4.21 A basic professional skill is to regularly review:
a. case briefs.
b. news sources.
c. legal dictionaries.
d. law journals.
ANS: B
REF: 75
LO: 1, 2, 3

4.22 To determine whether a particular case has been overturned or is still good law, you would:
a. remand it.
b. check popular literature.
c. shepardize the case.
d. brief it.
ANS: C
REF: 82
LO: 9

4.23 Many holdings of the Supreme Court are binding on the states through:
a. Marbury v. Madison
b. the Second Amendment
c. Article II of the U.S. Constitution
d. the Fourteenth Amendment
ANS: D
REF: 85
LO: 10

4.24 Which of the following information sources would not be classified as secondary?
a. popular literature.
b. scholarly literature.
c. law school publications, such as the *Harvard Law Review*.
d. state constitutions.
ANS: D
REF: 76
LO: 2, 3

4.25 A legal opinion usually contains all of the following *except*:
a. a description of the facts.
b. a statement of the legal issues presented for decision.
c. concurring or dissenting opinions of the plaintiff.
d. the relevant rules of law.
ANS: C
REF: 80
LO: 6

4.26 *Time* and *Reader's Digest* are examples of:
a. popular literature
b. professional literature
c. primary sources
d. scholarly literature
ANS: A
REF: 75
LO: 1

4.27 Which of the following would <u>not</u> be considered a source of primary information?
a. state legislation
b. state constitutions
c. specialized treatises
d. Congressional statutes
A: C
REF: 76
LO: 2

4.28 The final, official opinions of the Supreme Court of the United States are found only in the printed, bound volumes of:
a. the National Reporter System
b. Westlaw
c. SCOTUS blog
d. the United States Reports
A: D
REF: 78
LO: 2

4.29 *The Police Chief* magazine is an example of:
a. popular literature
b. professional literature
c. primary sources
d. scholarly literature
ANS: B
REF: 75
LO: 1, 3

4.30   Which of the following would *not* be included in a brief?
        a. case name and citation.
        b. summary of key facts.
        c. legal issues involved.
        d. copies of supporting articles.
        ANS: D
        REF: 80
        LO: 8

True/False

4.31   A concurring opinion is one written by a justice who disagrees with the holding and
        voted against the majority.
        ANS: F
        REF: 80
        LO: 6

4.32   One should never infer anything from the decisions made in a judicial opinion.
        ANS: F
        REF: 80
        LO: 7

4.33   Being able to "think in reverse" is a helpful skill in reading case law.
        ANS: T
        REF: 80
        LO: 7

4.34   Wikipedia is considered a reliable source for academic purposes.
        ANS: F
        REF: 75
        LO: 1, 10

4.35   The laws of the U.S. Congress are considered secondary sources.
        ANS: F
        REF: 76
        LO: 2

4.36   Basic legal research skills are as important as any of the more traditional job-related skills
        you pursue in the field of criminal justice.
        ANS: T
        REF: 74
        LO: 1

4.37 A basic rule of legal procedure is that there can be only one opinion written for each case decided in court.
ANS: F
REF: 80
LO: 6

4.38 Most legal encyclopedias make distinct efforts to be objective and noncritical by simply stating the propositions of law and providing an elementary introductory explanation.
ANS: T
REF: 77
LO: 3

4.39 The newspaper is not considered a legitimate source of information regarding the law.
ANS: F
REF: 75
LO: 1

4.40 Not all cases produce opinions, particularly at the trial court level.
ANS: T
REF: 79
LO: 6

Fill-In

4.41 The most authoritative information regarding the law is from a _____ source.
ANS: primary
REF: 76
LO: 2

4.42. *Anderson v. Smith* is an example of a case's _____.
ANS: caption
REF: 79
LO: 7

4.43 The _____ publishes regional sets of appellate opinions, as well as individual sets for specific states.
ANS: National Reporter System
REF: 79
LO: 5

4.44 Legal citations are usually followed by the _____.
ANS: date; date decided
REF: 78
LO: 4

4.45 Judge's thoughts in an opinion on issues not essential to the court's decision, looking at facts or issues other than those needed to determine the case are called _____ and are not binding on future courts.
ANS: dicta
REF: 81
LO: 6

4.46 The *UCLA Law Review,* being a compilation of recently decided cases pertinent to criminal justice professionals, is an example of a _____ information source.
ANS: secondary
REF: 76
LO: 3

4.47 The _____ of a case is the precise statement of the decision reached by a court.
ANS: holding
REF: 80
LO: 6

4.48 When a court agrees with a lower court ruling, they _____ the lower court's decision.
ANS: affirm
REF: 80
LO: 6

4.49 The _____ is an invaluable tool in researching the law and has made the law more readily accessible to the people it is intended to serve.
ANS: Internet
REF: 84
LO: 10

4.50 _____ information is only one part of information literacy; evaluating the validity of the information is also required.
ANS: Locating
REF: 85
LO: 10

Essay

4.51   Explain the difference between primary and secondary information sources, citing examples of each.

ANS: Primary sources present the raw data or the original information and include the U.S. Constitution, the constitutions of the 50 states, the laws of the U.S. Congress, the statutes of the 50 state legislatures, as well as appellate court decisions of the federal and state courts. Secondary sources present data or information based on the original information, and usually include analysis or comments by an author which explains the original or primary source material. Among the important secondary information sources for legal research are periodicals such as the *Harvard Law Review*, treatises and texts, encyclopedias such as *Corpus Juris Secondum*, and legal dictionaries such as *Black's Law Dictionary*.
REF: 76-77
LO: 2

4.52   List and describe the various components of a legal opinion.

ANS: A legal opinion usually contains (1) a description of the facts, (2) a statement of the legal issues presented, (3) the relevant rules of law, (4) the holding, and (5) the policies and reasons that support the holding.
REF: 80
LO: 6

4.53   List the six sections suggested for how to brief a case.

ANS: Most case briefs contain (1) case name and citation, (2) summary of key facts, (3) legal issues involved, (4) the court's decision, (5) the reasons for that decision, and (6) any separate opinions or dissents.
REF: 80-81
LO: 8

4.54   According to the author, what are the three skills required to read a case?

ANS: The skills and process needed to read case law are (1) thinking in reverse, as the opinion provides the end result of the deliberations and you must isolate what the dispute involved, what the trial court decided, how it proceeded, and what happened on appeal; (2) untangling the interplay of the basic components of a judicial opinion, as each affects the others in a complex process; and (3) drawing inferences from the decisions made, as not all of the elements of the judicial opinion may be included..
REF: 80
LO: 7

4.55 Explain what it means to *shepardize* a case and why it is important.

ANS: Shepardizing a case involves using *Shepard's Citations,* a reference that tracks cases so legal researchers can easily determine whether the original holding has been changed through any appeals. The resource provides a list of all the authorities citing a specific case, statute, or other legal authority. This is important because relying on a case that has been overturned or otherwise rendered invalid could prove disastrous.
REF: 82-83
LO: 9

Chapter 5
Equal Protection under the Law:
Balancing Individual, State and Federal Rights

LEARNING OBJECTIVES

Upon completing this chapter, the student will know:

1. What the Thirteenth Amendment provides. The Fourteenth Amendment?
2. How discrimination differs from prejudice.
3. The significance of the *Dred Scott* decision.
4. The Court's holding in *Plessy v. Ferguson*.
5. What Jim Crow laws are.
6. The legislation from the 1960s and 1970s that prohibited discrimination.
7. The intent of affirmative action programs.
8. What Equal Protection Clause violations have occurred in the criminal justice system.
9. How a right differs from a privilege.
10. What Fourteenth Amendment rights prisoners have.
11. How the incorporation doctrine prevents states from infringing on citizens' rights.

KEY TERMS

*   **affirmative action**—Programs created to spread equal opportunity throughout the diverse American population. [p. 100]

*   **American Dream**—The belief that through hard work anyone can have success and ample material possessions. [p. 102]

*   **contextual discrimination**—describes a situation in which racial minorities are treated more harshly at some points and in some places in the criminal-justice system but no differently than whites at other points and in other places. [p. 111]

*   **discrimination**—An action or behavior based on prejudice. [p. 97]

*   **disparate impact**—policies or practices that are not intended to discriminate but, in fact, have a disproportionately negative impact on minorities. [p. 103]

*   **disparate treatment**— *intentional* acts of employment discrimination based on race, color, religion, sex and national origin. [p. 103]

*   **disparity**—a difference, but one that does not necessarily invoke discrimination. [p.110]

- **due process of law**—The Fifth and Fourteenth Amendments' constitutionally guaranteed right of an accused to hear the charges against him or her and to be heard by the court having jurisdiction over the matter. It is the idea that basic fairness must remain part of the process, and it provides rules and procedures to ensure fairness to an individual and to prevent arbitrary actions by government. [p. 94]

- **equal protection of the law**—A constitutional requirement that the government give the same legal protection to all people: like people must be treated in like ways. [p. 94]

- **incorporation doctrine**—Holds that only the provisions of the Bill of Rights that are fundamental to the American legal system are applied to the states through the due-process clause of the Fourteenth Amendment. Also known as selective incorporation. [p. 118]

- **Jim Crow laws**—Laws that strictly segregated blacks from whites in schools, restaurants, streetcars, hospitals and cemeteries. Such laws passed in the American South in the 1800s to discriminate against blacks by restricting certain liberties were accepted by the Supreme Court until 1954, when separate was no longer considered equal. [p. 99]

- **movant**—a party making a motion to the court. [p. 103]

- **preemption**—federal law supersedes state law; if a state law stands as an obstacle to the purposes, objectives, and execution of the federal law, the supremacy clause *preempts* the state law. [p. 109]

- **prejudice**—A negative attitude regarding a person or thing. [p. 97]

- **privilege**—A claim that is not legally protected, in contrast to a right. [p. 116]

- **racial profiling**—The process of using certain racial characteristics, such as skin color, as indicators of criminal activity; acting on personal bias. Illegal race-based enforcement of the law. [p. 111]

- **reverse discrimination**—Giving preferential treatment in hiring and promoting to women and minorities to the detriment of white males. [p. 102]

- **right**—A legally protected claim, in contrast to a privilege. [p. 116]

- **SAR**—(suspicious activity report) an official documentation of observed behavior that may be indicative of intelligence gathering or preoperational planning related to terrorism, criminal or other illicit intention. [p. 95]

- **selective incorporation**—Holds that only the provisions of the Bill of Rights that are fundamental to the American legal system are applied to the states through the due-process clause of the Fourteenth Amendment. Also known as the incorporation doctrine. [p. 118]

- **summary judgment**—a request to the court to review the evidence and, without a trial, reach a decisions to dismiss a case against the movant because there is no dispute of material fact that a jury need resolve. [p. 103]

- **287(g)**—The program, called 287(g) for the section of the law authorizing it, is intended to help local law enforcement agencies assist in enforcing immigration laws by delegating federal immigration enforcement authority to state and local law enforcement agencies. [p. 107]

LECTURE OUTLINE

I. Introduction

II. The Thirteenth Amendment
    A. The Great Debate
    B. The Civil War
    C. The Emancipation Proclamation
    D. Amending the Constitution

III. The Fourteenth Amendment
    A. Preventing state infringement of Constitutional rights
    B. Section 1
        a. Due process of law
        b. Equal protection of the law

IV. The Nationwide Suspicious Activity Reporting (SAR) Initiative (NSI)

V. Familial DNA Database Searches

VI. Discrimination versus Prejudice

VII. The Roots of Racial Discrimination
    A. The *Dred Scott* decision
    B. *Plessy v. Ferguson*
        1. "Jim Crow laws"
    C. The Issue of "Separate but Equal"
        1. *Brown v. Board of Education of Topeka* (1954)
        2. 1964 Civil Rights Act

VIII. The Struggle for Equality
    A. Racial and Gender Discrimination
        1. Equal Pay Act of 1963
        2. Civil Rights Act of 1964

3. Equal Employment Opportunity Act of 1972
4. Title IX of the Education Amendments of 1972

IX. The Rise of Affirmative Action Programs
   A. "Affirmative action"
   B. *Regents of the University of California v. Bakke* (1978)
      1. Other affirmative action cases
   C. The American Dream

X. Reverse Discrimination
   A. Ricci v. Destefano (2009)
   B. Title VII of the Civil Rights Act
      1. Disparate treatment
      2. Disparate impact

XI. Racial and Gender Equality in the Twenty-First Century

XII. Other forms of discrimination
   A. People with disabilities
   B. Sexual orientation

XIII. The Immigration Issue
   A. Section 287(g) of the Immigration and Nationality Act
   B. The 2010 Arizona Immigration Law
      1. Preemption

XIV. Equal Protection in the Criminal Justice System
   A. Discrimination v. disparity
   B. Contextual discrimination
      1. Disproportionate minority contact (DMC)
   C. Discrimination in Law Enforcement
      1. Racial profiling
      2. Fourteenth Amendment Equal Protection Clause
   D. Discrimination in the Courts
      1. Jury selection
      2. Sentencing
         a. Disproportionate punishment
   E. Discrimination in Corrections
      1. The due process revolution
         a. Attica prison riot
         b. *Ex parte Hull* (1941)
         c. *Cooper v. Pate* (1964)
         d. Right v. privilege
         e. The Americans with Disabilities Act
      2. Disciplinary Hearings
      3. Access to Court

CHAPTER SUMMARY

To ensure "liberty and justice for all," two additional amendments were passed. The Thirteenth Amendment, ratified in 1865, abolished slavery. The Fourteenth Amendment, ratified in 1868, granted citizenship to all persons born or naturalized in the United States and forbids states to deny their citizens due process of law or equal protection of the law; that is, it made certain provisions of the Bill of Rights applicable to the states.

These amendments, however, did not eliminate prejudice and discrimination. Prejudice is an attitude; discrimination is a behavior. Racial discrimination in the United States has its roots in our nation's history of slavery. The *Dred Scott* decision (1856) ruled that a freed slave still did not enjoy the right to remain free in a territory where slavery was still legal. *Plessy v. Ferguson* (1896) showed the Court's desire to avoid civil rights issues, declaring discrimination to be outside the realm of the Court. Jim Crow laws strictly segregated Blacks from Whites in schools, restaurants, streetcars, hospitals and cemeteries.

The Court did not directly confront civil rights until the 1950s and 1960s. The Equal Pay Act of 1963, the Civil Rights Act of 1964, the Equal Opportunity Act of 1972 and Title IX of the Education Amendments of 1972 prohibit discrimination based on race, color, religion, sex or national origin in employment and education in public and private sectors at the federal, state and local levels. Affirmative action was created to spread equal opportunity throughout the diverse American population.

The equal protection clause of the Fourteenth Amendment to the Constitution applies to racial profiling. Race-based enforcement of the law is illegal. The equal protection clause also prohibits discrimination in jury selection on the basis of race or gender.

A right is a legally protected claim, whereas a privilege is not necessarily legally protected. For prisoners, cases based on Fourteenth Amendment rights involve equal protection on the basis of race, gender and the availability of facilities and services.

The doctrine of selective incorporation holds that only the provisions of the Bill of Rights that are fundamental to the American legal system are applied to the states through the due process clause of the Fourteenth Amendment. This area is evolving. In addition, controversial areas currently involving constitutional issues and federal powers include the immigration issue and the role of unions in public safety organizations.

SUGGESTED ANSWERS TO THE DISCUSSION QUESTIONS

1. Why was the Fourteenth Amendment necessary?

   Simply, to clearly limit government/police power.

2. Why has the entire Bill of Rights not been embraced by the Fourteenth Amendment?

   While some may argue that the Bill of Rights has, in effect, been applied to the states, the fact remains that the doctrine of "selected incorporation" has not summarily made the entire Bill of Rights directly applicable to the states, even via the Fourteenth Amendment. Perhaps the biggest reason is because the Bill of Rights was *not* drafted for application to the states. However, because of the importance of the majority of the Bill of Rights, they have, slowly but surely, found themselves applicable to state and local governments.

3. Were the framers of the Constitution racist?

   Probably a case could be made that people at that time were racist. For instance, slavery was in existence in the United States, and prominent figures involved in drafting the Constitution were slave owners. Cultures and societal expectations change with time, and it is interesting to note that even individuals who could well be considered racist then developed a basis of government that would help strive to eliminate racism.

4. Why are people prejudiced? Do you recognize your own prejudices?

   Some might argue that everyone is racist to a degree. While entire college courses and a multitude of research papers and other materials have been developed on the topic, people view the world around them based on their own experience. Limited experience, especially, produces limited perspective on differences.

5. Do you think employment quota laws improve things or worsen them? For whom?

   Students' answers may vary significantly. This question is a good class debate topic.

6. Is "separate but equal" possible?

   The U.S. Supreme Court has said no, and it would be interesting for students to argue to the contrary. Again, a possible debate subject.

7. Has the government "gone too far" by requiring all people to be treated equally? Can you think of instances in which different people might not be equally able to do a job?

   Responses to this question could be, and have been, far more extensive than time and space permit. Here we are encouraging students to consider whether, in the name of "equality," people have been encouraged to undertake tasks that they simply can't do.

8. What is your definition of the American Dream? Do you think it is within your reach?

The American Dream means different things to different people. Whether it be financial security, a home or physical security for one's family, the dream really does come down to "security." Whether one feels that it is within their reach is a matter of perspective worthy of discussion.

9. Can law shape attitude?

Definitely. Laws have the ability to directly state what is and isn't acceptable as a societal norm. Even if one disagrees with a particular law, to know that it is the accepted rule of the community makes a definitive statement.

10. Should inmates be allowed to file as many petitions as they please, or should a limit be placed so they would be more selective in bringing up their grievances? Is there a potential for corruption in either scenario?

Students' answers will vary. This question is a good class debate topic.

11. What are your views on the immigration issue?

Students' answers will vary. This question is a good class debate topic. See the student activity related to this question below.

STUDENT ACTIVITIES/ASSIGNMENTS

- Poll the class to determine the rates of support for and opposition to same-sex marriage. Have announced opponents explain why denial of such marriages does not violate the equal protection clause. Allow supporters to respond.

    a. Go to the Oyez Project, listen to the oral arguments, and discuss the ruling in the case of Loving v. Virginia at http://www.oyez.org/cases/1960-1969/1966/1966_395. Discuss how the Supreme Court might rule in a future case regarding this issue using Loving v. Virginia as precedent.
    b. Go to the Bill of Rights Institute and access 'The Defense of Marriage Act" lesson under "Current Events and the Constitution" at http://www.billofrightsinstitute.org/page.aspx?pid=780

- Moderate a class discussion of the question: "Does affirmative action violate the equal protection mandate of the 14th Amendment?"

- Go to the Bill of Rights Institute and access "The Arizona Immigration Law Countersuit" lesson under "Current Events and the Constitution" at http://www.billofrightsinstitute.org/page.aspx?pid=750

INTERNET CONNECTIONS

- Access Cornell Law School's **Legal Information Institute** web site at http://www.law.cornell.edu/wex/index.php/Equal_protection#Federal_Judicial_Decisions for a comprehensive overview of equal protection law.

- View President George W. Bush's Executive Order of December 12, 2002, entitled **Equal Protection of the Laws for Faith-Based and Community Organizations** at http://www.whitehouse.gov/news/releases/2002/12/20021212-6.html.

- Explore three recent Supreme Court cases dealing with "equal rights" at http://www.supremecourt.gov/.

CHAPTER 5 TEST BANK

Multiple Choice

5.1   The Thirteenth Amendment:
a. deals with the right to due process of law.
b. abolished slavery.
c. established prohibition.
d. guarantees equal protection.
ANS: B
REF: 93
LO: 1

5.2   Among other things, the Fourteenth Amendment:
a. permitted blacks to be citizens of the United States.
b. permitted states to determine the citizenship status of blacks.
c. abolished slavery in the territories.
d. overturned the Emancipation Proclamation.
ANS: A
REF: 93
LO: 1

5.3   The case of *Dred Scott v. Sandford* held that:
a. blacks had equal rights with whites.
b. the concept of "separate but equal" was unconstitutional.
c. freed slaves did not have the right to remain free in territory where slavery was still
   legal.
d. states could determine whether ex-slaves could be citizens.
ANS: C
REF: 92
LO: 3

5.4   After the *Plessy* decision, the concept of "separate but equal" became entrenched in the
Southern states through the enactment of:
a. the Civil Rights Act of 1964.
b. school desegregation.
c. Jim Crow laws.
d. the Fourteenth Amendment.
ANS: C
REF: 99
LO: 4, 5

5.5   "Due process of law" means:
       a. all state citizens have the right to a grand jury indictment.
       b. fairness of government actions.
       c. states must treat all citizens equally.
       d. federal law cannot usurp state rights.
       ANS: B
       REF: 94
       LO: 1

5.6   The fundamental provisions of the Bill of Rights have been applied to the states through
       the process of:
       a. stare decisis
       b. judicial activism
       c. summary judgment
       d. selective incorporation
       ANS: D
       REF: 118
       LO: 11

5.7   Which of the following has not been enacted to outlaw discrimination?
       a. the Civil Rights Act.
       b. the Equal Rights Amendment.
       c. the Voting Rights Act.
       d. the Equal Pay Act.
       ANS: B
       REF: 100
       LO: 2, 6

5.8   Which of the following was not one of the pressing issues that led to the Civil War?
       a. state banks and money versus national banks and currency.
       b. freedom versus slavery in the territories.
       c. federal aid versus state aid for improving highways and railways.
       d. racial segregation in the South.
       ANS: D
       REF: 92
       LO: 1

5.9   Title VII prohibits policies or practices that are not intended to discriminate but, in fact,
       have a disproportionately negative effect on minorities, also known as:
       a. disparate treatment.
       b. disparate impact.
       c. reverse discrimination.
       d. preemption.
       ANS: B
       REF: 103
       LO: 6

5.10 The Court acknowledged that virtual exclusion of African-Americans from juries constituted an equal protection violation in:
a. *Adarand v. Pena.*
b. *Norris v. Alabama.*
c. *Swain v. Alabama.*
d. *Batson v. Kentucky.*
ANS: B
REF: 113
LO: 8

5.11 A situation in which racial minorities are treated more harshly at some points and in some places in the criminal justice system, but no differently than whites at other points and in other places best describes:
a. pure discrimination.
b. systematic discrimination.
c. contextual discrimination.
d. discretionary discrimination.
ANS: C
REF: 111
LO: 8

5.12 Sentencing guidelines have reduced:
a. racial disparity.
b. ethnic disparity.
c. death sentences.
d. sentence disparity.
ANS: D
REF: 115
LO: 8

5.13 Which of the following holds that only the provisions of the Bill of Rights that are fundamental to the American legal system are applied to the states through the due process clause of the Fourteenth Amendment?
a. The incorporation doctrine
b. The equal justice clause
c. The selective preemption doctrine
d. The civil liberties proclamation
ANS: A
REF: 118
LO: 11

5.14 The Supreme Court ruling in *United States v. Virginia*, which held that exclusion of females was unconstitutional, involved denial of admission to a:
a. medical school.
b. golf tournament.
c. NASA astronaut training program.
d. military institute.
ANS: D
REF: 100
LO: 6

5.15 Perhaps one of the most fundamental constitutional rights of prisoners is:
a. access to the courts
b. freedom of religion
c. due process in disciplinary hearings
d. freedom of speech
ANS: A
REF: 117
LO: 10

5.16 Discrimination is:
a. an attitude.
b. not punishable by law.
c. a behavior.
d. an unconscious bias learned through socialization.
ANS: C
REF: 97
LO: 2

5.17 Which of the following amendments has most recently been held applicable to the states?
a. Second Amendment right to bear arms.
b. Fifth Amendment guarantee of criminal prosecution only on a grand jury indictment.
c. Seventh Amendment guarantee of a jury trial in a civil case.
d. Fourth Amendment right against unreasonable searches and seizures.
ANS: A
REF: 119
LO: 11

5.18 *Plessy v. Ferguson* held that:
a. our Constitution must be color blind.
b. discrimination was outside the realm of the Court.
c. it is up to legislation to eradicate prejudice.
d. the economic cost of segregation would be staggering.
ANS: B
REF: 99
LO: 4

5.19   The Constitution was originally drafted to limit the power of:
        a. the federal government.
        b. governments of the 13 independent colonial states.
        c. British rule over the colonies.
        d. Congress.
        ANS: A
        REF: 118
        LO: 11

5.20   A major issue facing the criminal justice system today is the growing population of and
        rising crime rates associated with:
        a. juveniles
        b. crack dealers
        c. illegal immigrants
        d. organized biker gangs.
        ANS: C
        REF: 106
        LO: 2, 8

5.21   In which case did the plaintiffs claim that they were being denied their right to equal
        protection of the law and that the laws of "separate but equal" were, in fact, not equal?
        a. *Marbury v. Madison*
        b. *Dred Scott v. Sanford*
        c. *Regents of the University of California v. Bakke*
        d. *Brown v. Board of Education of Topeka*
        ANS: D
        REF: 99
        LO: 5, 11

5.22   The Court's 1964 ruling in *Cooper v. Pate* held that:
        a. inmates retained all of their civil rights.
        b. inmates lost all of their civil rights.
        c. inmates could sue the warden for deprivation of basic rights.
        d. discarding inmates' petitions to the court was unconstitutional.
        ANS: C
        REF: 116
        LO: 10

5.23   State constitutions serve all of the following purposes *except* to:
        a. impose limitations on the exercise of state government's power.
        b. affirm the existence of certain powers.
        c. establish the supremacy of the state constitution over all federal laws and actions.
        d. establish the organization of a state's governing bodies.
        ANS: C
        REF: 118
        LO: 11

5.24   The section of the Civil Rights Act prohibits intentional acts of employment
        discrimination based on race, color, religion, sex, and national origin is:
        a. USC Section 1983
        b. Title VII
        c. Section 287(g)
        d. Title IX
        ANS: B
        REF: 100
        LO: 6

5.25   Prejudice is:
        a. an attitude.
        b. punishable by law.
        c. a behavior.
        d. deemed unconstitutional under the Fourteenth Amendment.
        ANS: A
        REF: 97
        LO: 2

5.26   Amenities such as cable television in prison are considered to be inmate:
        a. pampering.
        b. privileges.
        c. rights.
        d. sanctions.
        ANS: B
        REF: 117
        LO: 9, 10

5.27   Delegation of federal immigration enforcement to state and local law enforcement
        agencies so they may assist in enforcing federal immigration laws is allowed by:
        a. Section 1983 of the U.S. Code
        b. Congress
        c. Section 287(g) of the Immigration and Nationality Act
        d. The Department of Justice
        ANS: C
        REF: 107
        LO: 10

5.28   Inmates can sue for violation of their constitutional rights under:
        a. USC Section 1983
        b. the Civil Rights Act of 1964
        c. the Prisoner's Rights Act of 1992
        d. the Due Process Act of 1978.
        ANS: A
        REF: 116
        LO: 10

5.29 Women were granted the right to vote:
a. through the Emancipation Proclamation.
b. 50 years before discrimination based on race was prohibited.
c. at the same time discrimination based on race was prohibited.
d. 50 years after discrimination based on race was prohibited.
ANS: D
REF: 100
LO: 2

5.30 The landmark case in the issue of affirmative action is:
a. *United Steelworkers of America v. Weber* (1979).
b. *Regents of the University of California v. Bakke* (1978).
c. *United States v. Paradise* (1987).
d. *Fullilove v. Klutznick* (1980).
ANS: B
REF: 100-101
LO: 7

True/False

5.31 The Thirteenth Amendment granted citizenship to the freed slaves.
ANS: F
REF: 93
LO: 1

5.32 Unintentional acts of employment discrimination based on race, color, sex, religion, or national origin are prohibited by Title VII of the Civil Rights Act.
ANS: F
REF: 103
LO: 6

5.33 Affirmative action programs were created to spread equal opportunities throughout the diverse American population.
ANS: T
REF: 100
LO: 7

5.34 Rights and privileges are both legally protected.
ANS: F
REF: 116
LO: 9

5.35 Even after Lincoln issued the Emancipation Proclamation, slavery remained entrenched in the states.
ANS: T
REF: 93
LO: 1

5.36 Full due process rights are afforded to inmates in prison disciplinary proceedings.
ANS: F
REF: 117
LO: 9

5.37 The Bill of Rights was originally meant to apply only to the states, not the national government.
ANS: F
REF: 118
LO: 11

5.38 Jim Crow laws emerged across the south following the Supreme Court's ruling in *Plessy v. Ferguson* (1896).
ANS: T
REF: 99
LO: 4

5.39 Reverse discrimination consists of giving preferential treatment in hiring and promoting women and minorities to the detriment of white males.
ANS: T
REF: 102
LO: 2, 7

5.40 The Equal Protection Clause prohibits discrimination in jury selection only when it is based on race.
ANS: F
REF: 114
LO: 8

Fill-In

5.41 In the *Brown* decision, the Supreme Court ruled that "separate but equal" _____ were illegal.
ANS: schools
REF: 99
LO: 11

5.42 The _____ is the belief that through hard work anyone can have success and ample material possessions.
ANS: American Dream
REF: 102
LO: 7

5.43 _____ programs are sometimes referred to as ethnic-preference or gender-preference programs.
ANS: Affirmative action
REF: 100
LO: 7

5.44 The _____ guarantees that states shall not deny any person due process nor equal protection of the laws.
ANS: Fourteenth
REF: 94
LO: 1

5.45 After the Civil War, many southern states continued discrimination by passing _____ which forbade blacks to vote, serve on juries, hold certain jobs, move freely, own firearms, or gather in groups.
ANS: Black Codes
REF: 93
LO: 1

5.46 _____ is an attitude; discrimination is a behavior.
ANS: prejudice
REF: 97
LO: 2

5.47 _____ segregated blacks from whites in schools, restaurants, and even cemeteries.
ANS: Jim Crow laws
REF: 99
LO: 5

5.48 In *Dred Scott v. Sanford*, the Supreme Court ruled that even _____ could not be citizens and they had "no rights which a white man was bound to respect."
ANS: free blacks
REF: 92
LO: 3

5.49 The incorporation doctrine is also known as the doctrine of _____ incorporation.
ANS: selective
REF: 118
LO: 11

90

5.50   The contention that police single out subjects based solely on the color of their skin frequently leads to allegations of _____.
ANS: racial profiling
REF: 111
LO: 8

Essay

5.51   Discuss what alleged racial disparities exist within our criminal justice system.

ANS: Discrimination has been alleged to exist throughout the criminal justice system, including racial profiling by law enforcement, arrests, biased jury selection and sentencing decisions, and claims of prisoner rights violations in corrections. Minority youths in particular are perceived by many as being treated more harshly and are overrepresented at every decision point in the juvenile justice system.
REF: 110-118
LO: 8

5.52   Explain what the Fourteenth Amendment did and its effect on all U.S. citizens.

ANS: The Fourteenth Amendment granted citizenship to all persons born or naturalized in the United States. It also forbade the states to deny any persons due process or equal protection of the law. Through the process of selective incorporation, most of the provisions of the Bill of Rights have been made applicable to the states through the due process clause of the Fourteenth Amendment. The equal protection clause has had a profound impact on American society, providing the means by which all manner of discrimination has been challenged in the courts, leading to great strides in civil rights for all inhabitants of the U.S.
REF: 93-94
LO: 1

5.53   Describe what affirmative action programs are, where they are used, and discuss whether you feel they are effective. Are they appropriate? Are they fair?

ANS: Affirmative action programs were an attempt to cure or equalize the years of unequal treatment experienced by minorities and women and to prevent such discrimination in the future. They were/are used in employment and educational settings. Opinions regarding the appropriateness or fairness of such programs are highly subjective. Look for well thought-out and defended arguments in students' responses.
REF: 100-103
LO: 7

5.54   Explain the events leading up to the passage of the Thirteenth Amendment and how effective it was.

ANS: President Lincoln was elected on a promise to abolish slavery in the territories. Southern states feared, among other things, that Lincoln would abolish slavery in the states. Several states resolved to withdraw from the Union, thus beginning the Civil War. In 1862, Lincoln threatened to abolish slavery in the rebelling states if they did not return to the Union. They didn't, and Lincoln did, issuing the Emancipation Proclamation in 1863. The Proclamation had little effect. In 1864, an amendment abolishing slavery was proposed and in 1865, the Thirteenth Amendment was ratified. The Thirteenth Amendment, which abolished slavery, was not completely effective, as many southern states continued discrimination by passing "Black Codes," necessitating the passage of the Fourteenth Amendment in an attempt to prevent states from infringing upon the rights of the newly freed slaves.
REF: 92-93
LO: 1

5.55   Discuss the difference between prejudice and discrimination and give examples of each.

ANS: Prejudice is a negative attitude, how one thinks or feels about a specific person or group of people. Discrimination is behavior, overt actions based on prejudice. Examples of prejudice include thinking minorities are unintelligent or unmotivated; examples of discrimination include giving tickets to minority drivers but only warning citations to white drivers, sentencing minorities to hard time while giving white offenders probation for the same offenses, and giving minority inmates less access to reading material or exercise equipment.
REF: 97-98
LO: 2

Chapter 6
The First Amendment: Basic Freedoms

LEARNING OBJECTIVES

Upon completing this chapter, the student will know:

1. The basic freedoms guaranteed in the First Amendment.
2. Whether rights guaranteed in the First Amendment are absolute.
3. What freedoms are included in religious freedom.
4. What the establishment and free exercise clauses guarantee.
5. What freedom of speech guarantees.
6. What type of speech has been restricted by laws passed by Congress.
7. What the "imminent lawless action" test involves and when it is likely to be used.
8. When police officers' speech is protected under the First Amendment.
9. Whether symbolic acts are protected under the First Amendment.
10. What is included in freedom of the press.
11. What basic freedoms prison inmates have.

KEY TERMS

- **balancing test**—A position taken by the appellate courts to balance the needs of society for law and order and for effective law enforcement against the privacy rights of individuals. [p. 142]

- **"clear and present danger" test**—The test of whether words are so potentially dangerous as to not be protected by the First Amendment. Replaced by the "imminent lawless action" test. [p. 141]

- **"clear and probable danger" test**—The test of whether the gravity of the evil discounted by its improbability justifies an invasion of free speech necessary to avoid any danger. [p. 142]

- **establishment clause**—Clause in the First Amendment that states: "Congress shall make no law respecting an establishment of religion." That is, it cannot create a national church. [p. 131]

- **free exercise clause**—Clause in the First Amendment that declares: "Congress shall make no law . . . prohibiting the free exercise * [of religion]." [p. 134]

- **"imminent lawless action" test**—A three-part test that the government must meet if certain communication is not to be protected by the First Amendment: (1) the speaker subjectively intended incitement; (2) in context, the words used were likely to produce imminent, lawless action; and (3) the words used by the speaker objectively encouraged and urged incitement. This test replaced the "clear and present danger" test. [p. 142]

- **judicial activism**—Allowing judges to interpret the Constitution and its amendments. [p. 137]

- **preferred freedoms approach**—A position that stresses that civil liberties are to take precedence over other constitutional values because they are requisite to a democracy. Under this approach, the burden lies with the government to prove clear and present danger exists when a freedom is limited. [p. 143]

- **prior restraint**—A restriction on publishing certain materials; rare in the United States and most other democratic countries. [p. 154]

- **"rational basis" test**—The standard for analyzing not only First Amendment claims by prisoners but also other constitutional claims as well, containing these four criteria: (1) there must be a rational connection between the regulations and legitimate interest put forward to justify it; (2) alternative means of exercising the right must remain open to prison inmates; (3) the regulations must have only a minimal impact on correctional officers and other inmates; and (4) a less restrictive alternative must be available. [p. 161]

- **strict scrutiny**—the legal standard applied to due process analysis of fundamental rights, such as freedom of speech, in which the state must establish it has a compelling government interest that justifies and necessitates the law in question and that the law is narrowly tailored to fit that interest; a very high standard and difficult to defend. [p. 140]

- **symbolic speech**—a form of speech that expresses an idea or emotion without use of words, such as burning one's draft card, bra or flag, or picketing. [p. 148]

LECTURE OUTLINE

I. Introduction
    A. No rights absolute

II. Freedom of Religion
    A. The Establishment Clause
        1. *Hamilton v. Regents of University of California* (1934)
        2. Made applicable to the states in *Everson v. Board of Education* (1947)
        3. *Lemon v. Kurtzman* (1971) and "excessive entanglement"

94

B. The Free Exercise Clause
    1. Made applicable to the states in *Cantwell v. Connecticut* (1940)
    2. The Religious Freedom Restoration Act
    3. Conduct not protected by the freedom of religion clause
C. Interpretations
    1. Judicial activism

III. Freedom of Speech
A. Made applicable to the states in *Gitlow v. New York* (1925)
B. *Fogel v. Collins* (2008)—political rhetoric
C. *United States v. Stevens* (2010)—depiction of animal cruelty
D. *Holder v. Humanitarian Law Project* (2010)
    1. Strict scrutiny
E. Restrictions on Freedom of Speech
    1. The Alien and Sedition Acts of 1798
    2. Espionage Act (1917)
    3. "Clear and present danger" test
    4. "Clear and probable danger" test
    5. "Imminent lawless action" test
        a. Balancing test
        b. Preferred freedoms approach
    6. *Madsen v. Women's Health Center, Inc.* (1994)
    7. *Reno v. American Civil Liberties Union* (1997)

IV. First Amendment Expression Rights of Public Employees
A. The balancing test
B. *Garcetti v. Ceballos* (2006)
    1. Protected only if speech is unconnected to employment

V. Symbolic Expression
A. Flag Burning
    1. *Texas v. Johnson* (1989)
    2. Flag Protection Act of 1989
        a. Declared unconstitutional in 1990.
B. Cross Burning and Bias/Hate Crimes
    1. *R.A.V. v. City of St. Paul* (1992)
    2. *Virginia v. Black* (2003)
C. Nude Dancing
    1. *Barnes v. Glen Theatre* (1991)
D. Yard Signs
    1. *City of Ladue v. Gallileo* (1994)
E. Freedom of Speech and the Internet
    1. Reno v. American Civil Liberties Union (1997)
        a. "Virtual" child Pornography
    2. Child Online Protection Act
        a. Unconstitutional under "strict scrutiny" analysis
F. The Right to Photograph

95

CHAPTER SUMMARY

The First Amendment prohibits Congress from making any laws that abridge or restrict freedom of religion, freedom of speech, freedom of the press or the right to assemble peaceably and to request the government respond to complaints of its citizens. However, no rights are absolute, so government can regulate them when social interests outweigh that of the individual.

Religious freedom includes the freedom to worship, to print instructional material, to train teachers and to organize schools in which to teach, and to be free of government control or interference. The establishment clause of the First Amendment states: "Congress shall make no law respecting an establishment of religion." That is, Congress cannot create a national church or prescribed religion. The free exercise clause of the First Amendment declares that "Congress shall make no law . . . prohibiting the free exercise [of religion]."

Freedom of speech/expression includes the right to speak and the right to be heard. Congress has passed laws to limit speech that advocates overthrowing the government by force. The "clear and present danger" test was replaced by the "imminent lawless action" test to determine when speech should not be protected by the First Amendment. As public employees, law enforcement officers' speech is protected under the First Amendment only if it is (1) a matter of public concern or (2) unrelated to employment.

Symbolic acts are included within the protection of the First Amendment.

Freedom of the press applies to all types of printed and broadcast material, including books, newspapers, magazines, pamphlets, films and radio and television programs.

Prisoners' rights based on the First Amendment involve censorship of mail, expression within the institution, association within the institution, religion, appearance and visitation rights.

SUGGESTED ANSWERS TO THE DISCUSSION QUESTIONS

1. Is the First Amendment the most important amendment?

   This question deals with personal opinions and encourages students to prioritize the importance of various amendments. It would make a good debate subject.

2. Is free speech a right that should be absolute?

   No. The legal maxim that "you can't yell 'FIRE' in a crowded theater if there is no fire" is true. Like government power, our own rights are limited. It was never the intent that the Constitution grant absolute rights, only for people to be free from unreasonable interference from government. There are always reasonable limitations on what we can say and do.

3. Speaking from an historical perspective, why do you think the framers of the Constitution placed so much importance on the First Amendment?

   A likely perspective is that, for change to occur, one must be able to speak about problems they perceive with the government. Being able to say what is on one's mind and being able to hear the opinions of others is the basis for a strong and free society.

4. Should the government tolerate people speaking against or criticizing it?

   A strong government is one that is confident enough to permit people to criticize it, with the end result being an even stronger government. A government that does not tolerate criticism is one that becomes less and less responsive to the people it is meant to serve.

5. Should an amendment to ban burning the American flag be passed?

   This is a very personal, political question, one which requires the student to take a position. This question may provide insight into how sensitive such issues can be and how difficult, if not impossible, a definitive answer can be. Another possible class debate subject.

6. Imagine you are an attorney asked to defend nude dancing as an act of expression that should be allowed in a small-town bar. What would you say to represent your client's interests? Include an explanation of how nude dancing could ever be considered "speech."

This question encourages students to stretch their understanding of the First Amendment. Allow the class to discuss their views on this question.

7. Discuss whether Nazi Germany could have gone as far as it did if a similar First Amendment had been present in Germany.

This question requires students to assess the effectiveness of free speech. In Nazi Germany, as with dictatorships existing today, intimidation is a major reason why the government is able to continue unchallenged.

8. Should all schools, public and parochial, receive equal support from the government?

Another personal, political and religious question. The student of the Constitution is required to consider many aspects of the framework of our government in setting forth their personal opinion in response to this question.

9. Should there be any restrictions on public (i.e., government) employees' freedom of speech? Should it matter if the employee is speaking as a citizen on a matter of public concern? If yes, what would comprise an adequate justification from the employer to treat the employee differently than a regular citizen?

Students should relate their opinions to the *Pickering*, *Connick*, and *Garcetti* cases.

10. Discuss whether the U.S. government is hypocritical when, on the one hand, freedom of religion is guaranteed, but, on the other hand, Christianity is so obviously stated in the words of the Pledge of Allegiance, the fact that clergy are assigned to Congress and the like.

This is another possible debate topic. Students are encouraged to share their personal opinions and support it with what they now know about constitutional law.

STUDENT ACTIVITIES/ASSIGNMENTS

- Listen to the Supreme Court oral arguments in Texas v. Johnson at the Oyez Project at the IIT Kent-Chicago College of Law website at http://www.oyez.org/cases/1980-1989/1988/1988_88_155. Identify proponents and opponents of flag burning as a protected form of expression (free speech). Moderate a discussion of the opposing views.

- "Student Expression in the Age of Columbine" is available as a free PDF download from Vanderbilt University's First Amendment Center and would make an excellent topic for class discussion. http://www.firstamendmentcenter.org/publications

- Obtain a copy of the Sundance Channel/Court TV DVD *The First Amendment Project*. Show each of its three segments to the class and discuss each issue.

- Access the 18 minute CBS news clip "Should First Amendment Protection Include Corporations?" on YouTube at http://www.youtube.com/watch?v=n57Fsnd6Im8&feature=fvsr.

- Obtain a copy of the HBO documentary "Shouting Fire: Stories from the Edge of Free Speech" which "examines the balancing act between protecting both civil liberties and national security in a post-911 world." (HBO store)

INTERNET CONNECTIONS

- An intriguing example of free speech is available at the **Reporters Committee for Freedom of the Press** web page http://www.rcfp.org/index.php depicting its *First Amendment Handbook*, accessible at http://www.rcfp.org/handbook/index.html.

- The American Library Association presents Notable First Amendment Court Cases at http://www.ala.org/ala/aboutala/offices/oif/firstamendment/courtcases/courtcases.cfm

- More information regarding public employee First Amendment rights can be accessed at the "Exploring Constitutional Conflicts" page of the University of Kansas City, Missouri's "Exploring Constitutional Law" website at http://law2.umkc.edu/faculty/projects/ftrials/conlaw/publicemployees.htm.

CHAPTER 6 TEST BANK

6.1   The First Amendment specifically prohibits Congress from making any laws that restrict freedom of religion, speech, press, assembly, and:
        a. privacy.
        b. to petition the government.
        c. the presumption of innocence.
        d. travel.
        ANS: B
        REF: 128
        LO: 1

6.2   Protected forms of speech include all of the following, except:
        a. burning the American flag.
        b. protesting abortion clinics.
        c. advocating the violent overthrow of the government.
        d. swearing at a law enforcement officer.
        ANS: C
        REF: 142
        LO: 1, 2, 5

6.3   Which of the following is a permissible restriction on speech?
        a. Defamation.
        b. Political rhetoric
        c. Criticism of the government
        d. Depictions of animal cruelty
        ANS: A
        REF: 138-139
        LO: 6

6.4   As _____, law enforcement officers' speech is protected by the First Amendment only if it is a matter of public concern or unrelated to employment.
        a. officers of the court
        b. members of the Executive branch
        c. public employees
        d. private citizens
        ANS: C
        REF: 148
        LO: 9

100

6.5   The Supreme Court upheld prison regulations that are "reasonably related to legitimate penological interests" using the:
a. clear and present danger test
b. rational basis test
c. strict scrutiny test
d. clear and probable danger test
ANS: B
REF: 161
LO: 11

6.6   *Hamilton v. Regents of the University of California* (1934), involving compulsory military training, was one of the earliest cases regarding:
a. freedom of the press.
b. freedom of religion.
c. freedom of speech.
d. freedom to assemble.
ANS: B
REF: 131
LO: 3

6.7   In *Everson v. Board of Education* (1947), the Supreme Court cited Thomas Jefferson, stating that the _____ was intended to erect a "wall of separation between Church and State."
a. establishment of religion clause
b. free exercise clause
c. separation of parochial and secular schools
d. "excessive entanglement" test
ANS: A
REF: 132
LO: 1, 2, 4

6.8   Freedom of the press protects:
a. the right to publish information without governmental control.
b. magazine publishers from being told they can't print obscene material.
c. the public from the publication of offensive material.
d. press premises from being searched by law enforcement.
ANS: A
REF: 154
LO: 10

6.9   The Espionage Act, passed by Congress in 1917:
      a. empowered the President to expel "dangerous aliens."
      b. made it illegal to interfere with recruiting or drafting soldiers or any act that adversely
         affected military morale.
      c. made it illegal to write or speak "with the intent to defame" the government.
      d. made it illegal to provide material support to terrorist organizations.
      ANS: B
      REF: 141
      LO: 6

6.10 The 'Lemon' test regarding separation of church and state required that any law
      challenged under the establishment clause must meet all of the following criteria, except:
      a. have a primary secular purpose.
      b. have a principle effect that neither advances nor inhibits religion.
      c. have a principle effect that either advances or inhibits religion.
      d. not generate excessive entanglement between government and religion.
      ANS: C
      REF: 132
      LO: 4

6.11 The right to peaceful assembly:
      a. permits anyone to enter private property to assert protected speech.
      b. involves the right to assemble in public places.
      c. permits demonstrations on the property of private abortion clinics.
      d. cannot be restricted under any circumstances.
      ANS: B
      REF: 158-159
      LO: 1, 2

6.12 Which of the following is not subject to regulation by the state to protect societal interests
      under the free exercise clause?
      a. Performance of autopsies.
      b. Requiring Boy Scouts to promise to "Love God."
      c. Requiring Amish to put orange reflectors on their buggies.
      d. Ingestion of illegal drugs in religious ceremonies.
      ANS: B
      REF: 135-136
      LO: 2, 4

6.13   Control of the press during the Persian Gulf War was:
        a. absolute.
        b. close to 100 percent.
        c. fairly lax.
        d. nonexistent.
        ANS: B
        REF: 155
        LO: 10

6.14 . Under the First Amendment, there is an absolute freedom to:
        a. speak
        b. act
        c. protest
        d. believe
        ANS: D
        REF: 134
        LO: 1, 2, 3

6.15   Judicial activism is:
        a. unconstitutional.
        b. when judges interpret the Constitution and its amendments
        c. a violation of due process.
        d. all of the above.
        ANS: B
        REF: 137
        LO: 1, 2

6.16   The Supreme Court struck down a law banning computer-generated or "virtual" child
        pornography in:
        a. *Prewitt v. State of Arizona ex rel. Eyman* (1969).
        b. *Procunier v. Martinez* (1974).
        c. *City of Ladue v. Gilleo* (1994).
        d. *Reno v. American Civil Liberties Union* (1997).
        ANS: D
        REF: 152
        LO: 4, 5

6.17   The Supreme Court ruled that cities may not prohibit yard signs in:
        a. *Prewitt v. State of Arizona ex rel. Eyman* (1969).
        b. *Procunier v. Martinez* (1974).
        c. *City of Ladue v. Gilleo* (1994).
        d. *Reno v. American Civil Liberties Union* (1997).
        ANS: C
        REF: 152
        LO: 5, 9

6.18 The Smith Act (1940):
   a. banned nude dancing.
   b. made it unlawful to advocate overthrowing the government by force.
   c. established national standards for obscenity.
   d. established the 'clear and probable danger' test.
   ANS: B
   REF: 142
   LO: 6

6.19 In order for speech to be considered obscene, and thus not protected by the First Amendment, it must be all of the following *except*:
   a. the work arouses erotic sexual interest.
   b. the work taken as a whole appeals to the prurient interest in sex.
   c. it portrays sexual conduct in a patently offensive way.
   d. the work taken as a whole does not have a serious literary, artistic, political or scientific value.
   ANS: A
   REF: 146
   LO: 6

6.20 Which of the following is not part of the three-part test in determining "imminent lawless action"?
   a. The speaker subjectively intended incitement.
   b. In context, the words used were likely to produce imminent, lawless action
   c. the words used by the speaker objectively encouraged and urged incitement.
   d. the words used by the speaker caused excitement.
   ANS: D
   REF: 142
   LO: 7

6.21 Religious freedom includes all of the following, except:
   a. the freedom to worship.
   b. freedom to print instructional material.
   c. freedom to train teachers.
   d. prayer conducted in public schools.
   ANS: D
   REF: 131
   LO: 3

6.22   Freedom of the press was made binding on the states through the Fourteenth Amendment in *Near v. Minnesota* (1931), in which the Supreme Court ruled that:
a. no newspaper could be banned because of its contents, regardless how scandalous.
b. obscenity is not a constitutionally protected form of speech.
c. government may halt publication of books that endanger national security.
d. the press has no constitutional right to disregard promises of confidentiality.
ANS: A
REF: 155
LO: 10

6.23   "Whether the gravity of the evil discounted by its improbability, justifies such invasion of free speech as is necessary to avoid the danger" is called the:
a. clear and probable danger test
b. clear and present danger test
c. imminent lawless action test
d. imminent probable danger test
ANS: A
REF: 142
LO: 6

6.24   The Supreme Court justified the screening of inmate mail in:
a. *Prewitt v. State of Arizona ex rel. Eyman* (1969).
b. *Procunier v. Martinez* (1974).
c. *City of Ladue v. Gilleo* (1994).
d. *Reno v. American Civil Liberties Union* (1997).
ANS: A
REF: 161
LO: 11

6.25   The establishment clause of the First Amendment sets forth all of the following, except:
a. Congress shall make no law respecting an establishment of religion.
b. Congress is prohibited from establishing a national church.
c. Congress may establish a national church if three-fourths of the states vote to ratify.
d. government cannot show preference to any particular religion.
ANS: C
REF: 131
LO: 4

6.26 In the case of *Texas v. Johnson* (1989), the Supreme Court ruled: "If there is a bedrock principle underlying the First Amendment, it is that the government may not prohibit the expression of an idea simply because society finds the idea itself offensive or disagreeable." This case involved:
a. child pornography
b. flag burning
c. cross burning
d. nude dancing
ANS: B
REF: 150
LO: 9

6.27 The Supreme Court placed restrictions on the censorship of inmate mail in:
a. *Prewitt v. State of Arizona ex rel. Eyman* (1969).
b. *Procunier v. Martinez* (1974).
c. *City of Ladue v. Gilleo* (1994).
d. *Reno v. American Civil Liberties Union* (1997).
ANS: B
REF: 161
LO: 11

6.28 The Supreme Court held that obscenity is not a constitutionally protected form of free speech in:
a. *Near v. Minnesota*.
b. *Cohen v. Cowles Media Company*.
c. *Roth v. United States*.
d. the *Zenger* case.
ANS: C
REF: 155
LO: 6

6.29 Standards to define *obscenity* were set forth in:
a. *Near v. Minnesota*.
b. the *Zenger* case.
c. *Edwards v. City of Goldsboro, NC.*
d. *Miller v. California.*
ANS: D
REF: 155
LO: 10

6.30   The first guarantee to be made applicable to the states through incorporation was:
        a. freedom of religion.
        b. freedom to assemble.
        c. freedom of speech.
        d. freedom of the press.
        ANS: C
        REF: 138
        LO: 1

True/False

6.31   Many states apply a higher fighting words standard to law enforcement officers because
        they are expected to exercise a higher degree of restraint than the average citizen.
        ANS: T
        REF: 146
        LO: 7

6.32   In *Virginia v. Black,* the Supreme Court ruled the singular act of cross burning was not a
        form of free speech protected by the First Amendment.
        ANS: F
        REF: 151
        LO: 9

6.33   The Supreme Court has ruled that states cannot require children to pledge allegiance to
        the United States each day.
        ANS: T
        REF: 135
        LO: 1, 4

6.34   The Supreme Court has ruled that Americans have a free-speech right to pass out
        anonymous political pamphlets.
        ANS: T
        REF: 156
        LO: 10

6.35   The United States has been a model of religious tolerance throughout history.
        ANS: F
        REF: 130
        LO: 1

6.36   Any officer who speaks in public on an employment matter is not protected by the First
        Amendment.
        ANS: T
        REF: 148
        LO: 8

6.37 In the 1999 case of *Chicago v. Morales*, the Supreme Court upheld an "anti-loitering" ordinance, stating that the definition of illegal loitering as "to remain in any one place with no apparent purpose" was not unconstitutionally vague.
ANS: F
REF: 158
LO: 1

6.38 The court has <u>no</u> duty to protect those who come before it from undue adverse publicity.
ANS: F
REF: 157
LO: 10

6.39 In *Virginia v. Black* (2003), the Supreme Court held that a law banning cross burning as a hate crime itself is unconstitutional because the law presumes hate is the purpose—without more evidence, cross burning is deemed a protected form of speech.
ANS: T
REF: 151
LO: 9

6.40 Government's restriction of the press through use of prior restraint is rare in the United States and most other democratic countries.
ANS: T
REF: 154
LO: 10

Fill-In

6.41 The First Amendment provision that prohibits the government from creating a national church is the _____ clause.
ANS: establishment
REF: 131
LO: 4

6.42 The Religious Freedom Restoration Act of 1993 was declared _____ by the Supreme Court.
ANS: unconstitutional
REF: 162
LO: 11

6.43 In upholding the free speech right of anonymous pamphleteering, the Supreme Court held that "Anonymity is a shield from the tyranny of the _____."
ANS: majority
REF: 156
LO: 10

6.44   The act making it illegal to provide material support to any group that has been designated by the Attorney General as a "foreign terrorist organization" is the
_____.
A: USA Patriot Act, or Patriot Act
REF: 140
LO: 6

6.45   In determining when speech should not be protected, the courts replaced the clear and present danger test with the _____ test.
ANS: imminent lawless action
REF: 142
LO: 7

6.46   No rights are absolute, so government can regulate them when _____ outweigh those of the individual.
ANS: societal interests
REF: 129
LO: 2

6.47   The constitutionality of prison regulations that restrict prisoners' First Amendment rights are judged by using a _____ test.
ANS: rational basis
REF: 161
LO: 11

6.48   Balancing society's need for law and order and for effective law enforcement against the _____ of individuals is known as the balancing test.
ANS: privacy rights
REF: 142
LO: 7

6.49   The free exercise of religion involves both the freedom to believe and the freedom to
_____.
ANS: act
REF: 134
LO: 3, 4

6.50   Historically, freedom of the press has been attached to the general concept of
_____.
ANS: censorship
REF: 154
LO: 10

Essay

6.51   Rank the four basic freedoms guaranteed by the First Amendment in descending order of importance to you, then explain why you rank them as you do.

ANS: The four basic First Amendment freedoms addressed in this chapter include freedom of religion, freedom of speech, freedom of the press and freedom of peaceable assembly. Students' rankings and reasons will vary.
REF: 128
LO: 1

6.52   Discuss the delicate balance being struck by the Court in achieving the separation of church and state in schools.

ANS: Made applicable to the states in *Everson v. Board of Education* (1947), the Court ruled in this case that no constitutional violation occurred, as the reimbursement policy applied to parochial and public school students alike. Later cases ruled that reading Bible verses and moments of silence for meditation or voluntary prayer were unconstitutional. In the *Lemon* case, the Court found secular and religious education so tightly intertwined that supporting one without supporting the other would be virtually impossible. Laws requiring the posting of the Ten Commandments have been struck down, but students have been given the right to hold religious meetings in public high schools outside class hours. The issue is a case-by-case challenge to the Court and ultimately, no clear set of rules has been defined to determine the outcomes of these types of cases.
REF: 131-133
LO: 3, 4

6.53   Discuss the constitutionality of flag burning. Explain your feelings about this symbolic act and whether it should be constitutionally protected.

ANS: Although highly controversial, flag burning is *not* unconstitutional. Proposed constitutional amendments to ban flag desecration have been narrowly defeated several times. In its landmark *Texas v. Johnson* (1989) ruling, the Supreme Court held that burning an American flag as a political protest is "symbolic speech" protected by the First and Fourteenth Amendments. In response Congress passed the Flag Protection Act of 1989 which, in *United States v. Eichman* (1990), the Court struck down on the grounds set forth in *Johnson*. Students' opinions on this issue will vary.
REF: 150
LO: 9

6.54   Discuss the evolution of the "imminent lawless action" test.

ANS: Restrictions on freedom of speech began with the Alien and Sedition Acts of 1798. There followed the Espionage Act of 1917, and the Court's application of a "clear and present danger" test in 1925 and a "clear and probable danger" test in 1951. *Brandenburg v. Ohio* (1969) led to adoption of the "imminent lawless action" test, a three-part test to determine whether certain communication intentionally urges incitement and, thus, is not protected by the First Amendment. The approach has also been called the balancing test. Such a test might be used to determine if statements or other speech were used so as to create a threat to public safety or to incite others to commit lawless acts.
REF: 141-142
LO: 7

6.55   Discuss how protestors are protected and restricted by the First Amendment.

ANS: The First Amendment protects protestors' right to speak out about issues and to gather peacefully, on public or quasi-public property, to demonstrate their causes. It restricts their ability to infringe on others' privacy rights, to interfere with public access to businesses, or to engage in any unlawful activity in support of their demonstration (vandalism, noise ordinances, harassment, assault, etc.; refer to Table 6.2.)
REF: 157-159
LO: 1, 5, 6

Chapter 7
The Second Amendment: The Gun Control Controversy

LEARNING OBJECTIVES

Upon completing this chapter, the student will know:

1. Historically, who was included in the militia and what was required of them.
2. What a central controversy over the Second Amendment involves.
3. Whether the number of militia groups in the United States is growing or decreasing.
4. What opposing interpretations of the Second Amendment have clashed over the years.
5. Whether the Supreme Court has interpreted the Second Amendment right to bear arms as an individual or a state right.
6. If the Second Amendment has been incorporated into the Fourteenth Amendment and the case that determined this.
7. What the Brady Law accomplished.
8. What the Law Enforcement Officer's Safety Act (LEOSA) allows and what its three goals are.

KEY TERMS

- **castle law**—a legal claim based on English common law that designates one's place of residence (or, in some states, any place legally occupied such as one's car or place of work) as a place in which one enjoys legal protection from illegal trespassing and violent attack. [p. 178]

- **commerce clause**—section of the U.S. Constitution (Article 1, Section 8, Clause 3) that provides the legal foundation for much of the federal government's regulatory authority, including firearms. [p. 172]

- **demurrer**—A request that a suit be dismissed because the facts do not sustain the claim against the defendant. [p. 173]

- *dictum*—The statement by a court that does not deal with the main issue in the case, or an additional discussion by the court. [p. 176]

- **militia**—An armed group of citizens who defend their community as emergencies arise. [p. 169]

- **operative clause**—identifies the action to be taken or prohibited. [p. 172]

- **prefatory clause**—announces a purpose, but does not necessarily restrict the operative clause. [p. 172]

- **prohibited persons**—Individuals to whom, under the Gun Control Act, it is forbidden to sell firearms. [p. 181]

- **straw purchase**—an illegal transaction when a buyer uses an intermediary (the "straw man" to purchase a firearm(s) from a licensed firearms dealer and then sells the weapons(s) to individuals who cannot legally buy guns themselves, such as felons and the severely mentally retarded. [p. 190]

- **sunset clause**—A set ending time for legislation that is not renewed to prevent old law from remaining on the books. [p. 183]

LECTURE OUTLINE

I.   Introduction

II.   Historical Background
       A. Militia

III.   The Debate: Interpreting the Second Amendment
       A. Modern Day Militias in the United States
              1. Ruby Ridge
              2. Montana "Freemen"
              3. Dramatic increase in extremist groups

IV.   Balancing Individual and States' Rights
       A. Individual Rights
       B. States' Rights
              1. Commerce clause

VI.   Early Case Law Regarding the Second Amendment: A Slow Start
       A. *United States v. Cruikshank* (1875)
       B. *United States v. Miller* (1939)
       C. *Stevens v. United States* (1971)

VII.   A Shift in Interpretation: The *Heller* Decision
       A. *District of Columbia v. Heller* (2008)

VIII. Incorporation of the Second Amendment
       A. *Presser v. Illinois* (1886)
       B. *McDonald v. Chicago* (2010)
              1. Incorporated the Second Amendment to the states through the due process clause of the Fourteenth Amendment

CHAPTER SUMMARY

Historically, the militia was considered to be the entire adult male populace of a state. They were not simply allowed to keep arms, but were at times *required* to do so by law. A central controversy over the Second Amendment is whether people have a right to bear arms as individuals rather than only as part of a militia. The number of militia groups in the United States increased dramatically from 2008 to 2009.

The two opposing interpretations of the Second Amendment involve whether the amendment guarantees individuals' rights to keep and bear arms or whether it guarantees the states freedom from federal government infringement on this right. Judicial decisions over time reveal changes in how the Court has viewed Second Amendment guarantees. In *United States v. Miller* (1939) the court recognized a state right rather than an individual right to bear arms. In 1971 the courts ruled that there was no express right of an individual to keep and bear arms (*Stevens v. United States*). Both decisions have since been reversed.

In a landmark decision, the Supreme Court stated in *District of Columbia v. Heller* (2008) that the Second Amendment protects an individual's right to possess a firearm unconnected with service in a militia. In *McDonald v. Chicago* (2010) the Supreme Court, holding that the right to keep and bear arms was among those fundamental rights necessary to our system of ordered liberty, ruled that the Second Amendment *does* apply to the states and incorporated it under the Fourteenth Amendment.

The Brady Act, passed in 1993, contained the interim provision of a mandatory five-day waiting period on all handgun purchases. This provision was phased out and was replaced in 1998 with the permanent provision of an instant, computerized criminal background check of all handgun purchasers. Some states still impose a waiting period on firearms purchases.

The Law Enforcement Officers Safety Act allowing "qualified" active and retired law enforcement officers to carry concealed weapons anywhere in the United States has three goals: (1) to establish equality between local LEOs and their federal counterparts who already carry nationwide, (2) to create an unpaid homeland security force to help protect the nation, and (3) to allow qualified current and retired LEOs the means to defend themselves and families against criminals.

SUGGESTED ANSWERS TO THE DISCUSSION QUESTIONS

1. What makes gun control such a volatile issue?

   As one of the most heated political debates, many factors go into the gun control issue. With respect to those on one side or the other, this text does not take a position. However, certainly government control is an important issue here-what control should/does government have over restricting firearms possession?

2. Should the government control the possession of guns?

   Students' answers will vary. This question makes a good class debate subject.

3. Should the government restrict certain types of firearms?

   Rather than focus only on guns in this question, perhaps the question could be broadened to inquire whether government should restrict *any* activities. The answer would include whether government has certain legitimate needs to restrict such activities and how a balancing approach would need to be involved in such decisions.

4. Does the Brady Act serve a legitimate function?

   Again, students' responses will vary. Have the class discuss and debate this question.

5. Considering the history behind the drafting of the Second Amendment, can any original interpretations reasonably be used today? If so, how?

   This is an excellent question to encourage students to consider how the country, its people and its needs have changed over more than 200 years, if they've changed that much at all.

6. In Great Britain, police officers do not routinely carry firearms because, among other reasons, firearms are not considered the public threat they are elsewhere. Discuss whether you think this could ever occur in the United States.

   A philosophical question at least, this requires the student to consider whether "tradition" would influence America as it has in Great Britain. This question calls for personal, philosophical and political discussion. It may also be interesting to have students discuss, or actually research, what percentage of the American public owns firearms and any recent events involving public use of firearms.

7. Discuss whether gun control is crime control.

   Another good debate question.

8. Is a "cooling off" period for gun permits reasonable?

   At the root of this question is whether legislation is effective in controlling crime.

9. Does regulating handguns but not rifles and shotguns make sense?

   Again, a philosophical and perhaps political conclusion will need to be drawn by the student. Have the class discuss and debate their views.

10. Rewrite the Second Amendment as though you were asked to address contemporary concerns.

Considering the issues, history, needs and concerns of both sides, what better way can the student draft this amendment? It may be interesting to try allowing some individuals to rewrite this amendment and having other students work in groups to try and draft a new version. Is there more liberalism evident in the wording of either type of effort, singular or group?

STUDENT ACTIVITIES/ASSIGNMENTS

- Assign students questions to debate (or write essays on) from "A Right to Bear Arms?"at the "Exploring Constitutional Conflicts" page of the University of Kansas City, Missouri's "Exploring Constitutional Law" website at http://law2.umkc.edu/faculty/projects/ftrials/conlaw/beararms.htm.

- Research the concealed carry law, if any, for your state. If no concealed carry law exists, research any legislative bills that may have attempted to create legislation and the reasons they failed.

- Have students research state "castle laws"—nicknamed "Make My Day" and "Stand Your Ground" in some states. Have these laws been used in any cases of self-defense?

INTERNET CONNECTIONS

- Watch "Bowling for Columbine."

- See the **American Civil Liberty Union**'s stance on gun control at their web site, accessible at http://www.aclu.org/police/gen/14523res20020304.html.

- **about.com** offers a wide variety of articles and links on gun control, the Second Amendment, and gun control laws, available at http://usgovinfo.about.com/od/guncontrol/Gun_Control_and_the_Second_Amendment.htm.

CHAPTER 7 TEST BANK

Multiple Choice

7.1   In _____, a federal circuit court ruled in *Stevens v. United States* that there was no express Constitutional right of an individual to keep and bear arms.
a. 1801
b. 1871
c. 1921
d. 1971
ANS: D
REF: 174
LO: 4

7.2   A critical question regarding the interpretation of the Second Amendment is the definition of:
a. people.
b. a militia.
c. arms.
d. well-regulated.
ANS: B
REF: 169
LO: 4

7.3   The Southern Poverty Law Center documented a _____ in the number of active Patriot groups in 2009.
a. 244 percent increase
b. 58 percent decrease
c. 24 percent increase
d. 44 percent decrease
ANS: A
REF: 170
LO: 3

7.4   The central controversy of the Second Amendment has been whether:
a. the government should be involved in regulating the militia.
b. the militia should consist of professional soldiers or volunteers.
c. people have a right to bear arms as individuals rather than only as part of a militia.
d. arms are necessary for the proper functioning of a militia.
ANS: C
REF: 169
LO: 2

7.5   The first notable case involving the Second Amendment was the 1875 decision in:
        a. *Presser v. Illinois.*
        b. *United States v. Miller.*
        c. *United States v. Cruikshank.*
        d. *Stevens v. United States.*
        ANS: C
        REF: 173
        LO: 4

7.6   Which of the following is not one of the disqualifying criteria under federal gun control laws?
        a. Fugitive
        b. Drug user
        c. On terrorism watch list
        d. Convicted felon
        ANS: C
        REF: 182
        LO: 4

7.7   To date, federal courts have held that the Constitution:
        a. guarantees the absolute right of any American citizen to keep and bear arms.
        b. still does not guarantee an absolute right to keep and bear arms.
        c. is irrelevant in issues concerning private possession of firearms.
        d. the federal courts have not addressed the Second Amendment.
        ANS: B
        REF: 175
        LO: 5, 6

7.8   The law banning the manufacturing of 19 different semiautomatic guns with multiple assault-weapon features is the:
        a. Violent Crime Control and Law Enforcement Act of 1994.
        b. Brady Act.
        c. Omnibus Crime Control and Safe Streets Act.
        d. Federal Firearms Act.
        ANS: A
        REF: 183
        LO: 4

7.9   Individual rights proponents claim that:
        a. only military and law enforcement personnel have a right to possess firearms.
        b. citizens should be permitted to possess only a single, individual weapon, not an entire arsenal.
        c. the framers of the Constitution intended to preserve individual rights above state rights.
        d. during national emergencies, individuals should be allowed to choose whether they want to keep and bear arms to help defend the country.
        ANS: C
        REF: 172
        LO: 4

7.10   In *United States v. Lopez* (1995), the U.S. Supreme Court:
        a. affirmed the constitutionality of the Gun-Free School Zones Act.
        b. struck down the Gun-Free School Zones Act as being unrelated to interstate commerce and, therefore, unconstitutional.
        c. upheld a municipal ordinance banning all handguns, shotguns with barrels less than 18 inches and guns firing more than eight shots in repetition.
        d. struck down a municipal ordinance banning all handguns, shotguns with barrels less than 18 inches and guns firing more than eight shots in repetition.
        ANS: B
        REF: 178
        LO: 4, 5

7.11   During the colonial period, the militia was considered to be:
        a. the Continental Army.
        b. enlisted minutemen.
        c. the entire male populace of a state.
        d. the entire national population.
        ANS: C
        REF: 169
        LO: 1

7.12   States' rights proponents asserted that:
        a. everyone in the state has a right to keep and bear arms.
        b. gun control should not be the business of federal government.
        c. the Second Amendment was adopted with the primary purpose of preserving the state militia.
        d. gun control laws protect and modify Article 8, Section 23 of the Constitution, allowing the president to declare war on other nations.
        ANS: C
        REF: 172
        LO: 4

7.13   During the colonial period and the earliest years of the country, a permanent army was
        not possible due to:
        a. lack of citizen interest.
        b. a shortage of weapons.
        c. lack of funding and personnel, and organizational challenges.
        d. intense pressure from British authorities to cease and desist from such militarization.
        ANS: C
        REF: 169
        LO: 1

7.14   The Supreme Court held that "the Fourteenth Amendment incorporates the Second
        Amendment right, recognized in *Heller*, to keep and bear arms for the purpose of self-
        defense" in:
        a. *Adams v. Williams*
        b. *Presser v. Illinois*
        c. *McDonald v. Chicago*
        d. *U.S. v. Lopez*
        ANS: C
        REF: 176
        LO: 6

7.15   In *United States v. Emerson* (1999), U.S. District Judge Sam R. Cummings:
        a. placed a temporary moratorium on the purchase of small-caliber firearms pending
           results of a study by the Center to Prevent Handgun Violence.
        b. upheld a lower court's ruling that a convicted felon should not be allowed to possess
           firearms.
        c. handed down a landmark decision that permits specially trained and licensed
           individuals to carry concealed weapons.
        d. went against all federal court precedent and restored a domestic abuser's firearms,
           citing the Second Amendment as guaranteeing the individual's right to keep and bear
           arms.
        ANS: D
        REF: 174
        LO: 4

7.16   The Supreme Court stated that the Second Amendment protects an individual's right to
        possess a firearm unconnected with service in a militia in:
        a. *United States v. Miller*
        b. *District of Columbia v. Heller*
        c. *Presser v. Illinois*
        d. *Stevens v. United States*
        ANS: B
        REF: 175
        LO: 5

7.17   In the *Heller* decision, the Supreme Court specifically refrained from voicing an opinion on whether the Second Amendment applied to:
a. illegal immigrants.
b. the states.
c. private individuals.
d. certain misdemeanants.
ANS: B
REF: 176
LO: 5

7.18   Gun control opponents claim that gun control:
a. will prevent needless deaths and lower crime.
b. removes the role of local legislative bodies to be involved in the process.
c. will only put guns in the hands of criminals.
d. will force law-abiding citizens to seek alternate means of protection.
ANS: C
REF: 188
LO: 4

7.19   Which of the following gives a person the legal right to use deadly force to defend that place, and any other innocent persons legally inside it, from violent attack or an intrusion that may lead to violent attack?
a. The Fourth Amendment
b. The Brady Act
c. Castle laws
d. The Second Amendment
ANS: C
REF: 178-179
LO: 5, 6

7.20   The Law Enforcement Officers Safety Act of 2004, which allows off-duty officers and retired officers to carry concealed weapons throughout the country:
a. was ruled unconstitutional in *U.S. v. Miller*.
b. was strongly supported by the International Association of Chiefs of Police.
c. was strongly opposed by the International Association of Chiefs of Police.
d. provides for nationwide standards of use-of-force and firearms training.
ANS: C
REF: 183-184
LO: 8

7.21   Congress' power "to provide for the calling forth of the Militia to execute the laws of the Union" was granted by:
a. *United States v. Cruikshank*
b. Article I, Section 8 of the Constitution
c. The Third Amendment
d. The Omnibus Crime Control and Safe Streets Act
ANS: B
REF: 172
LO: 1, 4

7.22   The purpose of the Brady Act is to:
a. limit the number of firearms on American streets at any given time.
b. prevent prohibited persons from obtaining handguns.
c. ensure that those obtaining firearms receive training in proper use and storage of their weapon(s).
d. prevent accidental injury or death by firearms.
ANS: B
REF: 182
LO: 7

7.23   The Brady Act does *not* prohibit:
a. states from enacting longer waiting periods on firearms purchases.
b. instant, computerized background checks.
c. illegal aliens from purchasing firearms.
d. those dishonorably discharged from military service from purchasing firearms.
ANS: A
REF: 183
LO: 7

7.24   If members of the militia were called to service, they were to bring:
a. only their own arms. Ammunition was supplied by the government.
b. only their own ammunition. Arms were supplied by the government.
c. their own arms and ammunition.
d. nothing-the government supplied both arms and ammunition.
ANS: C
REF: 169
LO: 1

7.25 In 2010, nine suspects were arrested in a plot to kill police officers, then attack the funeral using homemade bombs in hopes of killing more law enforcement personnel. These people were tied to:
a. a Muslim terrorist group.
b. Al Quada.
c. the Branch Davidians.
d. a Midwest Christian militia.
ANS: D
REF: 171
LO: 2

7.26 The Supreme Court held that the right to keep and bear arms is fundamental to our scheme of ordered liberty and that it was clear that the framers of the Fourteenth Amendment deemed such a right as fundamental in:
a. *McDonald v. Chicago*
b. *District of Columbia v. Heller*
c. *Presser v. Illinois*
d. *Stevens v. United States*
ANS: A
REF: 176
LO: 6

7.27 *United States v. Miller* (1939):
a. is the case that set the precedent for the dozens of cases the Supreme Court hears every year concerning the issue of an individual's right to bear arms.
b. is a relatively insignificant case in the interpretation of Second Amendment rights.
c. was the first Supreme Court case that specifically addressed the scope of the Second Amendment.
d. is the basis upon which Congress passes federal gun control legislation.
ANS: C
REF: 173
LO: 4, 5

7.28 In District of Columbia v. Heller, the Supreme Court noted that the Second Amendment _____'s text and history demonstrate that it connotes an individual right to keep and bear arms.
a. operative clause
b. prefatory clause
c. sunset clause
d. demurrer
ANS: A
REF: 175
LO: 5

124

7.29   Justice Scalia noted that "the right…is not unlimited…Nothing in our opinion should be taken to cast doubt on longstanding prohibitions on the possession of firearms by felons and the mentally ill, or laws forbidding the carrying of firearms in sensitive places…or laws imposing conditions and qualifications on the commercial sale of arms" in:
a. *United States v. Miller*
b. *District of Columbia v. Heller*
c. *Presser v. Illinois*
d. *Stevens v. United States*
ANS: B
REF: 175
LO: 5

7.30   Until recently, courts throughout history:
a. have consistently rejected the individual rights view in favor of the states' rights interpretation.
b. have consistently rejected the states' rights view in favor of the individual rights interpretation.
c. rendered early decisions that favored the individual rights perspective but, since the 1970s, have progressively inclined more toward the states' rights perspective.
d. have continuously vacillated between the individual and states' rights perspectives, depending on the liberal or conservative orientation of the Supreme Court.
ANS: A
REF: 174
LO: 4

True/False

7.31   The central controversy over the Second Amendment is whether people have a right to bear arms as individuals rather than only as part of a militia.
ANS: T
REF: 169
LO: 2

7.32   *United States v. Miller* (1939) was a critical case because the court recognized an individual rather than a state right to bear arms.
ANS: F
REF: 173
LO: 4

7.33   The Second Amendment was drafted in a time when fear of tyranny from a strong central government was very strong.
ANS: T
REF: 169
LO: 1

7.34   The number of antigovernment "Patriot" groups has been declining in recent years.
        ANS: F
        REF: 170
        LO: 3

7.35   Research has found little evidence that increased in the number of citizens with concealed
        handgun permits reduce or increase rates of violent crime.
        ANS: T
        REF: 185
        LO: 4, 5

7.36   The Supreme Court ruling in *McDonald v. Chicago* prevents state and local governments
        from passing gun laws.
        ANS: F
        REF: 177
        LO: 6

7.37   The *Heller* decision has had a sweeping impact on gun control laws across the United
        States.
        ANS: F
        REF: 175
        LO: 5

7.38   There are no longer any national or state-sanctioned militias in the United States.
        ANS: F
        REF: 169
        LO: 2

7.39   A portion of the Omnibus Crime Control and Safe Streets Act of 1967 made possession
        of a firearm by convicted felons unlawful.
        ANS: T
        REF: 181
        LO: 4, 5

7.40   In *United States v. Cruikshank* (1875), the Supreme Court stated that only Congress was
        forbidden from infringing on the Second Amendment.
        ANS: T
        REF: 173
        LO: 4

Fill-In

7.41   In *McDonald*, the Supreme Court applied the Second Amendment to the states, recognizing a person's right "to keep and bear arms for the purpose of _____"
ANS; self-defense
REF: 176
LO: 6

7.42.   In *Presser v. Illinois* (1886), the Court refused to _____ the Second Amendment into the Fourteenth Amendment.
ANS: incorporate
REF: 175
LO: 6

7.43   The Second Amendment of the U.S. Constitution reads: "A well-regulated _____ being necessary to the security of a free state, the right of the people to keep and bear arms shall not be infringed."
ANS: militia
REF: 167
LO: 1

7.44   _____ rights proponents claim that the Second Amendment was adopted with the primary purpose of preserving the state militia.
ANS: States'
REF: 172
LO: 4

7.45   The Law Enforcement Officer's Safety Act allows "_____ active and retired law enforcement officers" to carry concealed weapons anywhere in the U.S.
ANS: qualified
REF: 183
LO: 8

7.46   According to the Brady Center, a gun is ___ times more likely to be used in a completed or attempted suicide, criminal assault or homicide, or unintentional shooting death or injury than to be used in a self-defense shooting.
ANS: 22, twenty-two
REF: 186
LO: 4, 5

7.47   The purpose of the _____ is to prevent prohibited persons from obtaining handguns.
ANS: Brady Act
REF: 182
LO: 7

7.48 Some activist groups argue that an _____ citizenry is the best defense against tyranny.
ANS: armed
REF: 172
LO: 4

7.49 A _____ is a set ending time for legislation that is not renewed, which is how the assault weapon ban in the Violent Crime Control and Law Enforcement Act of 1994 expired.
ANS: sunset clause
REF: 183
LO: 5

7.50 During the colonial period, the _____ was considered to be the entire male populace of a state.
ANS: militia
REF: 169
LO: 1

Essay

7.51 Explain the Second Amendment's current status, and how that status affects laws relating to gun ownership.
ANS: In 2008, the Supreme Court held in District of Columbia v. Heller that the Second Amendment protects an individual right to possess a firearm unconnected with service in a militia and use it for lawful purposes, such as self-defense within the home. In writing for the majority, Justice Scalia noted that the opinion should not cast doubt on longstanding prohibitions against possession of firearms by certain persons, or the carrying of guns in certain places, nor placing conditions on the sale of arms. The Second Amendment remained unincorporated until 2010, when McDonald v. Chicago held that the right of an individual to keep and bear arms was among those fundamental rights necessary to our system of ordered liberty and therefore applies to the states through the Fourteenth Amendment.
REF: 174-177
LO: 5, 6

7.52   Discuss the Brady Act.

ANS: The Brady Act is named for Jim Brady, press secretary to former president Ronald Reagan. Brady was shot during a 1981 assassination attempt on Reagan. The purpose of the law is to prevent prohibited persons from obtaining handguns. It took seven years for the Brady Bill to finally become law in 1993. The Act imposed a five-day waiting period on all handgun purchases and required law enforcement to conduct criminal background checks on all handgun purchasers. In 1998, the five-day waiting period was to be replaced by instant, computerized criminal background check, although some states retained the waiting period.
REF: 182-183
LO: 7

7.53   Discuss the authority and goals of the Law Enforcement Officers Safety Act of 2004. What are some concerns about the legislation?

ANS: The Law Enforcement Officers Safety Act allowing "qualified" active and retired law enforcement officers to carry concealed weapons anywhere in the United States has three goals: (1) to establish equality between local LEOs and their federal counterparts who already carry nationwide, (2) to create an unpaid homeland security force to help protect the nation, and (3) to allow qualified current and retired LEOs the means to defend themselves and families against criminals. The IACP strongly opposed the legislation due to concerns about officer and citizen safety, use-of-force and firearm training standards, officer identification and eligibility issues, supervision of retired police, liability, and a "fundamental belief that states and localities should determine who is eligible to carry firearms in their communities."
REF: 183-184
LO: 8

7.54   Discuss the two opposing interpretations of the Second Amendment that have clashed over the years. In light of current rulings, has either side won?

ANS: Proponents of individual rights (the first perspective) say the Second Amendment should be interpreted to guarantee the right of all citizens to bear arms, whether they are part of a militia or not). States' rights (the second perspective) proponents claim the Second Amendment was adopted with the primary purpose of preserving the state militia; thus, where there is no militia, there is no right to bear arms. Current rulings seem to have turned the tide away from states' rights toward individual rights, but state rights to regulate who can purchase firearms, where they can be sold, where they can be carried, who can carry them concealed, etc. appear not to be in jeopardy in light of current rulings.
REF: 172-177
LO: 4

7.55   Discuss the historical background of the Second Amendment.

ANS: Various key factors supported gun ownership at the time the Constitution was drafted, including: 1- widespread fear of tyranny from a strong central government; 2- the lack of a permanent army to provide for public defense; 3- the formation of state militias to provide for common defense; and 4- the fact that militia members, if called to service, were required to provide their own arms and ammunition.
REF: 169
LO: 1

Chapter 8
The Fourth Amendment:
An Overview of Constitutional Searches and Seizures

LEARNING OBJECTIVES

Upon completing this chapter, the student will know:

1. What the Fourth Amendment forbids and requires.
2. Who is governed by the Fourth Amendment.
3. What is established by the reasonableness clause of the Fourth Amendment.
4. Whether individuals are constitutionally guaranteed absolute freedom from government intrusion.
5. How probable cause relates to searches and arrests.
6. What is required for a search or arrest warrant.
7. What the knock and announce rule requires.
8. What a stop is and its purpose.
9. What a frisk is and when it is permitted.
10. What the law of stop and frisk deals with, and its precedent case.
11. What the *Terry* decision established.
12. The two consequences police face if they make an unconstitutional search or seizure.
13. What the exclusionary rule is and its precedent case.
14. The primary purpose served by the exclusionary rule.
15. The case that made the exclusionary rule applicable at the state level.
16. What happens to evidence obtained in ways that "shock the conscience."
17. What exceptions to the exclusionary rule exist.
18. Other consequences that may result from government agency misconduct.

KEY TERMS

- **articulable facts**—Actions described in clear, distinct statements. [p. 212]

- **bright-line approach**—Determining the reasonableness of an action according to a specific rule that applies to all cases, in contrast to the case-by-case method. [p. 202]

- **case-by-case method**—Determining the reasonableness of an action by considering the totality of circumstances in each case, in contrast to the bright-line approach. [p. 202]

- **continuum of contacts**—The almost limitless variations of contacts between the public and the police that illustrates how justification for police action increases as their reasons for thinking criminal activity is afoot build; how an individual's conduct can lead to sufficient probable cause and justify police in arresting the person, using force if necessary. [p. 209]

- **conventional Fourth Amendment approach**—Viewing the reasonableness clause and the warrant clause as intertwined, that is, all reasonable searches require a warrant. [p. 201]

- **exclusionary rule**—Judge-made case law promulgated by the Supreme Court to prevent police or government misconduct. It prohibits evidence obtained in violation of a person's constitutional rights from being admissible in court. [p. 215]

- **frisk**—A reasonable, limited pat down search for weapons for the protection of a government agent and others. A less intrusive search than a full search, but one that is still regulated by the Fourth Amendment. It is not automatically permitted with a stop, but only when the agent suspects the person is armed and dangerous. Any evidence or contraband may be seized. [p. 212]

- **fruit of the poisonous tree doctrine**—Evidence obtained as a result of an earlier illegality (a constitutionally invalid search or activity) must be excluded from trial. [p. 219]

- **furtive conduct**—Questionable, suspicious or secretive behavior. [p. 204]

- **good faith**—Officers are unaware that they are acting in violation of a suspect's constitutional rights. A standard by which one is assumed to have acted honestly in carrying out a legal duty. [p. 222]

- **harmless error**—Involves the admissibility of involuntary confessions: If no harm results, the confession should be admissible. Also, if the preponderance of evidence suggests a defendant's guilt, any "tainted" or illegal evidence not crucial to proving the case against the defendant will not cause the case to be dismissed. [p. 222]

- **inevitable discovery doctrine**—Exception to exclusionary rule deeming evidence admissible even if seized in violation of the Fourth Amendment when it can be shown that the evidence would have inevitably been discovered through lawful means. [p. 220]

- **litigious**—A tendency toward suing; a belief that most controversies or injurious acts, no matter how minor, should be settled in court. [p. 215]

- **magistrate**—A judge. [p. 206]

- **nightcap(ped) warrant**—Issued when officers wish to execute a warrant at night because that is when the suspected illicit activity is primarily occurring. [p. 208]

- **no-knock warrant**—Issued when officers want to make an unannounced entrance because they are afraid evidence might be destroyed or officer safety requires it. [p. 208]

- **probable cause**—Stronger than reasonable suspicion. The sum total of layers of information and the synthesis of what the police have heard, what they know and what they observe as trained officers. [p. 202]

- **reasonable**—Sensible, rational, justifiable. [p. 201]

- **reasonableness Fourth Amendment approach**—An interpretation of the Fourth Amendment that sees the reasonableness clause and the warrant clause as separate issues. [p. 201]

- **reasonable suspicion**—An experienced police officer's hunch or intuition, based on observed unusual conduct, which leads him reasonably to conclude that criminal activity may be afoot. [p. 213]

- **search**—an examination of a person, place or vehicle for contraband or evidence of a crime. [p. 195]

- **seizure**—a taking by law enforcement or other government agent of contraband, evidence of a crime or even a person into custody. [p. 196]

- **stop**—A brief detention of a person, short of an arrest, based on specific and articulable facts for the purpose of investigating suspicious activity. [212]

- *Terry* **stop**—An officer with articulable reasonable suspicion may conduct a brief investigatory stop, including a pat down for weapons if the officer has reason to suspect the person is armed and dangerous. [p. 213]

- **totality of circumstances**—The principle upon which a number of legal assessments are made, including probable cause; the sum total of factors leading a reasonable person (officer) to a course of action. [p. 203]

LECTURE OUTLINE

I.   Introduction
   A. Search and seizure
   B. The Fourth Amendment
      1. Overview of a Fourth Amendment Inquiry

II.   The Importance of the Fourth Amendment to Law Enforcement

III.   Who Is Regulated by the Fourth Amendment?
   A. Government agencies
   B. Private individuals

IV.   The Clauses of the Fourth Amendment
   A. Two Interpretations
      1. Conventional Fourth Amendment approach
      2. Reasonableness Fourth Amendment approach
   B. Reasonableness
      1. Bright-line approach
      2. Case-by-case method
   C. Probable Cause
      1. Totality of circumstances
   D. Sources of Probable Cause
      1. Observational probable cause
         a. furtive conduct
      2. Informational probable cause
         a. *Draper v. United States* (1959)
         b. *Aguilar v. Texas* (1964)
         c. *Spinelli v. United States* (1969)
         d. *Illinois v. Gates* (1983)
         e. *United States v. Sokolow* (1989)

V.   Search and Arrest Warrants
   A. Probable Cause
      1. Independent judge
   B. Knock-and-Announce Rule
      1. *Miller v. United States* (1958)
      2. *Wilson v. Arkansas* (1995)
      3. *United States v. Banks* (2003)
         a. 15-20 second wait satisfied the Fourth Amendment
   C. Special Conditions
      1. No-knock warrant
      2. Night-capped warrant
   D. Executing the Search Warrant
      1. *Illinois v. McArthur* (2001)

VI.   The Continuum of Contacts

CHAPTER SUMMARY

The Fourth Amendment forbids unreasonable searches and seizures and requires that any search or arrest warrant be based on probable cause. If a person is an employee of any governmental agency or is an agent of the government in any capacity, that person is bound by the Fourth Amendment. The Fourth Amendment does not apply to private parties.

The reasonableness clause of the Fourth Amendment makes warrantless searches and seizures valid and constitutional when they are sensible. The Constitution does not provide an absolute right to be free from government intrusion, only *unreasonable interference*.

Probable cause determines when officers may execute lawful searches and arrests, with or, in some cases, without a warrant. *Probable cause to search* means officers reasonably believe that evidence, contraband or other items sought are where police believe these items to be. *Probable cause to arrest* means officers reasonably believe that a crime has been committed by the person they seek to arrest. All warrants are to be based on probable cause. When executing a search or arrest warrant, the common law rule is that for an entry into a home to be constitutional, police must first knock and identify themselves and their purpose—the knock-and-announce rule.

A stop is a brief detention of a person based on specific and articulable facts for the purpose of investigating suspicious activity. A frisk is a limited pat down search for weapons for the protection of the government agent and others. It is not automatically permitted with a stop, but only when the agent suspects the person is armed and dangerous. The law of stop and frisk deals with that time frame during which officers follow up on their suspicions but before the time that the requisite probable cause is established to justify an arrest (*Terry v. Ohio*, 1968). The *Terry* decision established that, in what is termed a *Terry* stop, an officer with articulable reasonable suspicion that a crime is occurring, has occurred, or is about to occur, may conduct a brief investigatory stop, including a pat down for weapons if the officer has reason to suspect the person is armed and dangerous.

An unlawful search or seizure can have two serious consequences: (1) the evidence may be excluded from court and (2) internal sanctions as well as civil and criminal liability may be incurred. The exclusionary rule is judge-made case law promulgated by the Supreme Court to prevent police misconduct. It prohibits evidence obtained in violation of a person's constitutional rights from being admissible in court (*Weeks v. United States*). The primary purpose underlying the exclusionary rule is deterring government misconduct. *Mapp v. Ohio* made the exclusionary rule applicable at the state level. Evidence obtained in ways that *shock the conscience* will not be admissible in court. Among the exceptions to the exclusionary rule are the inevitable discovery doctrine, existence of a valid independent source, harmless error and good faith. Government misconduct could also result in departmental discipline against an officer, civil lawsuits and criminal charges.

SUGGESTED ANSWERS TO THE DISCUSSION QUESTIONS

1. Explain why the Fourth Amendment applies to the federal government and also to state, county and municipal governments.

   A concise answer is: the Fourteenth Amendment. All that the Fourth Amendment stands for has been determined, through common law, to be so essential to liberty that it applies to the states and all government agents-federal, state or local-and they must abide by its limitations.

2. Explain the meaning of search and seizure.

   The student is expected to recognize that the terms *search* and *seizure* have specific definitions within the realm of constitutional law. In this context, a search could involve the search of a person or property, as is the case with seizing a person or property as well.

3. How does a stop differ from an arrest?

The difference between a stop and an arrest should be understood by the student. In an arrest, the person is not considered free to go, while in a stop they are. Different criminal procedure issues apply to each, which should be articulated by the student, including that *Miranda* need not be given during a stop, and that search and seizure limitations are more extensive with the stop. While reasonable suspicion is necessary for a stop, probable cause is needed for an arrest.

4. How does a frisk differ from a search?

Frisk and search have been defined through common law, with each being justified through different standards and having different limitations. Remember that exceeding the limitations will result in the exclusionary rule prohibiting what may be obtained during these activities.

5. At what point does a stop and frisk develop into a search and seizure?

Simply put, when probable cause develops through the legal acquisition by the police of evidence to justify the arrest and subsequent search.

6. What restrictions does the Fourth Amendment put on private security guards, such as store detectives or private investigators?

Absolutely none. Private security personnel are not government agents.

7. In what ways can government agents be discouraged from violating the Fourth Amendment?

This question is really asking for students' thoughts on ways other than the exclusionary rule. Can you think of any (e.g., criminally charging police, perhaps fining them civilly, etc.)?

8. Should a case be dismissed because the one piece of evidence that would surely prove the defendant was guilty was not admitted due to a police error in obtaining it?

This situation has been put in the spotlight during recent high-profile cases, in which law enforcement didn't "play by the rules" and crucial evidence was thrown out. The procedures for obtaining evidence are in place to protect all citizens and follow the philosophy of "innocent until proven guilty." Unfortunately, there are times when everyone *knows* a person is guilty of a crime (whether through confessions, numerous witnesses, etc.) yet illegally obtained evidence was not allowed in trial and the verdict came back "not guilty." This question seems to push people's buttons about justice and makes a good class discussion subject.

9. To protect the public, can government ever really go "too far"?

This question calls for a conclusion by the student based on their personal and academic perspective at this point. Another good debate topic.

10. Why should a government agent try to get a warrant whenever possible?

Because once an independent judge has determined probable cause exists, the burden to argue otherwise lies on the defendant. When a government agent (e.g., police officer) makes a determination of probable cause, the burden is on that agent to justify the existence of probable cause.

STUDENT ACTIVITIES

- Invite your county prosecutor to address the class regarding the exclusionary rule.

- Use your classroom computer to play the 16-minute podcast of the Federal Law Enforcement Training Center's *Terry Stop and Frisk* training video, available at http://www.fletc.gov/training/programs/legal-division/podcasts/4th-amendment-roadmap-podcasts/Terry_Stop__Frisk.mp3/view.

- Listen to oral arguments in many of the cases discussed in this chapter at the United States Supreme Court Media "Oyez" site at http://www.oyez.org/search/apachesolr_search/exclusionary%20rule.

  Engage the class in a discussion of airport security. Access the lesson plan for "Airport Scanners and the Fourth Amendment" at the Bill of Rights Institute at http://www.billofrightsinstitute.org/page.aspx?pid=546.

INTERNET CONNECTIONS

- Access "Stop and Frisk Law: A Guide To Doctrines, Tests and Special Circumstances" at the Multimedia Education Resource for Learning and Online Teaching (MERLOT) at http://www.merlot.org/merlot/viewMaterial.htm?id=87167.

- Go to the Cato Institute's **Center for Constitutional Analysis** web site to read Timothy Lynch's article *In Defense of the Exclusionary Rule*, accessible at http://www.cato.org/pubs/pas/pa-319es.html.

- An opposing opinion of the exclusionary rule is presented in William Tucker's article *End of a Supreme Court Blunder?*, viewable on **The Weekly Standard** web site at http://www.weeklystandard.com/Content/Public/Articles/000/000/012/581mnsed.asp.

138

CHAPTER 8 TEST BANK

Multiple Choice

8.1 The law of stop and frisk deals with that time frame during which officers follow up on their suspicions but before the time that the requisite _____ is established to justify an arrest.
a. probable cause
b. reasonable suspicion
c. proof beyond a reasonable doubt
d. preponderance of the evidence
ANS: A
REF: 212
LO: 10

8.2 An unlawful search and seizure can include all of the following consequences, <u>except</u>:
a. departmental sanctions.
b. criminal liability.
c. evidence would be admissible in court.
d. civil liability.
ANS: C
REF: 225
LO: 12, 18

8.3 One way courts have determined reasonableness is the bright line approach, which:
a. considers the totality of circumstances in each individual case.
b. assigns points to each indicia of reasonableness.
c. compares a case to other similar cases.
d. considers a specific rule that applies to all cases.
ANS: D
REF: 202
LO: 3

8.4 The most commonly used method to determine reasonableness is the case-by-case method, which:
a. considers the totality of circumstances in each individual case.
b. assigns points to each indicia of reasonableness.
c. compares a case to other similar cases.
d. considers a specific rule that applies to all cases.
ANS: A
REF: 202
LO: 3

8.5 .. "Probable cause to search" means:
   a. having more evidence against a set of probabilities.
   b. officers reasonably believe that evidence, contraband or other items sought are where they believe them to be.
   c. that a reasonable person would believe the items may or may not be at a particular location.
   d. the officers have reasonable suspicion to think the items are where they wish to search.
   ANS: B
   REF: 203
   LO: 1, 5

8.6 The principle that looks at all available information to assess whether the sum total would lead a reasonable person to believe what the officers concluded is the:
   a. bright line approach
   b. totality of the circumstances
   c. individual circumstances
   d. overall assessment
   ANS: B
   REF: 203
   LO: 5

8.7 The section of the Fourth Amendment makes warrantless searches and seizures valid and constitutional when they are sensible is the:
   a. warrant clause
   b. probable cause clause
   c. reasonableness clause
   d. privacy clause
   A: C
   REF: 201
   LO: 3

8.8 The Supreme Court stated that the exclusionary rule operates as a judicially created remedy designed to safeguard Fourth Amendment rights generally through its deterrent effect, rather than a constitutional right of the person aggrieved in:
   a. *Mapp v. Ohio*
   b. *Weeks v. U.S.*
   c. *United States v. Leon*
   d. *Wolf v. Colorado*
   A: C
   REF: 215
   LO: 14

8.9   All warrants are to be based on:
       a. a preponderance of the evidence.
       b. reasonable suspicion.
       c. proof beyond a reasonable doubt.
       d. probable cause.
       ANS: D
       REF: 206
       LO: 1, 5, 6

8.10   The Fourth Amendment regulates the actions of all of the following, except the:
       a. Internal Revenue Service
       b. Secret Service
       c. United Parcel Service
       d. Food and Drug Administration
       ANS: C
       REF: 199
       LO: 2

8.11   The Supreme Court made the exclusionary rule applicable to the states, holding that "all
       evidence obtained by searches and seizures in violation of the Constitution are by the
       same authority inadmissible in state court" in:
       a. *Mapp v. Ohio*
       b. *Weeks v. U.S.*
       c. *United States v. Leon*
       d. *Wolf v. Colorado*
       A: A
       REF: 218
       LO: 15

8.12   What level of proof is required for a *Terry* stop?
       a. reasonable suspicion
       b. probable cause.
       c. preponderance of the evidence.
       d. no proof is required.
       ANS: A
       REF: 213
       LO: 11

141

8.13 In *Rochin v. California*, the Supreme Court held that searches that _____ are a violation of due process and any evidence so obtained will, therefore, be inadmissible.
a. offend liberty
b. violate privacy
c. show a heedless disregard for civil rights
d. shock the conscience
ANS: D
REF: 218
LO: 16

8.14 When executing a search or arrest warrant, the common law rule is that for an entry into the home to be constitutional, the police must first:
a. evacuate the immediate area.
b. knock and identify themselves and their purpose.
c. read the occupants their Miranda warnings.
d. obtain consent to enter.
ANS: B
REF: 207
LO: 7

8.15 All of the following are true of the exclusionary rule, except:
a. is used to discourage the police from violating a person's constitutional rights.
b. is judge-made law.
c. excludes illegally obtained evidence from trial.
d. it provides for criminal sanctions against the officer.
ANS: D
REF: 215
LO: 13

8.16 Which of the following is insufficient to support probable cause?
a. physical evidence
b. admissions
c. association with known criminals
d. failure to protest arrest
ANS: D
REF: 204
LO: 5

8.17   In *United States v. Banks*, the Court held that officers must wait a reasonable amount of time after knocking and before forcible entry and that, in this case, a _____ wait satisfied the Fourth Amendment.
   a. 1 to 2 minute
   b. 30 seconds to 1 minute
   c. 15 to 20 second
   d. 5 to 10 second
   ANS: C
   REF: 208
   LO: 7

8.18   "Where the facts and circumstances within the officers' knowledge and of which they had reasonably trustworthy information is sufficient to warrant a person of reasonable caution in the belief that an offense has been or is being committed" is the Supreme Court's definition of:
   a. reasonable suspicion
   b. probable cause
   c. a preponderance of the evidence
   d. beyond a reasonable doubt
   ANS: B
   REF: 202-203
   LO: 5, 6

8.19   The exclusionary rule:
   a. is a constitutional right under the Fourth Amendment
   b. is a Congressionally created remedy
   c. was promulgated by the Senate.
   d. safeguards rights through its deterrent effect.
   ANS: D
   REF: 215
   LO: 13

8.20   The _____ doctrine states that evidence obtained as a result of an earlier illegality must be excluded from trial.
   a. prior taint
   b. attenuation of the taint
   c. fruit of the tainted seizure
   d. fruit of the poisonous tree
   ANS: D
   REF: 219
   LO: 13

8.21   The exception to the exclusionary rule that deems evidence admissible even if seized in violation of the Fourth Amendment when it can be shown that the evidence would have been discovered through lawful means is:
a. harmless error doctrine
b. good faith exception
c. inevitable discovery doctrine
d. valid, independent source doctrine
ANS: C
REF: 220
LO: 17

8.22   The totality of the circumstances test made establishment of probable cause by use of _____ easier for police.
a. warrantless investigative stops
b. informants
c. victim reports
d. articulable reasonable suspicion
ANS: B
REF: 203
LO: 5

8.23   Which of the following would <u>not</u> prove exigent circumstances to justify entry by police without first announcing their presence and purpose?
a. A crime is in progress.
b. Illegal gambling is occurring at night.
c. Evidence would be destroyed
d. Making the officer's presence known would endanger them.
ANS: B
REF: 203
LO: 7

8.24   Federal lawsuits against police are filed under Title 42 of U.S. Code, Section 1983—Civil Action for Deprivation of _____.
a. Equal Protection
b. Due Process
c. Civil Rights
d. Human Rights
ANS: C
REF: 226
LO: 18

8.25   Deterring government misconduct is the primary purpose of the:
       a. good faith exception
       b. exclusionary rule
       c. Supreme Court
       d. citizen review board
       ANS: B
       REF: 215
       LO: 14

8.26   In *Segura v. United States* (1984), although evidence discovered during an illegal entry into an apartment was excluded, evidence later found in the apartment with a warrant obtained with information totally unconnected with the illegal entry was admissible under the:
       a. valid, independent source doctrine
       b. confidential source doctrine
       c. harmless error doctrine
       d. reliable informant exception
       ANS: A
       REF: 221
       LO: 17

8.27   In *Arizona v. Fulminante*, the Court ruled that the harmless error doctrine applies to cases involving admissibility of:
       a. spontaneous utterances
       b. involuntary confessions
       c. evidence that would have inevitably been discovered
       d. evidence obtained with an invalid warrant
       ANS: B
       REF: 222
       LO: 17

8.28   The exclusionary rule was established at the federal level in the 1914 case of:
       a. *Terry v. Ohio*.
       b. *Wolf v. Colorado*.
       c. *Mapp v. Ohio*.
       d. *Weeks v. United States*.
       ANS: D
       REF: 218
       LO: 13

8.29   The _____ is based on the belief that when an officer—innocent of misconduct—lawfully executes a warrant, the possibility that the warrant itself was issued without sufficient probable cause should not withhold valuable evidence from the trial.
a. harmless error doctrine
b. inevitable discovery doctrine
c. good faith exception
d. valid, independent source doctrine
ANS: C
REF: 222-223
LO: 17

8.30   The Constitution provides:
a. an absolute right to be free from government intrusion.
b. a right to be free from government intrusion unless a warrant has been issued.
c. a right to be free from unreasonable government intrusion.
d. a right against any form of intrusion by public or private parties.
ANS: C
REF: 202
LO: 1, 3

True/False

8.31   Probable cause to arrest means officers reasonably believe that a crime has been committed by the person whom they seek to arrest.
ANS: T
REF: 203
LO: 5

8.32   One consideration in determining whether a search or seizure is reasonable is whether a person's reasonable expectation of privacy has been violated by the government.
ANS: T
REF: 202
LO: 4

8.33   Furtive conduct may not be considered part of the totality of circumstances when establishing probable cause.
ANS: F
REF: 204
LO: 5

8.34   Evidence that has been seized illegally by an independently-acting private person and
        turned over to the police is inadmissible in court as fruit of the poisonous tree.
        ANS: F
        REF: 200
        LO: 2

8.35   The *Miranda* warning must be given during any stop.
        ANS: F
        REF: 212
        LO: 10

8.36   Any intrusion on a person's freedom, including stop-and-frisk situations, involves Fourth
        Amendment protections.
        ANS: T
        REF: 212
        LO: 1, 4, 10

8.37   Probable cause can be established after a search or arrest is made.
        ANS: F
        REF: 203
        LO: 5

8.38   Reasonable, articulable suspicion is the key determinant of whether a judge will grant
        officers a warrant to search or arrest.
        ANS: F
        REF: 206
        LO: 5

8.39   Airline employees inspecting luggage are not governed by the Fourth Amendment.
        ANS: F
        REF: 199
        LO: 2

8.40   A private store detective can search a shopper without first obtaining a warrant.
        ANS: T
        REF: 200
        LO: 2

Fill-In

8.41   The Fourth Amendment forbids _____ searches and seizures.
        ANS: unreasonable
        REF: 195
        LO: 1

8.42   A _____ is a limited pat down search for weapons for the protection of the
        government agent and others.
        ANS: frisk
        REF: 212
        LO: 9

8.43   The Fourth Amendment also requires that any search or arrest warrant be based on
        _____.
        ANS: probable cause
        REF: 206
        LO: 1, 6

8.44   The Constitution does not provide an absolute right to be free from government intrusion,
        only _____.
        ANS: unreasonable interference
        REF: 202
        LO: 1, 3

8.45   Issuing magistrates must be _____ and detached.
        ANS: neutral
        REF: 206
        LO: 6

8.46   Officers wanting to make an unannounced entrance to execute a warrant may request a
        _____ warrant.
        ANS: no-knock
        REF: 208
        LO: 7

8.47   A _____ is a brief detention of a person based on specific and articulable facts for the
        purpose of investigating suspicious activity.
        ANS: stop
        REF: 212
        LO: 8

8.48   The law of _____ was established in the landmark case of Terry v. Ohio.
        ANS: stop and frisk
        REF: 213
        LO: 11

8.49   Evidence seized in violation of a person's constitutional rights is prevented from being
        admitted into court by the _____.
        ANS: exclusionary rule
        REF: 215
        LO: 13

8.50   The exception to the exclusionary rule referring to instances in which the preponderance
        of evidence suggests the defendant's guilt and that the illegal evidence is not critical to
        proving the case is known as _____.
        ANS: harmless error
        REF: 222
        LO: 17

Essay

8.51   Explain reasonable suspicion.

        ANS: On the continuum between no suspicion and probable cause, "reasonable suspicion"
        is an experienced police officer's "hunch" or intuition that criminal activity may be taking
        place, though the officer must be able to articulate the facts and circumstances that led to
        their suspicion. In *Terry v. Ohio* (1968), the Court gave weight to "articulable reasonable
        suspicion" as being adequate justification for a brief investigatory stop and—if reasonable
        suspicion exists to believe the person is armed—a limited search of the person's outer
        clothing for weapons to protect themselves and others in the area.
        REF: 212-214
        LO: 111

8.52   Explain informational and observational probable cause.

        ANS: Probable cause is stronger than reasonable suspicion; is based on facts or
        observation; may lead a reasonable person to believe a crime is being or has been
        committed; and may justify more invasive action by officers (e.g., a search or an arrest).
        Observational probable cause is derived from a government agent's personal experiences—
        what officers perceive through their own senses. The physical actions of a person, such a
        furtive conduct, can be included in the totality of the circumstances when developing
        probable cause. Physical evidence and admissions may provide sufficient probable cause to
        arrest. Presence at a crime scene or association with known criminals are not sufficient by
        themselves to provide probable cause, but can contribute to it. Informational probable cause
        is information provided by official sources such as roll call, dispatch, police bulletins, and
        unofficial sources such as witnesses, victims, and informants.
        REF: 202-206
        LO: 5

8.53   Explain the law of stop and frisk and why it is needed.

        ANS: The law of stop and frisk applies to the "gray area" between "no illegal conduct/no
        police action" and "probable cause for illegal conduct/police power to arrest." It is based
        on officers' *reasonable suspicion* and allows a brief detention of a person, based on
        specific and articulable facts, to investigate suspicious activity. It is needed to balance the
        rights of an individual with the government's need for tools to carry out its job of
        protecting society from lawbreakers. *Frisk* is needed to allow officers to ensure their own
        safety and the safety of others by checking for concealed weapons.
        REF: 212-214
        LO: 10

8.54   Discuss the exclusionary rule.

ANS: The exclusionary rule is judge-made case law to prevent police misconduct. It prohibits the use of evidence obtained in violation of a person's constitutional rights. Essentially, it expresses the Court's unwillingness to support an unlawful act by an overzealous officer who *breaks* the law in a misguided effort to *enforce* the law. Originally applying only to the federal government in *Weeks v. United States*, it was applied to the states in the 1961 case of *Mapp v. Ohio*.
REF: 215-219
LO: 13, 14, 15

8.55   Describe two exceptions to the exclusionary rule.

ANS: The text presents four exceptions to the exclusionary rule: 1- The inevitable discovery exception holds that if the government can prove that evidence would have been obtained inevitably and, therefore, would have been admitted regardless of any overreach by police, there is no rational basis to keep that evidence from the jury in order to ensure the fairness of the trial proceedings. 2- The valid independent source exception holds that if evidence that might otherwise fall victim to the exclusionary rule is obtained from a valid, independent source, that evidence can be admitted. 3-The harmless error exception holds that an error that does not affect the outcome of a judicial proceeding will not cause the case to be dismissed. 4- The good faith exception holds that evidence is admissible if the police were acting on the belief that their search or arrest warrant was valid even if an error is made on the warrant by some other court entity (i.e., a clerical error or an error by the judge).
REF: 220-225
LO: 17

Chapter 9
Conducting Constitutional Seizures

LEARNING OBJECTIVES

Upon completing this chapter, the student will know:

1. Whether a stop constitutes an arrest.
2. What factors determine how long a stop may last.
3. When vehicles can be stopped.
4. Whether *Miranda* must be given during a traffic stop.
5. How a *seizure* and an *arrest* compare and whether a seizure always constitutes an arrest, or vice versa.
6. How *arrest* is usually defined.
7. What the elements of an arrest are.
8. When an arrest can legally be made.
9. Where arrests can be made.
10. How much force can be used in making an arrest.
11. When use of a Taser might be considered unreasonable and an excessive use of force.
12. The only justification for use of deadly force.
13. Who has immunity from arrests.

KEY TERMS

- **arrest**—The detention of an individual; the taking of a person into custody in the manner authorized by law for the purpose of presenting that person before a magistrate to answer for the commission of a crime. [p. 247]

- **citizen's arrest**—The detention by a nongovernment agent of one accused of an illegal act, with such detention being authorized by state statutes. [p. 264]

- *de facto* **arrest**—When a reasonable person would believe they are not free to leave while in the presence of the police, whether or not they have been told they are under arrest, have been handcuffed or are physically restrained. [p. 246]

- **fresh pursuit**—A situation in which police are immediately in pursuit of a suspect and may cross state jurisdictional lines to make an arrest of a felon who committed the felony in the officers' state and then crossed the border into another state. [p. 254]

- **Functional equivalent**—essentially the same or serving the same purpose. [p. 245]

- **hot pursuit**—The period during which an individual is being immediately chased by law enforcement. A period that influences Fourth Amendment search and seizure concerns; the person to be arrested knows an arrest is about to be made and is actively trying to escape it. [p. 254]

- **pretext stop**—Stopping a vehicle to search for evidence of a crime under the guise of a traffic stop. [p. 243]

LECTURE OUTLINE

I.   Introduction

II.   Intensity and Scope of a Seizure: Stop and Arrest Compared

III.   Investigatory Stops
       A. Establishing Reasonable Suspicion
       B. Informants and Anonymous Tips
          1. *Florida v. J.L.* (2000)
          2. *Harris v. Commonwealth* (2008)
       C. Flight from Police
          1. *Illinois v. Wardlow* (2000)
       D. Length of the Stop
       E. Protective Actions during Stops
       F. The Controversy over Pedestrian Stops
       G. Traffic Stops
          1. *Delaware v. Prouse* (1979)
          2. *Berkemer v. McCarty* (1984)
          3. *Pennsylvania v. Mimms* (1977)
          4. *Brendlin v. California* (2007)
          5. *Arizona v. Johnson* (2009)
          6. *Whren v. United States* (1996)
             a. pretext stop
       H. Roadblocks and Checkpoints
          1. *Brown v. Texas* (1979)
       I. Stops at International Borders

IV.   An Arrest or Not?
       A. Detention tantamount to arrest
          1. *Kaupp v. Texas* (2003)
          2. *Dunaway v. New York* (1979)
          3. *Michigan v. Chesternut* (1988)
       B. Community Caretaking Doctrine

152

153

CHAPTER SUMMARY

The *Terry* case established that the authority to stop and frisk is independent of the power to arrest. A stop is not an arrest, but it *is* a seizure within the meaning of the Fourth Amendment and, therefore, requires reasonableness. How long a stop may last depends on factors that indicate the suspect was not detained an unreasonably long time, including the purpose of the stop and the time and means the investigation required.

Officers may stop motorists only for violations of the law, which may include equipment violations, erratic driving or invalid vehicle registration. Because a traffic stop is brief and occurs in public, it is not considered an arrest, thus *Miranda* warnings need not be given.

A *seizure* occurs when a reasonable person believes he or she is not free to leave. An *arrest* is a formal restraint on one's freedom of movement. A seizure need not necessarily be an arrest, but all arrests are seizures. To arrest is to deprive a person of liberty by legal authority, taking the person into custody for the purpose of holding him or her to answer a criminal charge. The elements of an arrest are (1) intending to take a person into custody, (2) exercising authority to do so, (3) detaining or restraining the person to be arrested and (4) the arrestee understanding what is happening. Officers can usually make a lawful arrest for any crime committed in their presence, for any felony if they have probable cause, and with an arrest warrant.

Police may, without a warrant, arrest for any crime committed in their presence. Police may, without a warrant, arrest for an unwitnessed felony based on probable cause. Police may make a warrantless arrest based on probable cause in a public place or in a private place that a suspect has retreated to from a public place. Police may not make a nonconsensual, warrantless arrest inside a person's home or arrest a guest within that home without exigent circumstances.

When making an arrest, police officers can use only as much force as is reasonably necessary to overcome resistance and gain compliance. Excessive force may cause the officer to be sued. The use of a TASER might be considered unreasonable excessive force if the subject is not a flight risk, a dangerous felon, or an immediate threat (*Bryan v. McPherson*). The only justification for use of deadly force is self-defense or protecting the lives of others.

Foreign diplomats, including ambassadors, ministers, their assistants and attachés and their families and servants, have complete immunity from arrest. Foreign consuls and their deputies as well as some legislators and out-of-state witnesses may also have limited immunity.

SUGGESTED ANSWERS TO THE DISCUSSION QUESTIONS

1. Explain at what point a person is considered "under arrest."

   When a person would reasonably believe they were not free to go. This does not have to be under physical restraint, but merely requires the reasonable belief that they would be prevented from leaving by the police.

2. Explain the difference between a stop and an arrest.

   As discussed in a previous chapter, the differences between a stop and an arrest have been articulated through a series of criminal procedure cases decided by the Supreme Court

3. Why might states authorize probable cause arrests for certain unwitnessed misdemeanors?

   Keeping in mind that laws serve society by establishing norms in response to perceived needs, certain offenses may be deemed so important by society that it changes the requirement for the arrest (e.g., drunk driving, domestic assault, etc.).

4. How much force can be used by an officer when executing an arrest? How is it determined?

   Reasonable force may be used. Defining "reasonable" has been discussed previously and continues to serve as a great exercise for students of the Constitution.

5. When determining whether a stop or an arrest is lawful, how is the term *reasonable* determined? And, do the subject's subjective feelings enter the analysis of determining reasonableness?

   Reasonableness is determined by considering the totality (all) of the circumstances.

6. How does the entertainment industry portray arrest situations? Do you think this portrayal is generally realistic?

   This question used to be responded to from the personal perspective of the student, tying in an understanding of what is and isn't constitutional and how the media portray it. Some of today's "cop shows" are fairly realistic when portraying arrest situations. Others, trying to elevate the drama and entertainment value, carry the scene beyond reality.

7. Do you know anyone who has been arrested? If so, what did they have to say about it?

   Students' responses will vary. Encourage the class to discuss their experiences.

8. Should anyone be immune from arrest, for example, foreign diplomats?

   Immunity continues to be a subject of debate. Immunity for foreign diplomats often extends to their families and even to their hired help (drivers, valets, etc.). We grant foreign diplomats immunity in our country, in part, to protect our own diplomats abroad. And while diplomats are *supposed* to respect and obey the laws of the country, it is common knowledge that many of these diplomats flaunt their immunity and partake in blatant violations of the law. Several recent incidents in the United States have drawn attention to this practice, including the alleged multiple rapes by a diplomat's son and the drunk driving of another diplomat which resulted in the death of a young woman. This question makes a good class debate topic.

9. Should police officers who are doing their best to enforce the law ever be punished in any way if they are acting in "good faith?"

Students' responses will vary dependent on their personal beliefs. An excellent debate topic.

10. Under what circumstances is someone other than a law enforcement official authorized to make an arrest?

Here we are looking for students to explain their understanding of "citizen's arrest"—when the "average citizen" is permitted to enforce the laws of society.

STUDENT ACTIVITIES

- Have students research data relating to charges of excessive use of force by police in your city and your state. Discuss their findings in class.

- Invite a training officer or firearms instructor from your local law enforcement agency to address the class concerning use of force training and departmental policies. Ask him or her to include discussion of departmental actions taken upon receipt of a claim of excessive force by an officer or officers.

- Review the Use of Force Continuum, then view and discuss use of force scenario videos "What Force Option Would You Use?" on BluTube at PoliceOne.com at http://blutube.policeone.com/Topic/3513-Police-Use-Of-Force-Videos/.

- Listen to the Supreme Court oral arguments in the case of *Scott v. Harris* at the Oyez Project at the IIT Kent-Chicago College of Law website at http://www.oyez.org/cases/2000-2009/2006/2006_05_1631.

  Watch the in-car video of the incident at issue in *Scott v. Harris* on YouTube at http://www.youtube.com/watch?v=qrVKSgRZ2GY&playnext=1&list=PL51BD2E27 35E95FA6.

INTERNET CONNECTIONS

- Review **Bureau of Justice Statistics** data "Contacts Between the Police and the Public" at http://bjs.ojp.usdoj.gov/index.cfm?ty=pbdetail&iid=653.

- Compare **Bureau of Justice Statistics** contacts between police and public data with its data related to civilian complaints about police use of force, available at http://bjs.ojp.usdoj.gov/index.cfm?ty=pbdetail&iid=553.

- See the **National Center for Women and Policing**'s study *Men, Women, and the Police Use of Excessive Force: A Tale of Two Genders*, accessible at http://www.womenandpolicing.org/PDF/2002_Excessive_Force.pdf.

CHAPTER 9 TEST BANK

Multiple Choice

9.1   Which of the following, by itself, can be used as reasonable suspicion to conduct a stop?
a. anonymous tip
b. flight from police
c. general suspicion
d. existence of a wanted poster
ANS: D
REF: 234
LO: 1

9.2   The "fleeing felon" rule that allowed police officers to shoot any felon attempting an escape was invalidated by the Supreme Court's ruling in:
a. *Dunaway v. New York* (1979).
b. *Brown v. Texas* (1979).
c. *Tennessee v. Garner* (1985).
d. *State v. MacKenzie* (1965).
ANS: C
REF: 256-257
LO: 10, 12

9.3   All of the following delineate the point at which an arrest has actually occurred, except:
a. intending to take the person into custody.
b. exercising the authority to do so.
c. detaining or restraining the person to be arrested.
d. informing the arrestee of their rights.
ANS: D
REF: 247
LO: 7

9.4   Which of the following is not considered when determining if the length of an investigative stop was reasonable?
a. the purpose of the stop
b. whether force was used to stop and detain the suspect
c. the reasonableness of the time used to investigate
d. the reasonableness of the means of investigation
ANS: B
REF: 238
LO: 2

9.5   Searches at international borders:
       a. must be based on reasonable suspicion.
       b. must be based on probable cause.
       c. may be conducted without probable cause or a warrant.
       d. must be conducted randomly.
       ANS: C
       REF: 245
       LO: 3

9.6   Usually, officers *cannot* make a lawful arrest:
       a. for any crime committed in their presence.
       b. for any felony if they have probable cause.
       c. with an arrest warrant.
       d. for a misdemeanor committed outside their presence.
       ANS: D
       REF: 248
       LO: 8

9.7   In _____ the Supreme Court held that officers who were in hot pursuit of an armed
       robbery suspect acted reasonably when they entered the house and began to search for the
       man because "the Fourth Amendment does not require police officers to delay in the
       course of an investigation if to do so would gravely endanger their lives or the lives of
       others."
       a. *Payton v. New York*
       b. *Warden v. Hayden*
       c. *United States v. Watson*
       d. *Tennessee v. Garner*
       ANS: B
       REF: 254
       LO: 9

9.8   Which of the following is <u>not</u> one of the five legitimate uses of force ("Rules of
       Engagement")?
       a. effectuate an arrest
       b. prevent escape
       c. overcome resistance
       d. overcome objections
       ANS: D
       REF: 256
       LO: 10

9.9   The police may not make a nonconsensual warrantless arrest inside a person's home or
       arrest a guest within that home without:
       a. reasonable suspicion.
       b. information that meets the two-pronged test for reliability.
       c. justification under the community caretaker exception.
       d. exigent circumstances.
       ANS: D
       REF: 250
       LO: 8. 9

9.10   A study by Police One magazine found that the most commonly used less-than-lethal
       weapon is:
       a. a baton.
       b. OC spray.
       c. the Taser
       d. the bean bag round.
       ANS: C
       REF: 260
       LO: 10, 11

9.11   The use of a Taser might be considered unreasonable, excessive force if the subject is:
       a. verbally abusive.
       b. a flight risk.
       c. an immediate threat.
       d. a dangerous felon.
       ANS: A
       REF: 262
       LO: 11

9.12   Which of the following does *not* have complete immunity from arrest?
       a. Families of foreign diplomats
       b. Servants of foreign diplomats
       c. State legislators
       d. Foreign diplomats
       ANS: C
       REF: 265
       LO: 13

9.13   In which of the following scenarios would an officer <u>not</u> be able to make a lawful, warrantless arrest?
a. An officer smells marijuana emanating from the vehicle he just stopped.
b. An officer hears an assault taking place.
c.   An officer witnesses a petty larceny.
d. An officer hears a kid talking about the compact disc player he shoplifted last week.
ANS: D
REF: 248
LO: 8

9.14   A warrantless arrest that begins in a public place is valid:
a. only with good faith.
b. only with reasonable suspicion.
c. only if the officer witnesses the flight.
d. if probable cause exists, even if the arrestee retreats to a private place.
ANS: D
REF: 250
LO: 9

9.15   If police officers make a stop for a traffic violation and are reasonably suspicious that the situation is dangerous, they:
a. can order driver and passenger(s) out of the car, but not frisk them.
b. cannot order driver or passenger(s) out of the car or frisk them.
c. can order driver and passenger(s) out of the car and frisk them.
d. can order driver and passenger(s) out of the car; can frisk driver, but not passengers.
ANS: C
REF: 240-241
LO: 1, 3

9.16   A(n) _____ is a situation where the police take someone in for questioning in a manner that is, in reality, an arrest:
a. pretext arrest
b. ulterior motive seizure
c. *de facto* arrest
d. material witness seizure
ANS: C
REF: 246
LO: 1, 5, 6

161

9.17   A *Terry* stop requires:
        a. reasonable suspicion.
        b. informational probable cause.
        c. observational probable cause.
        d. corroborating information.
        ANS: A
        REF: 235
        LO: 1

9.18   In *Florida v. J.L.*, the Supreme Court ruled that *Terry* stops:
        a. can be justified by an anonymous tip.
        b. cannot be justified solely by an anonymous tip.
        c. only require probable cause.
        d. can be justified by an anonymous tip about deadly weapons only.
        ANS: B
        REF: 235
        LO: 1

9.19   Police may use deadly force against fleeing felons:
        a. if the pursuit enters another jurisdiction.
        b. if the police fear the felon would otherwise escape.
        c. only if the suspect presents an imminent danger to life.
        d. if state law requires it.
        ANS: C
        REF: 257
        LO: 12

9.20   In *Illinois v. Wardlow*, the Supreme Court ruled that unexplained flight from the police:
        a. is a constitutional right.
        b. does not, by itself, create reasonable suspicion
        c. in itself establishes reasonable suspicion.
        d. indicates, without exception, wrongdoing and establishes probable cause.
        ANS: B
        REF: 237
        LO: 1

9.21   In *United States v. Sharpe* the Court ruled that a stop:
        a. has no rigid time limit.
        b. has no time limit.
        c. can be no longer than 20 minutes.
        d. can be no longer than 75 minutes.
        ANS: A
        REF: 238
        LO: 2

9.22   When would a traffic stop require Miranda warnings?
        a. An officer is asking for consent to search the vehicle.
        b. The officer is going to arrest the driver.
        c. Miranda warnings are not required for traffic stops.
        d. A records check reveals an expired license.
        ANS: C
        REF: 240
        LO: 4

9.23   The Supreme Court held that "In terms that apply equally to seizures of property and to
        seizures of persons, the Fourth Amendment has drawn a firm line at the entrance to the
        house…Absent exigent circumstances, that threshold may not reasonably be crossed
        without a warrant" in:
        a. *Payton v. New York*
        b. *Illinois v. Wardlow*
        c. *United States v. Watson*
        d. *Tennessee v. Garner*
        ANS: A
        REF: 250
        LO: 8, 9

9.24   Officers must have a particularized and objective basis for suspecting the person stopped
        of criminal activity to demonstrate reasonable suspicion for an investigatory stop under
        the:
        a. totality of the circumstances test
        b. articulable probable cause test
        c. presumptively reasonable standard
        d. objectively reasonable standard.
        ANS: A
        REF: 234
        LO: 5

9.25   Roadblocks have been found to be constitutional if their purpose is to check for:
        a. drugs.
        b. drunk drivers.
        c. illegal weapons.
        d. criminal activity.
        ANS: B
        REF: 244
        LO: 3

9.26 A situation in which the police take someone in for questioning in a manner that is, in reality an arrest, but without the requisite probable cause (and therefore illegal) is called:

a. an augmented stop.
b. a seizure incident to arrest.
c. detention tantamount to arrest.
d. pre-arrest detention.

ANS: C
REF: 246
LO: 1, 5

9.27 Some states allow officers to arrest for a misdemeanor not committed in their presence in the case of:

a. domestic assault.
b. reckless driving.
c. drug possession.
d. illegal immigrants.

ANS: A
REF: 248
LO: 8

9.28 People who are arrested have the right to all of the following, except:

a. make a phone call.
b. know the charges against them.
c. appear before a magistrate without undue delay.
d. a reasonable expectation of privacy.

ANS: D
REF: 264
LO: 7

9.29 Police may make a warrantless arrest based on probable cause in all of the following circumstances, except:

a. felony committed in their presence.
b. an unwitnessed felony.
c. most misdemeanors occurring outside their presence.
d. any crime in their presence.

ANS: C
REF: 248
LO: 8

9.30   The circumstances in which officers leave their jurisdiction and enter another to make an arrest of a felon who committed the felony in the officers' jurisdiction and then fled across jurisdictional lines is called:
a. fresh pursuit
b. hot pursuit
c. continuous pursuit
d. unabated pursuit
ANS: A
REF: 254
LO: 3, 8, 9

True/False

9.31   An arrest is an informal restraint on a person's liberty of movement.
ANS: F
REF: 247
LO: 5, 6

9.32   A stop is a seizure of the person within the meaning of the Fourth Amendment.
ANS: T
REF: 233
LO: 1

9.33   A seizure is not necessarily an arrest, but all arrests are seizures.
ANS: T
REF: 246
LO: 5

9.34   The only justification for the use of deadly force is self-defense.
ANS: F
REF: 264
LO: 12

9.35   For an investigatory stop to be constitutional, the officer must have articulable probable cause.
ANS: F
REF: 234
LO: 1

9.36   An officer's hot pursuit of a suspect cannot legally continue past the threshold to a private residence without a warrant.
ANS: F
REF: 254
LO: 9

9.37   Officers may use deadly force to terminate a dangerous, high-speed vehicle pursuit.
        ANS: T
        REF: 255
        LO: 10

9.38   Miranda warnings must be given during traffic stops if information is about to reveal
        probable cause to arrest.
        ANS: F
        REF: 240
        LO: 4

9.39   De facto arrests are legal since officers are in the process of developing probable cause.
        ANS: F
        REF: 246
        LO: 8

9.40   Checkpoints at or near international borders require justification to stop all vehicles.
        ANS: F
        REF: 245
        LO: 1, 3

Fill-In

9.41   An estimated 95 percent of all arrests are made _____.
        ANS: without warrants; without a warrant
        REF: 248
        LO: 6

9.42   Police may not enter a private home without the appropriate warrant(s) to make a routine
        felony arrest unless _____ exist.
        ANS: exigent circumstances
        REF: 250
        LO: 9

9.43   The length of an investigative detention should be measured in _____.
        ANS: minutes
        REF: 238
        LO: 2

9.44   Stopping a vehicle to search for evidence of a crime under the guise of a traffic stop is
        called a _____.
        ANS: pretext stop
        REF: 243
        LO: 3

9.45 When a reasonable person believes he or she is not free to leave, a(n) _____ has occurred.
ANS: seizure
REF: 246
LO: 5

9.46 Common law has held that anyone witnessing certain crimes may make a(n) _____ and then turn that individual over to authorities.
ANS: citizen's arrest
REF: 264
LO: 6, 8

9.47 A situation in which the police take someone in for questioning in a manner that is, in reality, an arrest, but without the requisite probable cause is called _____.
ANS: detention tantamount to arrest; de facto arrest
REF: 246
LO: 1, 5, 6

9.48 A(n) _____ is the taking of a person into custody for the purpose of holding him to answer a criminal charge.
ANS: arrest
REF: 247
LO: 6

9.49 Police officers are allowed, without reasonable suspicion of any criminal acts, to approach and detain citizens for _____ purposes.
ANS: community caretaking
REF: 247
LO: 5

9.50 Police may arrest for an unwitnessed felony based on _____.
ANS: probable cause
REF: 248
LO: 8

Essay

9.51   Compare and contrast a stop and an arrest.

ANS: *Terry v. Ohio* (1968) established that the authority to stop is independent of the power to arrest. A stop is not an arrest, but it is a seizure within the meaning of the Fourth Amendment and, therefore, requires reasonableness. Students should articulate the basic differences between a stop and an arrest that are summarized in Table 9.1.
REF: 233
LO: 1

9.52   Explain when vehicles may be stopped and what officers can and cannot do.

ANS: Investigatory *Terry* stops may occur only when officer has articulable reasonable suspicion. Otherwise, officers may stop motorists only for violations of the law, which may include equipment violations, erratic driving, or invalid vehicle registration. An officer may order the driver and passenger(s) out of vehicle; frisk the driver and passenger(s) if reasonably believed to be armed; and stop vehicles for roadblock/checkpoint purposes. Officers may not conduct pretext stop with ulterior motives to search for drugs, etc.
REF: 239-246
LO: 3

9.53   Discuss the controversial topic of use of force and the landmark cases guiding officer behavior.

ANS: Officers may use only as much force as is needed to overcome resistance; pursuant to *Graham v. Connor* (1989), no resistance = no force. The Court set an "objective reasonableness" test in police use of force in *Tennessee v. Garner* (1985), reversing the "fleeing felon" rule and declaring that the only justification for use of deadly force is self-defense or protecting the lives of others. Students should articulate the various levels of force contained in the Use of Force Continuum as depicted in Figure 9.1.
REF: 255-264
LO: 12

9.54   List the elements of an arrest.

ANS: The elements of an arrest are: 1- intending to take a person into custody;
2- exercising authority to do so; 3- detaining or restraining the person to be arrested; and
4- the arrestee understanding what is happening.
REF: 247
LO: 7

9.55   Explain when an arrest may be made.

ANS: Officers may make a lawful arrest: 1- for any crime committed in their presence; 2- for any felony for which they have probable cause, whether witnessed by the officer or not; or 3- with an arrest warrant. Certain states also allow officers to arrest for specific misdemeanors that occur outside their presence, such as DWI, domestic assault, and shoplifting. State law may also authorize officers to arrest for misdemeanors that occur outside their presence if the subject might not be identified, might cause further harm to the victim, or might cause damage to property if not immediately arrested.
REF: 248-250
LO: 8

Chapter 10
Conducting Constitutional Searches

LEARNING OBJECTIVES

Upon completing this chapter, the student will know:

1. What fundamental constitutional rules apply to challenges under Fourth Amendment protection.
2. What limitation is placed on all searches. When general searches are legal.
3. What limitations are placed on searches with a warrant, with consent, in a frisk, and incident to a lawful arrest.
4. What exceptions to the warrant requirement have been established.
5. What the plain feel or plain touch ruling allows.
6. What the plain view doctrine is.
7. When a vehicle can be legally searched without a warrant and the precedent case.
8. What constitutes an exigent circumstance.
9. How reasonable expectation of privacy relates to searches of open fields, abandoned property, and public places.
10. How searches at international borders and airports are viewed under the Fourth Amendment.
11. Whether prison inmates, probationers and parolees have full Fourth Amendment protection.
12. How electronic surveillance is governed by the Fourth Amendment.
13. Whether a physical presence is required to constitute a search.
14. What relationship exists between electronic surveillance and one's reasonable expectations of privacy.
15. What is required to obtain an electronic surveillance warrant.

KEY TERMS

- **administrative warrant**—a search warrant issued to check private premises for compliance with local ordinances. [p. 277]

- **contemporaneous**—a concept that holds a search can be incident to an arrest only if it occurs at the same time of, and is confined to the immediate vicinity of, the arrest. [p. 287]

- **contraband**—anything that is illegal for people to own or have in their possession, for example, illegal drugs or illegal weapons. [p. 276]

- **curtilage**—the portion of property generally associated with the common use of land, for example, buildings, sheds, fenced-in areas and the like. The property around a home or dwelling that is directly associated with the use of that property. Because there is a reasonable expectation of privacy within the curtilage, it is protected by the Fourth Amendment. [p. 301

- **exigent circumstances**—emergency situations. [p. 296]

- **penumbra**—a type of shadow in astronomy with the principle extending to the idea that certain constitutional rights are implied within other constitutional rights. [p. 271]

- **plain feel**—Items felt during a lawful stop and frisk may be retrieved if the officer reasonably believes the items are contraband and can *instantly* recognize them as such. [p. 283]

- **plain touch**—same as plain feel. [p. 283]

- **plain view**—unconcealed evidence that officers see while engaged in a lawful activity may be seized and is admissible in court. [p. 285]

- **protective sweep**—a limited search made in conjunction with an in-home arrest when the searching officer possesses a reasonable belief based on specific and articulable facts that the area to be swept harbors an individual posing a danger to those on the arrest scene. It is not a full search of the premises, but a cursory inspection to determine if anyone else is present. [p. 289]

- **qualified immunity**—exemption of a public official from civil liability for actions performed during the course of his or her job unless they violated a "clearly established" constitutional or statutory right. [p. 276]

- **reasonable expectation of privacy**—a situation in which (1) a person has exhibited an actual (subjective) expectation of privacy and (2) that expectation is one that society is prepared to recognize as reasonable. [p. 271]

- **remoteness**—Regarding the unreasonableness and unlawfulness of searches of seized luggage or other personal belongings not immediately associated with the arrestee's body or under his or her immediate control if the search is distant in time and place from the arrest and, as such, is no longer an incident of the arrest, and if no emergency exists. [p. 288]

- **voluntariness test**—a determination as to whether one willingly and knowingly relinquished his or her constitutional rights, without pressure to do so, assessed by two factors: (1) the police conduct involved and (2) the characteristics of the accused. A determination that considers the totality of circumstances in assessing whether consent was obtained without coercion or promises and was, therefore, reasonable. [p. 281]

171

- **waiver test**—Citizens may waive their rights, but only if they do so voluntarily, knowingly and intentionally. The waiver is what makes the subsequent action reasonable. [p. 281]

- **wingspan**—the area within a person's reach or immediate control. [p. 287]

LECTURE OUTLINE

I.   Introduction

II.   Tenets of Fourth Amendment Search Analysis
    A. Reasonable expectation of privacy

III.   The Scope of Searches

IV.   Searches with a Warrant
    A. Executing the warrant
        1. Knock and announce rule
    B. Conducting the Search
    C. Administrative Warrants

V.   Searches without a Warrant
    A. Searches with Consent
        1. Standing
        2. Third party consent
        3. Voluntariness and waiver tests
    B. Frisks
        1. *Terry v. Ohio*
    C. Plain Feel/Plain Touch
        1. *Minnesota v. Dickerson* (1993)
    D. Plain View Evidence
        1. *Kyllo v. United States* (2001): infrared imaging
    E. Searches Incident to Lawful Arrest
        1. *Chimel v. California* (1969)
           a. wingspan
        2. Contemporaneous
        3. Remoteness: *United States v. Chadwick* (1977)
        4. Protective sweeps: *Maryland v. Buie* (1990)
        5. Use of Force in Searching an Arrested Person
        6. Searching People Other Than the Arrested Person
        7. Searching the Vehicle of an Arrested Person
           a. *Arizona v. Gant* (2009)
        8. Inventory Searches

CHAPTER SUMMARY

The fundamental constitutional rules that apply to challenges under Fourth Amendment protection are (1) there must be governmental action; (2) the person making the challenge must have standing, that is, the conduct violates the challenger's *reasonable expectation of privacy;* and (3) *general searches* are unlawful and restrict government from going beyond what is necessary. All searches must be limited in scope. General searches are unconstitutional and never legal.

Searches conducted with a warrant must be limited to the specific area and specific items described in the warrant. Although warrantless searches are presumed unreasonable, exceptions to the warrant requirement include the following: (1) with consent; (2) frisking for officer safety; (3) plain feel/view evidence; (4) incident to lawful, custodial arrest; (5) automobile exceptions; (6) exigent (emergency) circumstances; and (7) open fields, abandoned property and public places.

In the first exception, consent searches, the consent to search must be voluntary. The search must be limited to the area specified by the person granting permission. The person may revoke the consent at any time. In the second exception, stop-and-frisk situations, if a frisk is authorized by the circumstances of an investigative stop, only a limited pat down of the detainee's outer clothing for the officer's safety is authorized. In the third exception, plain feel/view, if, in the lawful course of a frisk, officers feel something that training and experience causes them to believe is contraband, there is probable cause to expand the search and seize the object—plain feel/touch. In addition, unconcealed evidence that officers see while engaged in a lawful activity may be seized and is admissible in court—plain view.

In the fourth exception, searches incidental to a lawful, custodial arrest, the search must be contemporaneous and must be limited to the area within the person's reach (*Chimel*). A search incident to lawful arrest allows seizure of property or containers not immediately connected with the arrestee's body, but under his or her immediate control, including backpacks, briefcases, luggage or other packages. In the fifth exception, the automobile exception, *Carroll v. United States* (1925) established that vehicles can be searched without a warrant provided (1) there is probable cause to believe the vehicle's contents violate the law and (2) the vehicle would be gone before a search warrant could be obtained. The sixth exception, exigent circumstances, includes danger of physical harm to officers or another person, danger of destruction of evidence, driving while intoxicated, hot-pursuit situations and individuals requiring "rescuing." The seventh exception, open fields, abandoned property and public places, involves the lack of expectation of privacy; therefore, the Fourth Amendment protection does not apply.

The Court has ruled that routine border searches and searches at international airports are reasonable under the Fourth Amendment. Prison inmates, probationers and parolees have limited Fourth Amendment rights because while under supervision, they should not expect the degree of privacy enjoyed by law-abiding citizens.

Electronic surveillance is a form of search and seizure and, as such, is governed by the Fourth Amendment. For a search to have occurred, government agents need not physically go onto someone's property. Information obtained whenever there is a reasonable expectation of privacy constitutes a search. The Fourth Amendment does not limit the use of electronic equipment that merely enhances officers' senses but does not interfere with a person's reasonable expectation of privacy. Lights, photography from aircraft and telescopes fall within this area. To obtain an electronic-surveillance warrant, probable cause that a person is engaging in particular communications must be established by the court, and normal investigative procedures must have already been tried.

SUGGESTED ANSWERS TO THE DISCUSSION QUESTIONS

1. Why is a "frisk" considered a search and an "arrest" considered a seizure?

   A frisk is a cursory search of an individual's person based on reasonable suspicion and is limited to a pat down of the outer clothing for the safety of the officer. The Fourth Amendment uses the term "search" which the Supreme Court has held to apply to a *frisk*. The term "seizure" applies to *arrest* (because the person is seized, i.e., not free to leave). The Supreme Court has interpreted these terms to maintain the spirit of the Constitution with regards to the variety of contacts government (i.e., police) have with the public.

2. What type of search were the framers of the Constitution prohibiting through the Fourth Amendment?

   General searches. Having experienced such abuse at the hands of the British government, the framers sought to prevent the same thing from happening in this country. They felt that searches by the government must be limited, with the reason for the search being held to a high standard of proof and the scope of the search being limited. To allow government to conduct general searches that exceed their purpose and need is unreasonable, which is why the Fourth Amendment was included in the Bill of Rights.

3. Provide your own definition of reasonable.

   Ask ten people to describe "reasonable" and you are likely to get ten different definitions. What a *reasonable person* would consider *reasonable* is what the Court looks towards. With direct reference to searches, what the Supreme Court has always looked for is overreaching or "unreasonableness" of government which the Constitution has sought to control.

4. Discuss the advantages to obtaining a warrant.

   Two primary benefits of obtaining a warrant are an independent magistrate's determination that probable cause exists, placing the burden of proving otherwise with the defense, and removing the officer from the determination in cases that are uncertain or politically volatile.

5. Why are searches of homes different from searches of motor vehicles?

   The basic reason for the automobile exception to the warrant requirement is the ease with which motor vehicles may be moved during the time a warrant would be sought. A diminished expectation of privacy surrounds the automobile. A vehicle is used for transportation and not as a residence or repository of personal belongings. The vehicle's occupants and contents are in plain view. Vehicles are necessarily highly regulated by the government. A person has a greater expectation of privacy in their home. The Fourth Amendment specifically mentions "houses" and the Court has consistently held that non-consensual, warrantless entry into one's home is what the Fourth Amendment was created to prevent.

6. Provide your own definition of *reasonable expectation of privacy.*

   Students' definitions will likely vary. Here we are looking to the student to provide an understanding of when a person does *not* have this expectation of privacy. Examples could include all of the exceptions that make warrantless searches reasonable, including displaying something in public or before police officers, abandoning or throwing away something or telling the police that they may proceed with their search without a warrant.

7. Do you think the U.S. Supreme Court has been supportive of law enforcement through its rulings in cases involving the Fourth Amendment?

   Students' responses will vary dependent on their personal beliefs. An excellent debate topic.

8. Draft a scenario in which an innocent, routine interaction between a citizen in a public place and the police could result in a continuing escalation through reasonable suspicion to probable cause, and what the results to each party would be.

   Students' scenarios will vary considerably. For example, an officer might have an innocuous contact with someone such as stopping to assist them with their flat tire along the highway. The demeanor of the vehicle operator might lead the officer to suspect he or she has been consuming alcohol, possibly to the point of being impaired. The officer would then have justification for keeping the person there to conduct a brief investigatory stop to determine if, indeed, they are under the influence, and if this were the case and probable cause was established, that person might be placed under arrest (considering variations in state laws).

9. Is the exclusionary rule effective in limiting potential abuse of the Fourth Amendment by police when searching? Could another means be more effective?

   Students' responses will vary dependent on their personal beliefs. An excellent debate topic.

176

10. How do you think the Fourth Amendment will be held to apply to e-mail and other data transmitted over the Internet?

This is an excellent question for students because, as of the date this text was published, there is no answer. In forming their response students should consider issues of whether others could freely access this data, who might realistically and lawfully have access to it, etc. This is the type of technology that the framers of the Constitution could never have anticipated, and yet they successfully drafted a document which could, eventually, address such developments.

STUDENT ACTIVITIES

- Ask if any students have experienced a search at a border crossing or airport or other security checkpoint (visiting a prison, etc.). If so, ask them to describe the circumstances, including the actions of the searching agents and their own reaction to being searched.

- Moderate a class discussion on privacy. In particular, pose this question: Given that terrorists use existing privacy protections to mask their activities in preparation for an attack, should Americans be more tolerant of privacy invasions in the interest of assisting law enforcement in their efforts to preempt such attacks?

- Access the lesson plan on "Airport Scanners and the Fourth Amendment" at the Bill of Rights Institute at http://www.billofrightsinstitute.org/page.aspx?pid=546.

- Have students research cases involving abandoned property and the Fourth Amendment and discuss the examples that they find. When making and explaining the assignment, use the humorous example of "Trash Might Be Abandoned Property, "Butt" Not If The Detective Kicks It Off The Patio" (referencing State v. Reed, N.C.App. No. COA06-400) at the Fourth Amendment and FDCPA website at http://fairdebtlawyer.blogspot.com/2007/03/trash-might-be-abandoned-property-butt.html.

INTERNET CONNECTIONS

- Privacy issues reign supreme at the **privacy.org** web site, accessible at http://www.privacy.org/.

- The **Electronic Privacy Information Center** provides comprehensive information on the subject at http://www.epic.org/.

- **Loyola of Los Angeles Law Review**: "Are Emerging Technologies in Airport Passenger Screening Reasonable Under the Fourth Amendment?" by Sara Kornblatt at: http://llr.lls.edu/docs/41-1kornblatt.pdf.

- Access a listing of key cases involving "exigent circumstances" at the **Case Law 4 Cops** website at http://www.caselaw4cops.net/searchandseizure/exigent.htm.

CHAPTER 10 TEST BANK

Multiple Choice

10.1   The Supreme Court ruled that unannounced cell searches or shakedowns did not require warrants, did not violate inmates' Fourth Amendment rights, and were justified by the need to maintain order in:
a. *Morrissey v. Brewer*
b. *Bell v. Wolfish*
c. *Gideon v. Wainwright*
d. *Griffin v. Wisconsin*
ANS: B
REF: 307
LO: 11

10.2   Searches with a warrant:
a. are presumed to be unreasonable.
b. must be executed within 36 hours to be valid
c. are presumed to be reasonable.
d. are unlimited in scope.
ANS: C
REF: 272
LO: 3

10.3   General searches are:
a. routinely done by police.
b. never constitutional.
c. permitted if authorized by a warrant.
d. permitted in cases where the suspect is found to be armed.
ANS: B
REF: 272
LO: 2

10.4   Which of the following would not be a legitimate factor contributing to the decision to frisk?
a. suspect who flees
b. suspicion a suspect possesses dangerous drugs
c. being in known high-crime area
d. suspect's hand is concealed in pocket
ANS: B
REF: 282
LO: 3

10.5 Which of the following would be considered a violation of a subject's reasonable expectation of privacy, requiring a warrant?
a. Police put a "beeper" on a vehicle to monitor its location.
b. Undercover officer converses with suspects and uses information in court.
c. Taking photographs of curtilage from an aircraft.
d. Placing listening device in public telephone booth to monitor conversations.
ANS: D
REF: 312
LO: 14

10.6 Searches of vehicles incident to the arrest of an occupant area allowed only if the officer has a reasonable belief that the arrestee can gain access to the vehicle or _____ will be found in the vehicle.
a. contraband
b. weapons
c. evidence of the crime of arrest
d. evidence of any crime
ANS: C
REF: 291
LO: 3, 4, 7

10.7 For which of the following does Title III require a warrant?
a. Electronic surveillance (wiretap)
b. Recording phone conversations with consent of one of the two parties to the conversation.
c. Using a pen register to obtain the numbers dialed from a telephone.
d. Randomly intercepting cordless and cellular phone conversations.
ANS: A
REF: 313-314
LO: 14

10.8 A search can be incident to arrest only if it is substantially _____ with the arrest and is confined to the immediate vicinity of the arrest.
a. extemporaneous
b. noncontemporary
c. contemporaneous
d. asynchronous
ANS: C
REF: 287
LO: 3

10.9   Officers can conduct a limited protective search incident to in-house arrest _____ that anyone dangerous is hiding in the home.
a. without any suspicion
b. with reasonable suspicion
c. with probable cause
d. with specific, articulable facts
ANS: A
REF: 289
LO: 3, 4

10.10   The Supreme Court reduced law enforcement's authority to search the passenger compartment of a vehicle incident to arrest in:
a. *Arizona v. Gant*
b. *Carroll v. United States*
c. *United States v. Simmons*
d. *New York v. Belton*
ANS: A
REF: 290
LO: 3, 4, 7

10.11   *Robbins v. California* specified all of the following justifications for warrantless vehicle searches, except:
a. mobility produces exigent circumstances.
b. vehicles occupants are in plain view.
c. diminished expectation of privacy in a vehicle.
d. vehicle searches do not require the probable cause necessary for a warrant.
ANS: D
REF: 294
LO: 7

10.12   Routine searches at our national borders require:
a. reasonable suspicion.
b. consent.
c. probable cause.
d. no justification.
ANS: D
REF: 303
LO: 10

10.13 Electronic surveillance:
a. is governed by the Fourth Amendment.
b. never requires a warrant.
c. produces no intrusion on one's reasonable expectations of privacy.
d. requires a warrant only when entry on premises is necessary to conduct the surveillance.
ANS: A
REF: 311
LO: 12

10.14 Which of the following would not constitute a lawful warrantless search?
a. dumpster-diving
b. looking at curtilage from the air
c. using a thermal imaging device to find a "grow" room
d. covert involuntary DNA sampling
ANS: C
REF: 299-302
LO: 9

10.15 When government agents are lawfully executing a warrant they:
a. must obtain another warrant if they find additional illegal items.
b. can seize any contraband, even if not specified in the warrant.
c. can continue searching the premises after what was specified in the warrant is found.
d. can take anything they want for any reason.
ANS: B
REF: 276
LO: 3

10.16 Which of the following is not one of the criteria that must be met for plain view?
a. The original intrusion is legal only because it is pursuant to a valid warrant.
b. The items are plainly observed while in the permissible scope of the original intrusion.
c. The original intrusion is legal because the officers are present legally.
d. The items are immediately recognizable as evidence or contraband.
ANS: A
REF: 285
LO: 6

10.17 Which of the following is not one of the fundamental constitutional rules that apply to Fourth Amendment cases?
a. There must be governmental action.
b. General searches are unlawful.
c. The person making the challenge must have a reasonable expectation of privacy.
d. There must be law enforcement action.
ANS: D
REF: 271
LO: 1

10.18 Relationships where third-party consent to search is allowed include all *except*:
a. parent/child.
b. employer/employee.
c. landlord/tenant.
d. host/guest.
ANS: C
REF: 280
LO: 4

10.19 To obtain an electronic surveillance warrant, or wiretap order, probable cause that a person is engaging in particular communications must be established by the court and _____ must have already been tried.
a. random interception of communications
b. normal investigative procedures
c. an attempt to obtain one-party's consent
d. a trap and trace device
ANS: B
REF: 313
LO: 15

10.20 When conducting inventory searches of a vehicle, it is important to have:
a. probable cause to trigger the automobile exception.
b. a standard operating procedure.
c. a warrant because the vehicle is no longer mobile.
d. a systematic method for conducting the search..
ANS: B
REF: 296
LO: 7

10.21 All searches must be:
a. with a warrant.
b. with consent.
c. limited in scope.
d. general in nature.
ANS: C
REF: 272
LO: 2

10.22 When a person is handcuffed after being arrested, officers may search:
a. only their person.
b. the area that has been under the immediate control of the suspect prior to being arrested.
c. only where the suspect could reach while handcuffed.
d. all areas where the suspect could have hidden evidence.
ANS: B
REF: 287
LO: 3

10.23 Which of the following have lower courts not yet recognized as analogous to plain view?
a. plain feel
b. plain smell
c. plain hearing
d. plain taste
ANS: D
REF: 283-285
LO: 5, 6

10.24 In which of the following situations are school officials justified in searching without a warrant or probable cause if they have reasonable suspicion to believe contraband exists?
a. University dorm rooms
b. Students and student lockers at public and private schools
c. Students and student lockers at public schools
d. Adult students
ANS: C
REF: 306
LO: 4, 9

10.25 The Supreme Court has said that a Fourth Amendment _____ is a governmental infringement of a legitimate expectation of privacy.
a. search
b. seizure
c. arrest
d. investigative stop
ANS: A
REF: 271
LO: 1

10.26   The precedent case for searches incidental to a lawful arrest is:
        a. *Minnesota* v. *Dickerson.*
        b. *Terry* v. *Ohio.*
        c. *New Jersey* v. *T.L.O.*
        d. *Chimel* v. *California.*
        ANS: D
        REF: 287
        LO: 3, 4

10.27   Limited searches conducted in accordance with constitutional guidelines serve society's needs while:
        a. protecting the individual.
        b. preserving the admissibility of any discovered evidence.
        c. preventing improper conduct by overzealous law enforcement agents.
        d. serving to protect against a successful appeal of a conviction.
        ANS: A
        REF: 272
        LO: 3

10.28   The precedent for warrantless searches of vehicles came from:
        a. *Carroll* v. *United States.*
        b. *Chambers* v. *Maroney.*
        c. *Robbins* v. *California.*
        d. *South Dakota* v. *Opperman.*
        ANS: A
        REF: 293
        LO: 7

10.29   The Fourth Amendment applies:
        a. only to police investigating criminal activity.
        b. only to state and federal law enforcement agencies.
        c. to the actions of both public officials and private citizens.
        d. to all government workers.
        ANS: D
        REF: 272
        LO: 1

10.30   Exigent circumstances include all of the following, *except*:
        a. driving while intoxicated.
        b. a person fleeing upon seeing an officer approach.
        c. rendering emergency aid.
        d. danger of destruction of evidence.
        ANS: B
        REF: 296
        LO: 8

True/False

10.31 Officers are required to inform people that they have the right to refuse consent to search.
ANS: F
REF: 278
LO: 3, 4

10.32 For a search to have occurred, government agents must make physical entry into someone's property.
ANS: F
REF: 312
LO: 13

10.33 When both occupants are present and one consents to a search and one objects, the consent "overrides" the refusal and officers can legally search.
ANS: F
REF: 280
LO: 3, 4

10.34 The maxim that it is unreasonable for officers to search for "an elephant in a matchbox" means the size of the item(s) sought determines where officers may reasonably search.
ANS: T
REF: 272
LO: 2, 3

10.35 A person's reasonable expectation of privacy determines when Fourth Amendment protections apply.
ANS: T
REF: 271
LO: 1, 9

10.36 If a warrant states that one specific item is sought, the search may still continue after it is found.
ANS: F
REF: 276
LO: 3

10.37 "Open fields" is a federal concept only; some states hold that "No Trespassing" signs establish a right of privacy requiring a warrant.
ANS: T
REF: 301
LO: 9

10.38 Since they are not incarcerated, probationers and parolees enjoy the same Fourth
       Amendment rights as law-abiding citizens.
       ANS: F
       REF: 308
       LO: 11

10.39 Seizures of items from a suspect's body, such as hair samples, are typically allowed
       without a warrant incident to arrest if painless reasonable procedures are used.
       ANS: T
       REF: 288
       LO: 3, 4

10.40 A person's refusal to give consent to search can be used to establish probable cause.
       ANS: F
       REF: 281
       LO: 3, 4

Fill-In

10.41 General searches are _____.
       ANS: unconstitutional; never legal
       REF: 272
       LO: 2

10.42 Courts typically justify the consent exception by two separate tests: the _____
       test and the _____ test.
       ANS: voluntariness, waiver
       REF: 281
       LO: 4

10.43 _____ includes anything that is illegal for people to own or have in their possession.
       ANS: Contraband
       REF: 276
       LO: 1, 3

10.44 The area within a person's reach or immediate control is called the person's _____.
       ANS: wingspan
       REF: 287
       LO: 3

10.45 When officers arrest someone in a home, they are allowed to make a _____ for
       their safety.
       ANS: protective search; protective sweep
       REF: 289
       LO: 3

10.46 Vehicles may often be searched without a warrant because of their _____.
ANS: mobility
REF: 293
LO: 7

10.47 The _____ doctrine allows officers who feel something that they immediately identify as contraband, it can be lawfully seized based on probable cause.
ANS: plain feel; plain touch
REF: 283
LO: 5

10.48 Driving while intoxicated and hot pursuit situations are examples of _____.
ANS: exigent circumstances; emergencies
REF: 296
LO: 8

10.49 The property around a home or dwelling directly associated with use of that property is called the_____.
ANS: curtilage
REF: 301
LO: 9

10.50 After a person has _____ property, he or she has no reasonable expectation of privacy relative to that property.
ANS: abandoned; discarded
REF: 301
LO: 9

Essay

10.51 Discuss at least five exceptions to the search warrant requirement.

ANS: Exceptions to the warrant requirement include:
- Consent search.
- Frisks.
- Plain feel/plain view.
- Incident to arrest.
- Automobile exception.
- Exigent (emergency) circumstances.
- Open fields, abandoned property, and public places.

Students should reference appropriate cases and examples in their answers.
REF: 278-303
LO: 4

10.52 List three fundamental constitutional rules for searches and discuss their importance.

ANS: The fundamental constitutional rules for searches are that: 1- unreasonable searches and seizures are not allowed; 2- people's reasonable expectation of privacy determines when Fourth Amendment protections apply; and 3- general searches are unlawful and restrict government from going beyond what is necessary. These rules are important because they protect the right of individuals to be free from unreasonable invasion of privacy by the government while permitting necessary governmental intrusion under limited and specific circumstances.
REF: 271
LO: 1

10.53 Discuss the relationship between electronic surveillance and one's reasonable expectation of privacy.

ANS: Electronic surveillance is a form of search and seizure and is governed by the Fourth Amendment. A search occurs whenever information is obtained from a location where one holds a reasonable expectation of privacy. The Fourth Amendment does not limit the use of electronic equipment that merely enhances officers' senses (e.g., lights, telescopes, or aerial photography) but does not interfere with a person's reasonable expectation of privacy.
REF: 311-316
LO: 14

10.54 Discuss what might constitute exigent circumstances. Give specific examples.

ANS: Emergency situations that might justify a warrantless search under exigent circumstances include threats to life or safety (e.g., hot-pursuit situations, drivers under the influence of alcohol or drugs, unconscious individuals, or suspects thought to be armed), possible destruction or removal of evidence, or the potential escape of a suspect.
REF: 296-299
LO: 8

10.55 Explain the justifications for the automobile exception to the requirement for a warrant.

ANS: The mobility of automobiles creates the circumstance whereby it would be unreasonable to expect suspects to voluntarily remain in place while the officer returns to the station to obtain a warrant and then find a judge to sign it. Likewise, it would be unreasonable to detain a suspect for the length of time needed to obtain a signed warrant. A diminished expectation of privacy surrounds the automobile. A vehicle is used for transportation and not as a residence or repository of personal belongings. The vehicle's occupants and contents are in plain view. Vehicles are necessarily highly regulated by the government (*Robbins v. California*).
REF: 293-294
LO: 7

Chapter 11
The Fifth Amendment:
Obtaining Information Legally

LEARNING OBJECTIVES

Upon completing this chapter, the student will know:

1. What the Fifth Amendment prohibits the government to do and what it guarantees.
2. How the Supreme Court has extended the elements of due process.
3. What factors determine the voluntariness of a confession.
4. The primary modern case for analyzing confessions.
5. What four warnings are included in *Miranda*.
6. When the *Miranda* warning must be given.
7. What constitutes a valid waiver of *Miranda* rights.
8. Whether private security officers need to recite the *Miranda* warning before interrogating suspects.
9. What the public safety exception allows police officers to do.
10. How expectations of privacy are related to statements, including confessions.
11. What rights in addition to due process are guaranteed by the Fifth Amendment.
12. Which rights are not incorporated.
13. How the USA PATRIOT Act enhances government's ability to gather information related to suspected terrorist activities.

KEY TERMS

- **beachheading**—the unconstitutional approach of purposely withholding the *Miranda* warnings until after a confession is obtained and then giving *Miranda* to re-ask the question. [p. 342]

- **custodial interrogation**—Questioning by law-enforcement officers after a person has been taken into custody or otherwise deprived of freedom of action in any significant way. [p. 334]

- **double jeopardy**—A prohibition against the government from trying someone twice for the same offense. [p. 354]

- **due process**—The Fifth and Fourteenth Amendments' constitutionally guaranteed right of an accused to hear the charges against him or her and to be heard by the court having jurisdiction over the matter. It is the idea that basic fairness must remain part of the process, and it provides rules and procedures to ensure fairness to an individual and to prevent arbitrary actions by government. [p. 325]

- **entrapment**—The act of government officials or agents (usually police) that induce a person to commit a crime that the person would not have otherwise committed. [p. 350]

- **grand jury**—A group of citizens who determine whether sufficient evidence exists to send an accused to trial. [p. 352]

- **harmless error doctrine**—Involves the admissibility of involuntary confessions: If no harm results, the confession should be admissible. Also, if the preponderance of evidence suggests a defendant's guilt, any "tainted" or illegal evidence not crucial to proving the case against the defendant will not cause the case to be dismissed. [p. 328]

- **indictment**—A formal accusation of a defendant, usually by a grand jury, that sends the defendant on to trial for prosecution. [p. 353]

- **interrogation**—the formal, systemic, express questioning by law enforcement of a person suspected of criminal activity, as well as the functional equivalent of express questioning (any words or actions by the police, other than those normally attendant to arrest and custody, that the police should know are reasonably likely to elicit an incriminating response from the suspect). [p. 337]

- **just compensation**—The requirement that property owners be paid fair market value by the government when government takes their property. [p. 355]

- **procedural due process**—Constitutionally guaranteed rights of fairness in how the law is carried out or applied. [p. 325]

- **public safety exception**—Allows officers to question suspects without first giving the *Miranda* warning if the information sought sufficiently affects the officers' and the public's safety. [p. 347]

- **substantive due process**—Requires laws themselves to be fair. [p. 326]

- **USA PATRIOT Act**—legislation that significantly improves the nation's counterterrorism efforts by (1) allowing investigators to use the tools already available to investigate organized crime and drug trafficking, (2) facilitating information sharing and cooperation among government agencies so they can better "connect the dots," (3) updating the law to reflect new technologies and new threats and (4) increasing the penalties for those who commit or support terrorist crimes. [p. 356]

- **waiver**—A purposeful and voluntary giving up of a known right. [p. 338]

LECTURE OUTLINE

I.   Introduction

II. Government's Need to Know

III. The Right against Self-Incrimination

IV. Due Process of Law
    A. Procedural due process
    B. Substantive due process

V.   The Fifth Amendment and Confessions
    A. Voluntariness of Confessions
        1. *Brown v. Mississippi* (1936)
        2. *Fikes v. Alabama* (1957)
            a. due process voluntariness test
    B. Police Conduct
        1. *Arizona v. Fulminante* (1991)
            a. harmless error doctrine
    C. Characteristics of the Accused
    D. A Standard for Voluntariness
    E. False Confessions

VI. *Miranda v. Arizona*
    A. The Case
    B. The *Miranda* Warning
        1. The wording
            a. *California v. Prysock* (1981)
            b. *Duckworth v. Egan* (1989)
            c. *Florida v. Powell* (2010)
            d. "Soft" *Miranda* warnings
    C. Premature *Miranda* Warnings
    D. When the *Miranda* Warning Must Be Given
        1. Custodial interrogation
        2. Custody
            a. Suspect under Arrest
            b. Suspect at the Police Station
            d. Suspect Is in Custody for Another Offense
            e. Other Factors Indicating a Custodial Situation
        3. Interrogation
            a. *Rhode Island v. Innis* (1980)
    E. Waiving the Rights
        1. Waiver
        2. Right to Remain Silent
            a. *Michigan v. Mosley* (1975)

CHAPTER SUMMARY

The Fifth Amendment protects against self-incrimination and guarantees citizens due process of law by limiting the federal government's actions: "No person shall . . . be compelled in any criminal case to be a witness against himself" and "No person shall . . . be deprived of life, liberty, or property, without due process of law." The Supreme Court has extended the elements of due process through case law beyond the words of the Constitution but in keeping with its spirit. Voluntariness of a confession is determined by (1) the police conduct involved and (2) the characteristics of the accused.

Miranda remains the precedent case referred to by courts analyzing confession issues. The four warnings included in Miranda are (1) you have the constitutional right to remain silent, (2) anything you say can and will be used against you in court, (3) you have the right to talk to a lawyer now and have him present now or at any time during questioning, and (4) if you cannot afford a lawyer, one will be appointed for you without cost. The *Miranda* warning must be given to a suspect interrogated in police custody, that is, when the suspect is not free to leave. If after hearing an officer read the *Miranda* warning, a suspect remains silent, the silence is not a waiver. To waive their rights, suspects must state, orally or in writing, that (1) they understand their rights and (2) they will voluntarily answer questions without a lawyer present.

Private security officers are not required to advise suspects of their *Miranda* rights. The public safety exception allows police officers to question suspects without first giving the *Miranda* warning if the information sought sufficiently affects the officers' and the public's safety. Further statements, including confessions, will not be admissible in court if they were obtained while a person's Fourth Amendment right to a reasonable expectation of privacy was being violated.

In addition to the right not to incriminate oneself, the Fifth Amendment also guarantees the right to a grand jury indictment, the prohibition against double jeopardy and the right to receive just compensation when government takes private property. The right to a grand jury is the only unincorporated clause of the Fifth Amendment (*Hurtado v. California*, 1884).

The USA PATRIOT Act strengthened the ability of the Justice Department and the FBI to monitor suspected terrorists or their associates and significantly improves the nation's counterterrorism efforts.

SUGGESTED ANSWERS TO THE DISCUSSION QUESTIONS

1. Why should government be limited on how and when it asks questions?

   Because government inherently has so much authority that coercion must be a consideration. Again, limitation of government is at the basis of this issue.

2. How do you feel about police "encouraging" suspects to talk by threatening or using physical force or otherwise intimidating them?

   Students' responses will vary dependent on their personal beliefs. An excellent debate topic.

3. Does the *Miranda* decision impede police work?

   Students' responses will vary dependent on their personal beliefs. An excellent debate topic.

4. Would a different result occur, given exactly the same circumstances of an interrogation, for what a private security officer could do as opposed to what a city police officer must do?

   Students' responses will vary dependent on their personal beliefs. An excellent debate topic.

5. Why shouldn't a stop require *Miranda*?

   This is a difficult, even tricky question: *Would* the police just allow a person to drive off or walk away during an investigatory stop? Would that not escalate the situation by causing the police to consider probable cause to be present? Or is this is an example of legal fiction brought about by the Court to reach a predetermined outcome?

6. Referencing Justice Holmes' proposition that it is better that some criminals escape rather than have the government involved in playing an ignoble part, what logic can you see in releasing a suspect who has confessed to a crime under circumstances that prohibit use of that admission, when the police know that person committed the crime? Where is the fairness here?

   Students' responses will vary dependent on their personal beliefs. An excellent debate topic.

7. What do you think motivates informants, and should their information be considered reliable?

   Students' responses will vary dependent on their personal beliefs. An excellent debate topic.

8. Why would it be wise for an officer to read the *Miranda* rights from a card?

   Inevitably, the defense attorney will ask the officer on the stand whether they read the Miranda warning from a card or recited it from memory. If the response is "from memory," the questions sure to follow will be "How do you know you covered everything?", "Have you ever forgotten anything at anytime in your life?" and "Why don't you recite it for us right now, before the judge, jury and everyone in court?"

9. Why might trickery, innuendo or even falsehoods asserted by police during questioning not be Fifth Amendment violations?

Techniques that do not bring about intimidation might be considered simply that-techniques, and not a violation of due process rights. Do you think due process is violated by trickery?

10. Considering the USA PATRIOT Act, do you think Americans could ever sacrifice too many rights in exchange for national security?

Many people believe that only those with something to hide would invoke the Fifth Amendment. Students' answers will likely vary on this question.

STUDENT ACTIVITIES

- Test the impact of television and the movies! Have your students close their books, then hold a contest to see if anyone can accurately recite the *Miranda* warnings.

- Moderate a class discussion of these questions: Do you think it implies guilt when a defendant invokes his or her right to not answer any questions or testify during his or her trial? Would such action by the defendant cause you to doubt their innocence if you were on their jury in a criminal trial?

- Discuss the recent use of the "public safety" exception to the *Miranda* warnings in the "Times Square Bomber" case and the resulting debate over the *Miranda* warnings at The Washington Post website at http://www.washingtonpost.com/wp-dyn/content/article/2010/05/06/AR2010050603380.html.

- Go to TruTV's "True Crime Library" and access the information on "Coerced False Confessions During Police Interrogations" featuring the false confession case of Michael Crowe at http://www.trutv.com/library/crime/notorious_murders/not_guilty/coerced_confessions/6.html.

- Go to the PBS video site to view the Frontline documentary "The Confessions" regarding four innocent men who confessed to a crime they didn't commit at http://video.pbs.org/video/1637166286.

- Listen to the oral arguments for *Dickerson v. United States* at the Oyez Project website at http://www.oyez.org/cases/1990-1999/1999/1999_99_5525.
  Then go to the Bill of Rights Institute lesson on the case and have students complete the activity and answer the "Comprehension and Critical Thinking" questions. The lesson plan can be accessed at http://www.billofrightsinstitute.org/page.aspx?pid=631.

INTERNET CONNECTIONS

- Access Stephanos Bibas's University of Iowa College of Law research paper entitled *The Rehnquist Court's Fifth Amendment Incrementalism* by navigating to http://papers.ssrn.com/sol3/papers.cfm?abstract_id=830724, then downloading the paper from the **Social Science Research Network** site.

- Read the U.S. Supreme Court's ruling in **Haynes v. U.S. (1968)**—to say the least, a unique interpretation of the Fifth Amendment protection against self-incrimination— accessible at http://www.firearmsandliberty.com/cramer.haynes.html.

- Peruse Fifth Amendment Takings Clause issues at the **Exploring Constitutional Conflicts** site; http://www.law.umkc.edu/faculty/projects/ftrials/conlaw/takings.htm.

CHAPTER 11 TEST BANK

<u>**Multiple Choice**</u>

11.1   Which of the following is not guaranteed or prohibited by the Fifth Amendment?
   a. right against self-incrimination
   b. trial by jury
   c. double jeopardy
   d. just compensation
   ANS: B
   REF: 352
   LO: 1

11.2   The exclusionary rule prohibits the use of confessions obtained in violation of a person's
   constitutional rights and those that are otherwise coerced for all of the following reasons,
   except:
   a. they are inherently unreliable.
   b. to do otherwise would be a violation of due process.
   c. of a need to hold government accountable by holding such confessions inadmissible.
   d. the concern for public safety is not a Fifth Amendment issue.
   ANS: D
   REF: 327
   LO: 3, 4

11.3   The U.S. Supreme Court held that confessions obtained through brutality and torture by
   law enforcement officials are violations of constitutionally protected due process rights
   in:
   a. *Brown v. Mississippi*
   b. *Fikes* v. *Alabama*
   c. *Katz v. United States*
   d. *Dickerson v. United States*
   ANS: A
   REF: 327
   LO: 3

11.4   No *Miranda* warning is required if there is no seizure of the person as long as the police
   do not:
   a. convey the message that compliance is required.
   b. secretly intend to arrest the person at a later time.
   c. ask the person any incriminating questions.
   d. let the person voluntarily come to the police station.
   ANS: A
   REF: 334
   LO: 6

11.5 When considering the characteristics of the accused, all of the following would apply, except:
a. if the accused is of low intelligence.
b. if the accused is mentally ill.
c. if the accused is intoxicated.
d. if the accused is remorseful.
ANS: D
REF: 329
LO: 3

11.6 The U.S. Supreme Court established the right to counsel during police interrogation for all criminal suspects in:
a. *Escobedo* v. *Illinois*
b. *Miranda* v. *Arizona*.
c. *Dickerson* v. *United States*
d. *Fikes* v. *Alabama*
ANS: B
REF: 330
LO: 4

11.7 The USA PATRIOT Act improves counter-terrorism efforts by all of the following, *except*:
a. allowing investigators to use tools already available to investigate organized crime and drug trafficking.
b. facilitating information sharing and cooperation among government agencies.
c. increasing penalties for those who support or commit organized crime.
d. Updating the law to reflect new technologies and new threats.
ANS: C
REF: 356
LO: 13

11.8 The Supreme Court effectively set an expiration date on the right to counsel invocation by announcing a new "14 day break in custody" rule in:
a. *Edwards v. Arizona*
b. *Arizona v. Roberson*
c. *United States v. Dunn*
d. *Maryland v. Shatzer*
ANS: D
REF: 340, 349
LO: 6, 7

11.9 Which of the following statements would probably constitute an invocation of *Miranda* rights?
a. "I think I may have said too much."
b. "If I don't like your questions, it's lawyer time."
c. "I'll talk, but I'm not signing that waiver form."
d. "I'm done talking to you."
ANS: D
REF: 342
LO: 7

11.10 The *Miranda* warning must be given:
a. immediately upon arresting an individual.
b. only to those suspects interrogated in the custody of police.
c. to all witnesses who may be called upon to testify in court.
d. to anyone being interrogated by the police.
ANS: B
REF: 334
LO: 6

11.11 *Miranda* warnings must be given to a suspect interrogated in police custody, defined as when the suspect is:
a. under arrest.
b. facing criminal charges.
c. not free to leave.
d. reasonably free to leave the situation.
ANS: C
REF: 334
LO: 6

11.12 At issue in *Dickerson v. United States* was Section 3501 of the Omnibus Crime Control and Safe Streets Act of 1968 which stated that the admissibility of statements should turn only on whether they were voluntarily made, and not only on whether:
a. coercive tactics were used.
b. Miranda warnings had been given.
c. custodial interrogation had occurred.
d. the statement was made without an attorney present.
ANS: D
REF: 344
LO: 6, 7

11.13 In which scenario would *Miranda* warnings be required?
    a. Suspect in custody for an unrelated offense.
    b. When suspect appears to testify before grand jury.
    c. undercover officer poses as inmate and asks incriminating questions.
    d. during line-ups, show-ups, and photographic identifications.
    ANS: A
    REF: 335
    LO: 6

11.14 Police actions that would "shock the conscience" were found to violate due process in:
    a. *Miranda v. Arizona.*
    b. *Rochin v. California.*
    c. *In re Gault.*
    d. *Katz v. United States.*
    ANS: B
    REF: 325
    LO: 2

11.15 The first confession case decided by the Supreme Court was:
    a. *Miranda v. Arizona.*
    b. *In re Gault.*
    c. *New York v. Quarles.*
    d. *Brown v. Mississippi.*
    ANS: D
    REF: 327
    LO: 3

11.16 The due process voluntariness test is "whether the totality of the circumstances that preceded the confession deprived the defendant of his…":
    a. reasonable expectation of privacy
    b. power of resistance
    c. self-incrimination rights
    d. determination to remain silent.
    ANS: B
    REF: 327
    LO: 2, 3

11.17 It is *not* unconstitutional to obtain a confession by:
    a. deprivation of food, drink, and sleep
    b. psychological coercion
    c. trickery and deceit
    d. threats, but not acts, of violence
    ANS: C
    REF: 328
    LO: 3

11.18   You are the on-duty desk sergeant. A man walks in and says "I killed someone and want to confess." You grab your digital voice recorder and direct the man to a chair at your desk. He sits down and tells the tale of what turns out to be a first-degree murder. You record every word, including the numerous instances in which you said "Uh-huh" and "I see." Satisfied that the subject did, indeed, commit a murder, you place him under arrest. The confession is:
   a. inadmissible because recording it was a violation of the subject's reasonable expectation of privacy.
   b. inadmissible because the subject was in a coercive environment (police station), was therefore in custody for purposes of *Miranda,* and the encouragement to continue was interrogation.
   c. admissible under the "public safety" exception to *Miranda* as the subject was a danger to the officer and public.
   d. admissible as a voluntary statement when the subject was neither in custody nor interrogated for purposes of *Miranda*.
   ANS: D
   REF: 335
   LO: 6

11.19. In order for a confession to be admissible it must be:
   a. voluntary.
   b. true.
   c. independently corroborated.
   d. in writing.
   ANS: A
   REF: 327
   LO: 3

11.20   The conception and planning of an offense by an officer and his procurement of its commission by one who would not have perpetrated it except for the trickery, persuasion, or fraud of the officer is:
   a. ensnarement
   b. entrapment
   c. framing
   d. a set up
   ANS: B
   REF: 350
   LO: 2, 10

11.21   The precedent case for analyzing confession issues is:
a. *Terry* v. *Ohio*.
b. *Miranda* v. *Arizona*.
c. *Escobedo* v. *Illinois*.
d. *Massiah* v. *United States*.
ANS: B
REF: 330
LO: 4

11.22   Statements, including confessions, will not be admissible in court if obtained while violating a person's right to reasonable expectation of privacy under the:
a. Fourth Amendment
b. Fifth Amendment
c. Sixth Amendment
d. Fourteenth Amendment
ANS: A
REF: 349
LO: 10

11.23   Which of the following is not a part of the *Miranda* warning?
a. You have the right to remain silent.
b. If you cannot afford a lawyer, one will be appointed for you without cost.
c. You may stop answering questions at any time you choose.
d. Anything you say can and will be used against you in court.
ANS: C
REF: 332
LO: 5

11.24   The public safety exception was established in:
a. *Jacobson* v. *United States*.
b. *Katz* v. *United States*.
c. *New York* v. *Quarles*.
d. *Illinois* v. *Perkins*.
ANS: C
REF: 347
LO: 9

11.25   Which of the following is not true about grand juries?
a. Choice of jurors determined by state law.
b. Does not make a determination of guilt.
c. May initiate investigations.
d. Different jury for each case.
ANS: D
REF: 353
LO: 11, 12

11.26 The only unincorporated right guaranteed by the Fifth Amendment is the right to:
a. be a witness against oneself.
b. a grand jury indictment.
c. due process of law.
d. just compensation when government takes private property.
ANS: B
REF: 353
LO: 12

11.27 In prisoners' rights cases the Fifth Amendment arises:
a. infrequently.
b. quite often, involving nearly half of all lawsuits filed by prisoners.
c. very often, involving more than 80 percent of all lawsuits filed by prisoners.
d. never—prisoners are not protected by the Fifth Amendment.
ANS: A
REF: 355
LO: 11

11.28 *In re Gault* assured juveniles:
a. the right to a jury trial.
b. due process in the legal system.
c. the right to be tried as an adult in certain cases.
d. the right against self-incrimination.
ANS: B
REF: 325-326
LO: 2

11.29 The Fifth Amendment privilege against self-incrimination comes into play:
a. whenever a law enforcement officer questions a suspect, whether in custody or not.
b. only during custodial interrogation.
c. only at trial.
d. whenever incriminating information is being communicated.
ANS: C
REF: 346
LO: 1

11.30 Which of the following would not violate the right against double jeopardy?
a. A second prosecution for the same offense after acquittal.
b. More than one punishment for the same offense.
c. Independent trials for an offense in both state and federal courts.
d. Lesser-included offenses tried after initial trial.
ANS: C
REF: 354
LO: 11

True/False

11.31 When a person on the witness stand "pleads the Fifth," they are asserting their right against self-incrimination.
ANS: T
REF: 324
LO: 1

11.32 A suspect who has invoked only his right to silence cannot be re-approached to seek a waiver on a different case.
ANS: F
REF: 338, 348
LO: 5, 7

11.33 The Fifth Amendment requires just compensation when the government takes property.
ANS: T
REF: 355
LO: 11

11.34 The prohibition against double jeopardy prevents a second trial for the same offense for any reason.
ANS: F
REF: 354
LO: 11

11.35 Lying by the police to obtain a confession is a violation of the Fifth Amendment.
ANS: F
REF: 328
LO: 3

11.36 Since their actions can ultimately result in arrest, private security officers must inform suspects of their *Miranda* rights prior to interrogation.
ANS: F
REF: 347
LO: 8

11.37 The precedent case for analyzing confessions issues is *Miranda* v. *Arizona*.
ANS: T
REF: 330
LO: 4

11.38 A "soft" *Miranda* warning recited less harshly and directly than is imprinted on most Miranda cards is permissible if all four warnings are adequately conveyed to the suspect.
ANS: T
REF: 332
LO: 5

11.39 A waiver of *Miranda* is valid even if the suspect thought the questioning was going to be about a minor crime and the questioning switched to a more serious crime.
ANS: T
REF: 339
LO: 7

11.40 The *Miranda* warning must be given during lineups, show-ups, and photographic identifications.
ANS: F
REF: 346
LO: 6

Fill-In

11.41 _____ due process is constitutionally guaranteed rights of fairness in how the law is carried out or applied.
ANS: Procedural
REF: 325
LO: 2

11.42 Statements are not admissible in court if obtained while violating a person's Fourth Amendment right to a reasonable _____.
ANS: expectation of privacy
REF: 349
LO: 10

11.43 The voluntariness of a confession is determined by the _____ and the characteristics of the accused.
ANS: police conduct involved
REF: 328
LO: 3

11.44 The requirement that laws themselves be fair and not just how laws are enforced refers to _____ due process.
ANS: substantive
REF: 326
LO: 2

11.45 False confession cases in which the suspect acquiesces to escape from a stressful situation, to avoid punishment, or gain a promised or implied reward are called _____ confessions.
ANS: compliant
REF: 330
LO: 3

206

11.46 A purposeful, voluntary giving up of a known right is a _____.
ANS: waiver
REF: 338
LO: 7

11.47 _____ is questioning initiated by law enforcement officers after a person has been taken into custody or otherwise deprived of his freedom of action in a significant way.
ANS: Interrogation; Custodial interrogation
REF: 333
LO: 6

11.48 The _____ exception allows police to questions suspects without first giving Miranda warnings if information sought sufficiently affects the officers' and the public's safety.
ANS: public safety
REF: 347
LO: 9

11.49 The _____ Act strengthens the ability of the Justice Department and the FBI to monitor suspected terrorists and their associates.
ANS: USA PATRIOT; Patriot
REF: 356
LO: 13

11.50 _____ is a deliberate "end run" around Miranda by purposely withholding warnings until after a confession is obtained and then giving Miranda to re-ask the question (and is unconstitutional).
ANS: Beach-heading
REF: 342
LO: 7

Essay

11.51   Describe at least eight instances in which *Miranda* need not be given.
        ANS: Generally, the *Miranda* warning need not be given:
- When the officer asks no questions.
- During general on-the-scene questioning.
- When the statement is volunteered.
- When questioning a suspect about identification.
- When questioning witnesses.
- In stop-and-frisk cases.
- When asking routine questions of drunken driving suspects and videotaping the proceedings.
- During lineups, showups or photographic identification.
- When the statement is made to a private person.
- When the suspect appears before a grand jury.
- When there is a threat to public safety

REF: 346
LO: 6

11.52   Explain the public safety exception to the *Miranda* warnings.
        ANS: In *New York v. Quarles* (1984), the U.S. Supreme Court held that officers may question suspects without giving the *Miranda* warning if the information sought sufficiently affects the officers' and the public's safety. The need to have the suspect talk takes precedence over the requirement to read the defendant his rights.
        REF: 347
        LO: 9

11.53   Describe the challenge to *Miranda* presented in *Dickerson v. United States* (2000) and the Supreme Court's ruling.
        ANS: Dickerson was indicted for bank robbery using a firearm. His attorney moved to suppress a statement he made to the FBI based on their not reading the *Miranda* warning prior to interrogation. The government, however, relied on a portion of the Omnibus Crime Control and Safe Streets Act (§3501), which made the admissibility of such statements turn solely on whether they were made voluntarily. The Fourth Circuit acknowledged that, although Dickerson had not received *Miranda* warnings, his statement was admissible because it satisfied the requirements in §3501. This court concluded that *Miranda* was not a constitutional holding, and that, therefore, Congress could by statute have the final say on the admissibility question. The Supreme Court, however, reversed and, referring to *Marbury v. Madison* (1803), held: "*Miranda,* being a constitutional decision of this Court, may not be in effect overruled by an Act of Congress. . . ." The Court went on to assert: "*Miranda* has become embedded in routine police practice to the point where the warnings have become part of our national culture."
        REF: 343-344
        LO: 6

208

11.54 Discuss the USA PATRIOT Act, its elements, and how it aims to improve the nation's counter-terrorism efforts.

ANS: The United and Strengthening America by Providing Appropriate Tools Required to Intercept and Obstruct Terrorism (USA PATRIOT) Act, signed into law on October 26, 2001, enables government to access information more readily. Its elements include: 1- allowing investigators to use the tools already available to investigate organized crime and drug trafficking; 2- facilitating information sharing and cooperation among government agencies so they can better "connect the dots;" 3- updating the law to reflect new technologies and new threats; and 4- increasing the penalties for those who commit or support terrorist crimes.
REF: 356-359
LO: 13

11.55 Explain *Miranda* requirements as they relate to private security.

ANS: The Constitution exists to regulate the *government's* authority. The regulations set forth by the Constitution apply to government agents, not to private individuals. This stipulation means private security personnel are <u>not</u> bound by constitutional restraints. Thus, private security officers may conduct a legal interrogation without providing *Miranda* warnings, and information they obtain from the suspect during such legal interrogation will be admissible at trial.
REF: 347
LO: 8

Chapter 12
The Sixth Amendment: Right to Counsel and a Fair Trial

LEARNING OBJECTIVES

Upon completing this chapter, the student will know:

1. The two requirements set forth for a trial in the Sixth Amendment.
2. The four factors to be considered in determining whether a trial is sufficiently "speedy."
3. Where the trial is to be held.
4. The two requirements for juries established by the Sixth Amendment.
5. Which guarantee of the Sixth Amendment extends beyond the trial.
6. What precedent case supports the right to have an attorney present during trial.
7. What happens if a defendant facing "deprivation of liberty" cannot afford to hire an attorney, and the precedent case.
8. When or whether a defendant accused of a misdemeanor offense has the right to an attorney.
9. When the Sixth Amendment right to counsel exists.
10. What is required at a lineup.
11. Whether there is a Sixth Amendment right to a lawyer during pre-indictment identification procedures.
12. How the court will view pretrial identification procedures to determine whether they are unconstitutional.
13. How many appeals through which the right to counsel may be invoked.
14. What the Sixth Amendment right to counsel presumes about the attorneys.
15. What is required to waive the right to counsel.
16. If people can defend themselves in a criminal trial.
17. Whether juveniles have Sixth Amendment rights.
18. How the Sixth Amendment affects corrections.

KEY TERMS

- **adversarial judicial system**—A legal system such as that used in the United States, which places one party against another to resolve a legal issue, stipulating that only in an actual conflict will a judicial body hear the case. Also called adversary system. [p. 372]

- **arraignment**—Usually the first court appearance by a defendant during which the accused is advised of his or her rights, advised of the charges and given the opportunity to enter a plea. [p. 383]

- **blind line-up**—one conducted by someone who does not know who the suspect is. [p. 380]

- **Brady Rule**—The suppression by the prosecution of evidence favorable to an accused upon request violates due process when the evidence is material either to guilt or to punishment, irrespective of the good faith or bad faith of the prosecution. [p. 384]

- **compulsory process**—Permits a defendant to require witnesses to appear in court, usually under the issuance by the court of a subpoena. [p. 381]

- **court trial**—When a case is heard before only the bench (or judge) without a jury. [p. 369]

- **critical stage**—any step during a criminal prosecution where the accused's rights may be affected by the absence of legal representation. [p. 376]

- **cross-racial identification**—suggests that people of one race have difficulty recognizing facial attributes of other races. [p. 379]

- **deliberate elicitation**—the Massiah standard that violates the Sixth Amendment by purposefully, yet covertly, drawing out incriminating statements from a suspect whose Sixth Amendment right to counsel has attached but who has not waived the right. [p. 378]

- **detainer**—Document filed against inmates who have other criminal charges pending against them, ensuring their appearance before the prosecuting jurisdiction for the next trial after their current sentence is complete. [p. 391]

- **hearsay**—Testimony made in court about something heard outside of court offered as proof of the matter asserted; a statement made by someone other than the person who actually said it. [p. 378]

- **indigent**—Poor, unable to afford a lawyer. [373]

- **jury nullification**—ability of a jury to acquit a defendant even though they believe that person is guilty; occurs because the jury either feels the circumstances make it unfair to convict or they disagree with the law. [p. 369]

- **lineup**—Occurs when the victim or witness is shown several people, including the suspect. [p. 380]

-

- **offense specific**—the Sixth Amendment right to counsel applies only to the specific charges for which the defendant has been indicted or arraigned. [p. 386]

- **peremptory challenges**—A specific number of allowances given to each side in a case so that they may assert to remove a potential juror for any reason whatsoever. [p. 368]

211

- **preliminary hearing**—A critical stage of criminal proceedings when it is determined if probable cause exists to believe a crime has been committed and that the defendant committed it. [p. 383]

- *pro se*—Appearing in court without an attorney, representing oneself. Latin meaning "for himself." [p. 390]

- **showup**—When only one individual is shown to the victim or witness. [p. 380]

- **subpoena**—Requires an individual to appear in court to testify or to bring documents or other physical evidence to the court. [p. 371]

- **venue**—The geographical area in which a specific case may come to trial, and the area from which the jury is selected. [p. 367]

- *voir dire*—The process of questioning potential jurors to determine their impartiality. [p. 368]

LECTURE OUTLINE

I.   Introduction
      A. The Star Chamber

II.   Speedy and Public Trial
      A. Speedy Trial: *Barker v. Wingo* (1972)
            1. Four factors considered
      B. Public Trial: *Gannet Co. v. DePasquale* (1979)
            1. Balancing Sixth and First Amendments

III. Where the Trial Is Held

IV.   An Impartial Jury
      A. Voir dire
            1. Peremptory challenges
            2. Challenges for cause
      B. Jury Nullification

V.   Being Informed of the Accusation

VI.   The Right to Confront Witnesses
      A. *Coy v. Iowa* (1988) and closed-circuit televisions
      B. *Melendez-Diaz v. Massachusetts* (2009)
            1. "Certificates of Analysis"
      C. Hearsay

VII.   Compulsory Process

VIII.   Right to Counsel
    A. Extends beyond the Trial
    B. The Role of Counsel
        1. Adversarial judicial system
    C. Development of the Right to Counsel
        1. *Powell v. Alabama* (1932)
            a. Assistance of lawyer is basic, fundamental right
            b. Decided under due process clause of Fourteenth Amendment
        2. *Gideon v. Wainwright* (1963)
            1. Indigent defendants accused of a felony
        3. *Argersinger v. Hamlin* (1972) and misdemeanor offenses
    D. Current Developments

IX.   Right to Counsel at Critical Stages of Criminal Proceedings
    A. Critical Stages during the Criminal Investigation
        1. *Massiah v. United States* (1964)
        2. *Miranda* versus *Massiah*
        3. *Brewer v. Williams* (1977)
            a. Deliberate elicitation
    B. Rights during Identification
        1. Mistaken eyewitness identifications
        2. Cross-racial identification
        3. Show-up
        4. Line-up
        5. Blind line-up
        6. *Wade-Gilbert* rule
        7. *Neil v. Biggers* (1972)
            a. Five factors to determine witness reliability
    C. Critical Stages at Hearings, Trials and Appeals
        A. Preliminary hearing
        B. Arraignment
        C. *Douglas v. California* (1963)
            a. Through the first appeal of right
        D. The *Brady* rule
        E. *Texas v. Cobb* (2001)
            a. Right to counsel "offense-specific"

X.   The Presumption of Effective Counsel
    A. *Strickland v. Washington* (1984)
        1. Two-pronged test to establish claim of ineffective assistance of counsel

XI.   Waiver of Sixth Amendment Right to Legal Counsel

XII.   The Right to Act as One's Own Counsel

CHAPTER SUMMARY

The Sixth Amendment requires a speedy and public trial. Whether a trial is sufficiently "speedy" is determined by (1) the length of the delay, (2) the reason for the delay, (3) the defendant's assertion of this right and (4) the harm caused (*Barker* v. *Wingo*). The Sixth Amendment also requires that the trial occur in the district in which the crime was committed and that defendants have the right to an impartial and representative jury. The confrontation clause requires that witnesses be present in court so the defendant can confront them.

The right to counsel is the only Sixth Amendment guarantee that extends beyond the trial. Denying legal counsel for a defendant at trial is clearly a denial of due process (*Powell* v. *Alabama*). *Gideon* v. *Wainwright* established that indigent defendants are to be provided lawyers when faced with a "deprivation of liberty." Beyond that, when police inquiry has begun to focus on a particular suspect, custodial interrogation at the police station entitles a suspect to legal representation (*Escobedo* v. *Illinois*).

The Sixth Amendment right to legal counsel occurs at every critical stage of a criminal proceeding, including during the investigation, at hearings and during the trial. After a defendant has been charged with a crime and retained an attorney, that attorney must be present during any subsequent questioning. *Miranda* invokes both the Fifth Amendment right against self-incrimination and the Sixth Amendment right to counsel. The exclusionary rule will prohibit confessions obtained in violation of these rights from being used in court.

In the *Wade-Gilbert Rule,* the Court held that pretrial lineups invoke Sixth Amendment protection and require that the suspect have a lawyer. Lineups may not be arranged in such a manner as to make the defendant stand out from the others in any unnecessarily suggestive ways. Preindictment (before being formally charged) identification procedures are *not* critical stages of criminal proceedings, so there is no Sixth Amendment right to a lawyer. The court will view pretrial identification procedures in the totality of circumstances when determining whether they were constitutional. Any hearing or trial through the first appeal invokes the Sixth Amendment right to counsel.

The Sixth Amendment right to counsel presumes counsel is effective. A waiver of one's Sixth Amendment right to counsel must be knowing and voluntary. Individuals can appear in court without attorneys, representing themselves, that is, *pro se. In re Gault* applied Sixth Amendment rights to juveniles, including the right against self-incrimination, to receive notice of the charges, to confront and cross-examine witnesses and the right to counsel. Finally, for prisoners, cases based on the Sixth Amendment involve the right to a speedy trial and the detainer problem.

SUGGESTED ANSWERS TO THE DISCUSSION QUESTIONS

1. Does having a lawyer present during a trial ensure fairness?

    With the complexity of court proceedings, it is curious why anyone would *not* want a lawyer present. It's a little like asking why someone wouldn't want a dentist around while getting a cavity filled. However, there is no law requiring representation by an attorney. And even with a lawyer present, not all lawyers are competent. Furthermore, even if they are good at one area of the law, it doesn't mean they are good in the courtroom. Presumably, a trial attorney will know enough to oversee the process and advocate on behalf of their client to ensure a fair trial. Remember that the other side will be pursuing success as aggressively as possible, too, and would be unlikely to "back off" because of any inability on the part of the opposition. Hopefully the judge would be watching over the proceedings, too, but the purpose of a lawyer is to watch out for one client and one client only.

2. Why would people want to represent themselves in court *pro se?* Would you think more or less of those representing themselves? Why?

    This, again, is hard to say, except that some people distrust *everyone* who is a part of the system, including an attorney who might represent them. Students may have other reasons for why a person would choose to not have an attorney represent them.

3. With the complexity of law, should there be a right to self-representation?

    Certainly it would be odd for a system based on freedom to say one *must* have legal representation even if they don't want it.

4. When has the line been crossed between a public trial at which the media are present and a "trial by media"? Could this problem ever justify barring the media from attending trials? Do the media ever have that much influence on the public or jurors?

    This is an excellent class debate topic.

5. Why would someone choose to be a defense attorney? A prosecutor?

    Each of these roles holds appeal for different reasons. No other areas provide similar courtroom experience. Most lawyers are seldom in court--defense lawyers and prosecutors are there daily. For any lawyer wanting to practice law "in the trenches," this is the place to be. Some prosecutors, as well as some defense attorneys, simply feel they are "on the right side," and working on that side of the system is the only place they wish to be. Some see it as a professional challenge to hold either position and are comfortable doing so. Others do

    both, prosecuting in one jurisdiction part-time and doing defense work in another the rest of the time.

6. Do public defenders provide less of a defense than would a private attorney? What might a private attorney with a wealthy client be capable of that a public defender with an indigent client would not?

A public defender is absolutely no less a legal advocate than is a private attorney. In fact, some argue that those who choose public defense have a level of commitment that produces even better advocacy.

What money buys could really be considered resources. For example, the O.J. Simpson defense team had resources in the form of investigators, experts, research assistants and other sources which helped them provide an impressive defense. But so did the prosecution. Money may buy an experienced lawyer who will be able to devote more time to one client's case, but it is not true to say that money simply buys justice.

7. Why is the adversary system of law a necessity to produce just results?

Our legal system is based on the premise that justice is best served when both the accuser and the accused are allowed to give their all during a legal conflict. Because a crime is defined as a wrong against society, and society is represented in court by the government, the adversarial system is seen as a way to keep the government from infringing on individuals' rights. To achieve the just and proper result, the parties to the action must pursue their position aggressively (within the confines of legal rules of procedure) so that all aspects of the case and legal arguments are considered and addressed. Anything less would leave more questions than answers.

8. Why could one attorney not represent *both* sides in a trial by providing objective facts?

The job of an attorney—to win for his or her client using all legal means—requires defeating the opposing side. Common sense explains the rest.

9. Does the adversary system today encourage, or even demand, that attorneys represent their clients "too vigorously?"

When it is you standing trial in a court of law, there is no such thing as being represented "too vigorously."

10. If you were a lawyer, would you prefer to represent the prosecution or the defense? Why?

Lead a class discussion of this question.

STUDENT ACTIVITIES

- Obtain and show the 1979 film ***Gideon's Trumpet***, which depicts the U.S. Supreme Court's landmark ruling in the case entitled *Gideon v. Wainwright* (1963). After the film, discuss the case with your students.

- Have students research the case of *Sheppard v. Maxwell* (1966) and discuss how this case compares to recent high-profile cases. Refer them to the University of Missouri at Kansas City "Famous Trials" website at http://law2.umkc.edu/faculty/projects/ftrials/sheppard/Sheppard.htm.

- Go to the Constitutional Rights Foundation's "The American Jury: Bulwark of Democracy" website for lesson plans and activities regarding the right to trial by jury at http://www.crfc.org/americanjury/right_accused.html.

- Have students research cases involving speedy trial violations and discuss the cases in class. (For example, the case of "Speedy-trial violation frees man convicted of molesting daughter" from the Cleveland Plain Dealer newspaper 05/15/2008) at http://blog.cleveland.com/metro/2008/05/speedytrial_violation_frees_ma.html.

- Have students research the case of *Maryland v. Craig* (1990) regarding the Confrontation Clause. Listen to the oral arguments at the Oyez Project at http://www.oyez.org/cases/1980-1989/1989/1989_89_478/.

INTERNET CONNECTIONS

- An excellent discussion of the scope of the Sixth Amendment is available at http://www.answers.com/topic/amendment-vi-to-the-u-s-constitution.

- See Findlaw.com's Sixth Amendment overview with annotations at http://caselaw.lp.findlaw.com/data/constitution/amendment06/.

- See Lawbrain.com's Sixth Amendment overview with annotations at http://lawbrain.com/wiki/Sixth_Amendment.

CHAPTER 12 TEST BANK

Multiple Choice

12.1   The first prong of the two-pronged test to establish a claim of ineffective counsel requires the defendant to show:
a. representation falling below an objective standard of reasonableness.
b. representation whose incompetence "shocks the conscience."
c. representation falling below community standards of excellence.
d. representation that resulted in an unfavorable outcome.
ANS: A
REF: 387
LO: 14

12.2   *Escobedo v. Illinois* (1964) held that:
a. no *Miranda* warning is required during a stop and frisk.
b. *Miranda* does not need to be given by private police.
c. an individual being investigated by police may not be denied counsel.
d. indigent defendants are entitled to a lawyer when seeking an appeal.
ANS: C
REF: 374
LO: 9

12.3   The Star Chamber was:
a. the old Supreme Court chamber located in the U.S. Capitol.
b. an English court that tried people in secret with no regard to due process.
c. a group of highly revered lawyers who drafted the Sixth Amendment.
d. an 1880s theatrical group that taught the public the true meaning of "due process."
ANS: B
REF: 365
LO: 1

12.4   *Massiah v. United States* (1964) held that a critical stage requiring a lawyer includes when a defendant is:
a. made aware a crime has been committed.
b. approached by the police.
c. determined to be indigent.
d. charged with a crime.
ANS: D
REF: 377
LO: 9

12.5 A statement obtained in violation of a person's constitutional rights will only be permitted in court to:
a. corroborate the defendant's protestations of innocence.
b. impeach the defendant's perjured testimony at trial.
c. impeach defense witnesses during cross-examination.
d. provide aggravating factors in the sentencing phase.
ANS: B
REF:386
LO: 9

12.6 In *Brewer v. Williams*, the Christian Burial Speech case (involving the search for the body of a missing girl), the Supreme Court determined there was:
a. an inevitable articulation exception to the Sixth Amendment.
b. a deliberate elicitation of an incriminating statement.
c. the functional equivalent of interrogation.
d. intimidation resulting in an involuntary statement.
ANS: B
REF: 378
LO: 9

12.7 The Supreme Court has interpreted the Sixth Amendment to mean that an accused has the constitutional right to counsel at:
a. every critical stage during a criminal proceeding.
b. any critical stage, excluding post-trial appeals.
c. every critical stage after arraignment.
d. any stage in the criminal investigation.
ANS: A
REF: 376
LO: 6, 9

12.8 *Mempa v. Rhay* held that a convicted offender has the right to assistance of counsel at _____ in which the sentence has been referred.
a. inmate disciplinary hearings
b. probation revocation hearings
c. hearings before a parole board
d. inmate grievance boards
ANS: B
REF: 391
LO: 18

12.9   A waiver of one's Sixth Amendment right to counsel must be all of the following, except:
       a. in writing.
       b. knowing.
       c. voluntary.
       d. intelligent.
       ANS: A
       REF: 390
       LO: 15

12.10 Ineffective assistance of counsel claims can be based on the:
       a. gravity of the offense charged.
       b. accessibility of witnesses for the defense.
       c. failure to take normal and routine steps before trial.
       d. counsel's inexperience compared to the complexity of the case.
       ANS: C
       REF: 388
       LO: 14

12.11 Whether a trial is sufficiently speedy is determined by the length of the delay, the reason
       for the delay, _____, and the harm caused.
       a. court review of the facts
       b. the prosecution's waiver of the right
       c. the relevance of the delay
       d. the defendant's assertion of this right
       ANS: D
       REF: 366
       LO: 2

12.12 One Sixth Amendment guarantee is:
       a. the defendant's right to confront adverse witnesses.
       b. having all court proceedings on the record.
       c. having an independent investigation.
       d. indictment by a grand jury.
       ANS: A
       REF: 370
       LO: 1

12.13 The case establishing that indigent defendants accused of a felony must be provided a
       lawyer was:
       a. *Barker v. Wingo.*
       b. *Powell v. Alabama.*
       c. *Gideon v. Wainwright.*
       d. *Argensinger v. Hamlin.*
       ANS: C
       REF: 373
       LO: 9

12.14 Which is not one of the reasons the Sixth Amendment requires a speedy trial:
a. uncertainty about the outcome causes undue stress.
b. some defendants remain in jail because they cannot afford or have been denied bail.
c. the government incurs additional expenses.
d. cases generally improve with more time.
ANS: D
REF: 366
LO: 2

12.15 The test used by courts when determining whether pretrial identification procedures were constitutional is the:
a. harmless error test
b. totality of the circumstances test
c. preponderance of the evidence test
d. undue influence test
ANS: B
REF: 382
LO: 12

12.16 The Sixth Amendment guarantees a right to counsel during:
a. civil proceedings.
b. hostile contractual negotiations.
c. criminal proceedings.
d. any and all court proceedings
ANS: C
REF: 376
LO: 9

12.17 The Supreme Court has never incorporated this segment of the Sixth Amendment to apply to the states, although it does fall within the due process clause of the Fourteenth Amendment.
a. Being informed of the accusation.
b. Right to a jury trial.
c. Right to compulsory process.
d. Confrontation rights.
ANS: A
REF: 370
LO: 1

12.18 The case establishing that indigents must be provided an attorney if they have been accused of misdemeanor offenses and the penalty could include incarceration is:
a. *Barker v. Wingo*.
b. *Powell v. Alabama*.
c. *Gideon v. Wainwright*.
d. *Argensinger v. Hamlin*.
ANS: D
REF: 374
LO: 8

12.19 *Gideon v. Wainwright* established that indigent defendants are to be provided lawyers when faced with a(n):
a. custodial interrogation
b. deprivation of liberty
c. period of incarceration exceeding one year
d. adversary criminal proceeding
ANS: B
REF: 374
LO: 7

12.20 The Supreme Court held that denying legal counsel for a defendant at trial in a capital case was a denial of due process in:
a. *Barker v. Wingo*
b. *Powell v. Alabama*.
c. *Gideon v. Wainwright*.
d. *Argensinger v. Hamlin*.
ANS: B
REF: 373
LO: 6

12.21 Which of the following is not a "critical stage" requiring the Sixth Amendment right to counsel?
a. At sentencing.
b. At the arraignment.
c. During post-indictment identifications
d. Investigation prior to suspect being charged.
ANS: D
REF: 376
LO: 9

12.22   Potential jurors are questioned by both sides to determine impartiality in a process called:
a. peremptory challenging
b. jury nullification
c. voir dire
d. habeus juris
ANS: C
REF: 368
LO: 4

12.23   A peremptory challenge seeks to remove a potential juror for:
a. lack of knowledge or intelligence.
b. bias for the defendant.
c. bias against the defendant
d. any reason whatsoever.
ANS: D
REF: 368
LO: 4

12.24   In *Douglas v. California* the Court held that the right to counsel extends to:
a. the first appeal at all levels.
b. the first appeal at the state level only.
c. the first appeal at the federal level only.
d. all appeals.
ANS: A
REF: 384
LO: 13

12.25   Which is *not* one of the factors a court would use in determining witness reliability in show-up identifications?
a. Opportunity to view defendant during crime.
b. Level of attention witness was paying.
c. Level of intelligence the witness demonstrates.
d. The witness' level of certainty in his or her identification.
ANS: C
REF: 382
LO: 12

12.26   Which is not one of the three conditions set forth in *Faretta v. California* that must be met before a person can represent him or herself?
a. awareness of the right to counsel.
b. valid waiver
c. competency
d. legal knowledge
ANS: D
REF: 390
LO: 16

12.27 The Sixth Amendment right to a public trial requires a balance with the public's
        _____ rights.
        a. First Amendment
        b. reasonable access.
        c. the Fifth Amendment.
        d. compelling public interest
        ANS: A
        REF: 366
        LO: 1

12.28 The Wade-Gilbert Rule requires that a lawyer be present during:
        a. post-indictment lineups.
        b. the arraignment.
        c. the preliminary hearing.
        d. pre-indictment lineups.
        ANS: A
        REF: 380
        LO: 11

12.29 For prisoners, cases based on Sixth Amendment rights involve the right to a speedy trial
        and the problem of:
        a. extradition
        b. detainer
        c. incarceration
        d. inter-facility transfer
        ANS: B
        REF: 391
        LO: 18

12.30 The Supreme Court applied Sixth Amendment rights to juveniles in:
        a. *In re Winship*
        b. *California v. Hodari D*
        c. *In re Gault*
        d. *Brewer v. Williams*
        ANS: C
        REF: 390
        LO: 17

True/False

12.31 The Sixth Amendment embodies the concept of due process.
        ANS: T
        REF: 365
        LO: 1

12.32   Perhaps the most important "speedy trial" issue is whether the defendant was unduly harmed by the delay.
ANS: T
REF: 366
LO: 1

12.33   In *Codispoti v. Pennsylvania* (1994), the Supreme Court has held that only more serious offenses require a jury trial, which means if *any* period of incarceration is a possibility.
ANS: F
REF: 368
LO: 4

12.34   The United States operates its juvenile justice system under the parens patriae model where juveniles have no constitutional rights during adjudication.
ANS: F
REF: 390
LO: 16

12.35   Representing oneself does not preclude a later claim of ineffective assistance of counsel.
ANS: F
REF: 390
LO: 16

12.36   The Sixth Amendment right to counsel is violated if police intentionally create a situation likely to result in an incriminating statement when that right has not been waived.
ANS: T
REF: 377
LO: 9

12.37   The right to counsel attaches when a person faces custodial interrogation.
ANS: T
REF: 376
LO: 9

12.38   The right to counsel extends not only to the trial, but to all subsequent appeals.
ANS: F
REF: 384
LO: 13

12.39   The right to counsel is the only Sixth Amendment guarantee which extends beyond the trial.
ANS: T
REF: 372
LO: 5

12.40 The Sixth Amendment requires that the trial occur in the district in which the crime was
committed.
ANS: T
REF: 367
LO: 3

Fill-In

12.41 The first two requirements for a criminal trial are that it be speedy and _____.
ANS: public
REF: 365
LO: 1

12.42 The Sixth Amendment provides the accused with an attorney not only during trial but
also at every _____ of the criminal prosecution.
ANS: critical stage
REF: 376
LO: 9

12.43 The geographic location of a trial is known as its _____.
ANS: venue
REF: 367
LO: 3

12.44 Individuals may appear in court without an attorney, representing themselves, the Latin
term for which is _____.
ANS: pro se
REF: 390
LO: 16

12.45 The Sixth Amendment right to counsel presumes counsel is _____.
ANS: effective
REF: 387
LO: 14

12.46 Impaired _____ identification is a situation in which people of another race
have difficulty recognizing facial attributes of other races.
ANS: cross-racial
REF: 379
LO: 12

12.47 In *Texas v. Cobb*, the Supreme Court ruled that the Sixth Amendment right to counsel is
_____-specific, applying only to the crime charged.
ANS: offense
REF: 385-386
LO: 9

12.48 A document filed against an inmate who has other criminal charges filed against him or
her is called a _____.
ANS: detainer
REF: 391
LO: 18

12.49 A _____ identification procedure is when only one individual is shown to the victim
or witness.
ANS: show-up
REF: 380
LO: 10

12.50 The Sixth Amendment requires an impartial and _____ jury.
ANS: representative
REF: 367
LO: 4

Essay

12.51 Discuss the evolution of the right to be represented by an attorney during a criminal trial.
ANS: Though important enough to be included in the Bill of Rights, initially the right to
counsel only meant that counsel could not be denied, not that counsel would be provided.
This left the "right" to counsel to be available only to those who could afford it. That
changed in 1932 with the Supreme Court ruling in *Powell v. Alabama*. The Supreme
Court held that the right to an attorney is a basic, fundamental right and those who are
charged with *capital crimes* shall have counsel appointed if they are indigent. Three
decades later, the right for indigent defendants to have appointed counsel was extended to
those charged with felonies in *Gideon v. Wainwright*. Subsequent cases have further
extended the right to appointed counsel to include indigent defendants charged with any
crime which would result in incarceration (*Argersinger v. Hamlin; Scott v. Illinois*).
REF: 372-376
LO: 6

12.52 List the five factors used to determine witness reliability in pre-trial identification procedures.

ANS: In *Neil v. Biggers* (1972), the Supreme Court set forth five factors courts should consider in determining a witness's reliability: (1) the opportunity of the witness to view the defendant during the crime; (2) the level of attention the witness was paying to the defendant; (3) the accuracy of any descriptions of the defendant made by the witness prior to the identification procedure; (4) the witness' level of certainty in his or her identification; (5) the time between the crime and confrontation.
REF: 382
LO: 12

12.53   List the rights guaranteed by the Sixth Amendment.

ANS: (1) A speedy and (2) public trial, (3) by an impartial jury of the state and district wherein the crime was committed, ; (4) to be informed of the nature and cause of the accusation; (5) to be confronted with witnesses against him; (6) to have compulsory process for obtaining witnesses in his favor; and (7) to have the assistance of counsel in his defense."
REF: 363
LO: 1, 3, 9

12.54 Discuss how the Sixth Amendment interacts with the First Amendment.

ANS: A defendants' Sixth Amendment right to an open, public trial must be balanced against the public's First Amendment rights concerning media coverage of trials (*Gannett Co. v. De Pasquale* {1970}); but the Sixth Amendment does not permit the public, including the press, to attend every trial (*Richmond Newspapers, Inc. v. Virginia* {1980}: the public has the right to attend trials unless there is a compelling government interest in doing otherwise. Excessive media coverage of high profile cases may disrupt court proceedings to the extent that defendant can claim deprivation of due process.
REF: 366
LO: 1

12.55 Explain what factors are considered when a defendant waives the right to counsel.

ANS: A court will consider the totality of the circumstances regarding how the waiver was obtained, the competency and age of the person, as well as issues of intelligence, health and ability to understand the language. The waiver must be knowing, voluntary, and intelligent. It does not need to be in writing, though it is obviously preferable.
REF: 388-390
 LO: 15

Chapter 13
The Eighth Amendment: Bail, Fines and Punishment

LEARNING OBJECTIVES

Upon completing this chapter, the student will know:

1. The three rights protected by the Eighth Amendment.
2. The purposes bail serves.
3. Whether the Eighth Amendment guarantees the right to bail, and if it applies to the states.
4. What was established by the Bail Reform Act of 1984.
5. What case attempted to define excessive bail and the limits it established.
6. If the prohibition against excessive bail and excessive fines applies to the states.
7. What may be seized under asset forfeiture laws.
8. What restriction is placed on the amount that can be seized through forfeiture.
9. Where the meaning of "cruel and unusual punishment" must come from.
10. What the general Eighth Amendment rule is regarding punishments.
11. The precedent cases that addressed the constitutionality of capital punishment.
12. What is required of proceedings that may involve the death penalty.
13. Under what age most states do not consider capital punishment for a juvenile.
14. Whether the mentally retarded can be executed.
15. The Eighth Amendment rights that prisoners often claim.

KEY TERMS

- **asset forfeiture**—The seizure by the government, without compensation, of money and property connected with illegal activity. [p. 402]

- **bail**—Money or property pledged by a defendant for pretrial release from custody that would be forfeited should the defendant fail to appear at subsequent court proceedings. [p. 398]

- **bifurcated trial**—A two-step trial for capital cases. The first step is determination of innocence or guilt; the second step is determination of whether to seek the death penalty. [p. 412]

- **commercial bail**—Using the services of a bail-bond person to post a defendant's bail for a fee. [p. 400]

- **compensatory damages**—Reimbursement of the plaintiff for actual harm done, such as for medical expenses or lost business. [p. 401]

- **corporal punishment**—Causing bodily harm through physical force, for example, whipping, flogging or beating. [p. 406]

- **preventive detention**—The right of judges to consider the potential criminal conduct of those accused of serious offenses and deny bail on those grounds. [p. 399]

- **proportionality analysis**—In essence, making the punishment fit the crime. Sentences must be proportional or directly related to the crime committed. [p. 404]

- **punitive damages**—Fines above and beyond the actual economic loss to punish the defendant in a civil trial. [p. 401]

- **ROR**—Released on their own recognizance, meaning that the court trusts defendants to show up in court when required. No bail money is required. Also called RPR. [p. 399]

LECTURE OUTLINE

I. Introduction

II. A Brief History of Punishment

III. Bail
   A. The Evolution of Legislation and Case Law on Bail
   B. The Bail Reform Act of 1966
   C. The Bail Reform Act of 1984
       1. Preventive detention
       2. *United States v. Salerno* (1987)
   D. *Stack v. Boyle* (1951)
   E. Commercial bail

IV. Fines
   A. Prohibition against excessive fines does not apply in civil area
       1. Compensatory damages
       2. Punitive damages
   B. Asset Forfeiture and the Prohibition against Excessive Fines
       1. *United States v. Bajakajian* (1998)
           a. Forfeiture must bear some relation to value of illegal enterprise
       2. *United States v. Ursery* (1996)
           a. Forfeiture not double jeopardy
       3. Civil Asset Forfeiture Reform Act of 2000

V. Cruel and Unusual Punishment
A. Cases
1. *Trop v. Dulles* (1958)
a. Evolving standards of decency
2. *Solem v. Helm* (1983)
a. Proportionality analysis
3. *Ewing v. California* (2003) and "three-strikes laws"
4. *Graham v. Florida* (2010)
a, Juvenile convicted of nonhomicide crime
b. Life without parole unconstitutional
5. *Ingraham v. Wright* (1977) and corporal punishment
B. Punishment Options
C. Physical Forms of Punishment

VI. Capital Punishment
A. Means of Execution
B. Is Capital Punishment Cruel and Unusual?
1. *Furman v. Georgia* (1972)
2. *Gregg v. Georgia* (1976)
a. Bifurcated trial required
C. Lengthy Delays in Execution as Cruel and Unusual
D. Who Can Be Executed?
1. Age
2. Race
3. Mental Retardation
4, The Mentally Ill
E. Appeals
F. Costs of the Death Penalty
G. Juries and Capital Punishment Cases
1. *Ring v. Arizona* (2002)
H. Continuing Controversy

VII. The Eighth Amendment and Corrections
A. Prisoner Treatment and the Eighth Amendment
1. "Deliberate indifference"
2. Chain gangs

VIII. Summary

CHAPTER SUMMARY

The Eighth Amendment protects three rights: a prohibition against excessive bail, excessive fines and cruel and unusual punishment. Bail serves two purposes. First, it helps ensure the appearance of the accused at court proceedings. Second, it maintains the presumption of innocence by allowing individuals not yet convicted of a crime to avoid continued incarceration. The Constitution does not guarantee a right to bail; it only prohibits excessive bail, which it does not define. The Eighth Amendment does not apply to the states.

The Bail Reform Act of 1984 established the practice of preventive detention for individuals deemed a threat to society or likely to flee, as well as other options to incarceration. Bail set at a figure higher than an amount reasonably calculated to fulfill its purpose is excessive under the Eighth Amendment (*Stack v. Boyle*, 1951). The excessive bail prohibition has never been formally incorporated to apply to the states under the Fourteenth Amendment, allowing states to deal with it through their constitutions, legislation and case law. Likewise, the prohibition against excessive fines has not been incorporated, so it does not apply to the states.

One type of fine is asset forfeiture. Property connected with illegal activity may be forfeited when used as a "conveyance" (including aircraft, ships and motor vehicles) to transport illicit drugs. Real estate used in association with a crime and money or other negotiable instruments obtained through the criminal activity also can be seized, and such seizure is considered a civil sanction by the government. The amount seized through asset forfeiture must bear some relation to the value of the illegal enterprise.

In *Trop v. Dulles* (1958) Chief Justice Warren stated that the cruel and unusual punishments clause "must draw its meaning from the evolving standards of decency that mark the progress of a maturing society." The general rule under the Eighth Amendment is that punishment must be proportional or directly related to the crime committed.

Although capital punishment may appear to be cruel and unusual, the Supreme Court has not held this to be the case. However, in certain instances, the Court has found states to be in violation of its citizens' due process protection. *Furman v. Georgia* (1972) was the landmark case in which the Supreme Court called for a ban on the death penalty in Georgia, ruling its law was capricious and, hence, cruel and unusual punishment. In *Gregg v. Georgia* (1976) the Supreme Court reinstated the Georgia death penalty by sustaining its revised death penalty law. The death penalty itself is not cruel and unusual punishment, but a capital case requires two proceedings: one to determine guilt or innocence and the other to determine the sentence (*Gregg v. Georgia*, 1976). Most states will not consider the death sentence for anyone younger than 15 years of age. In addition, the Supreme Court has prohibited executing mentally retarded individuals.

For prisoners, cases based on Eighth Amendment rights involve cruel and unusual punishment, such as overcrowding, solitary confinement, corporal punishment, physical abuse and use of force; treatment and rehabilitation; the right not to be treated; and the death penalty.

SUGGESTED ANSWERS TO THE DISCUSSION QUESTIONS

1. What historical background do you suspect led to the Eighth Amendment being included in the Bill of Rights?

   The cruelty that may inevitably result when only one person is in control and another challenges that person. The framers of our Constitution had no intention of tolerating any form of leadership that could permit the unfairness that they experienced under British rule and the cruelty that accompanied it.

2. Why has the Eighth Amendment not been fully incorporated?

   Students' answers will vary. The Court has never explained why this amendment remains only partially incorporated, thus speculation remains and may fuel an interesting class debate.

3. If the Bill of Rights does not guarantee the right to bail, how can bail be assured for those accused of crimes?

   What *is* assured is that bail will not be exceedingly high, nor will people be detained for an unreasonable time.

4. Explain the basic need for bail.

   For people to defend themselves, they need to be freed to organize their defense and carry out other necessary business. Because people are presumed innocent until proven otherwise, it is generally impermissible to detain them without the possibility of bail.

5. Does the bail system discriminate against the poor?

   If someone can't pay, it could be said that the poor do not have access to that which those with money do.

6. How would you define cruel and unusual punishment? Can you think of any currently lawful punishments you believe are cruel and unusual?

   The students' varied responses should demonstrate to the class the difficulty the courts have had in establishing such a definition.

7. Do you support the death penalty? Why or why not? Could you be an executioner or witness to an execution?

   Use this question as the basis for a class debate.

8. Should juveniles or mentally retarded individuals who have committed capital crimes be executed?

   Herein lies the opportunity provided by the framers of the Constitution to assess how the law is to affect whom, recognizing that different societies at different times may view circumstances differently. This is one major reason the Constitution itself has continued to serve society during major changes over generations.

9. Does the death penalty deter murder? Why or why not?

   Some believe the death penalty does nothing to deter crime for those acting in the "heat of passion" or for those individuals who believe they can "beat the system." Does the threat of punishment deter you from acting as you otherwise might? For example, does it keep you from committing traffic offenses, lying on your taxes, etc.? At what point does the severity, and surety, of punishment become high enough to prevent one from acting illegally?

10. Should fines be the same for the poor and the wealthy?

    Have students discuss this issue, pointing out the principle of day fines and other "sliding scale" fine systems.

STUDENT ACTIVITIES

- Using your classroom computer to access related links below, moderate a class discussion of the pros and cons of three-strikes laws.

- Have students research the effect of the death penalty on homicide rates. Is it a deterrent? Discuss the results in class.

- Research corporal punishment laws in your state and policies in your school district. Is corporal punishment allowed? How widespread is its use across the United States?

- Discuss the ruling in *Brown v. Plata* (2011) the Supreme Court ruling declaring overcrowding in California prisons to be unconstitutional.

- Go to PBS and access the Frontline Documentary "Death by Fire: Did Texas Execute an Innocent Man?" (55 minutes) at http://video.pbs.org/video/1618590505.

INTERNET CONNECTIONS

- Compare the attitudes and opinions expressed in the **Three Strikes and You're Out** web site (available at http://www.threestrikes.org/), which strongly supports this sentencing innovation with…opposing views expressed in the **FACTS (Families to Amend California's Three Strikes)** web site at http://facts1.live.radicaldesigns.org/.

- **The Death Penalty Information Center** site, at http://www.deathpenaltyinfo.org/, is the place to go to find answers about this highly controversial punishment.

- **Findlaw's Prisoner Rights and Resources** contains links to a variety of national resources related to corrections and the rights of those incarcerated and can be accessed at: http://criminal.findlaw.com/crimes/criminal_help/prisoners.html.

CHAPTER 13 TEST BANK

Multiple Choice

13.1   At the end of 2009, all 36 states with the death penalty authorized _____ as a method of execution.
        a. the gas chamber
        b. lethal injection
        c. the electric chair
        d. hanging
        ANS: B
        REF: 410
        LO: 11

13.2   The Supreme Court held that any amount of bail exceeding that necessary to ensure a return to trial violated the Eighth Amendment in:
        a. *Stack v. Boyle*
        b. *Gregg v. Georgia*
        c. *Solem v. Helm*
        d. *Ingraham v. Wright*
        ANS: A
        REF: 400
        LO: 5

13.3   In *Wilson v. Seiter*, the Supreme Court ruled that prisoners must not only prove prison conditions are objectively cruel and unusual but also show that they exist because of officials':
        a. culpable negligence
        b. deliberate indifference
        c. criminal negligence
        d. willful disregard of the conditions.
        ANS: B
        REF: 419
        LO: 15

13.4   Under asset forfeiture, the most frequently seized assets are:
        a. firearms
        b. real estate
        c. vehicles
        d. electronics
        ANS: C
        REF: 402
        LO: 7

13.5 The Bail Reform Act of 1984 established the practice of:
   a. preventive detention for people deemed a threat or likely to flee.
   b. assigning lawyers with the responsibility of seeing to it that their clients appear when directed.
   c. permitting a property bond in lieu of cash.
   d. third-party custody.
   ANS: A
   REF: 399
   LO: 4

13.6 Courts have used all of the following in assessing what constitutes cruel and unusual punishment, except whether the punishment:
   a. "shocks the general conscience" of a civilized society.
   b. is specifically prohibited in the Eighth Amendment.
   c. is unnecessarily cruel.
   d. goes beyond legitimate penal aims.
   ANS: B
   REF: 404
   LO: 10

13.7 The Supreme Court" "proportionality analysis" of sentences includes all of the following, except:
   a. the gravity of the offense and the harshness of the penalty.
   b. the sentences imposed on other criminals in the same jurisdiction.
   c. the sentences imposed for the commission of the same crime in other jurisdictions.
   d. an analysis of punishments for the same offense from an historical perspective.
   ANS: D
   REF: 404-405
   LO: 10

13.8 Bail is forfeited when:
   a. the defendant is found guilty.
   b. the defendant is acquitted.
   c. the defendant doesn't appear in court.
   d. the defendant has to be apprehended by a bail agent.
   ANS: C
   REF: 398
   LO: 3

13.9   Bail may not be denied in:
        a. capital cases.
        b. cases involving the death penalty.
        c. when the accused has threatened trial witnesses.
        d. all homicide cases.
        ANS: D
        REF: 398
        LO: 2

13.10   Which is not a purpose of bail?
        a. Maintain the presumption of innocence.
        b. Guarantee the appearance of the accused in court.
        c. Sanction the offender.
        d. Allow the accused to organize their defense.
        ANS: C
        REF: 398
        LO: 2

13.11   The Eighth Amendment's prohibition against excessive fines:
        a. applies to states because of the Fourteenth Amendment.
        b. applies to states because it is an important part of our system of justice.
        c. does not apply to any states.
        d. does not apply to all states, but does apply to some.
        ANS: C
        REF: 401
        LO: 6

13.12   Which has not been held to be cruel and unusual punishment?
        a. Execution of anyone under 18 when they committed a capital offense.
        b. Execution of the mentally ill or mentally retarded.
        c. Execution method presenting substantial risk of serious harm.
        d. Execution by firing squad.
        ANS: D
        REF: 409, 413-415
        LO: 10, 11

13.13   The prohibition against excessive fines:
        a. has been incorporated to apply to the states.
        b. does not apply in civil cases.
        c. limits punitive damages in civil cases
        d. does not apply in criminal cases.
        ANS: B
        REF: 401
        LO: 6, 8

13.14 The general rule under the Eighth Amendment is that punishments must be:
    a. consistent with international standards.
    b. approved by a unanimous jury.
    c. proportional or directly related to the case.
    d .in adherence with the biblical standard of "an eye for an eye."
    ANS: C
    REF: 405
    LO: 10

13.15 Though in the past some states have approved of executing offenders as young as 15, the Supreme Court has held that no one who was under ____ when they committed a capital offense shall be sentenced to death.
    a. 16
    b. 17
    c. 18
    d. 19
    ANS: C
    REF: 414
    LO: 13

13.16 The practice established for individuals deemed a threat to society or likely to flee is:
    a. Involuntary commitment
    b. The Bail Reform Act of 1966
    c. Preventive detention
    d. Protective custody
    ANS: C
    REF: 399
    LO: 4

13.17 Bail set at a figure higher than an amount "reasonably _____" is excessive under the Eighth Amendment.
    a. calculated to fulfill its purpose
    b. affordable for the defendant to produce
    c. necessary to sanction the defendant
    d. designed to make pretrial release possible
    ANS: A
    REF: 400
    LO: 5

13.18 In *United States v. Salerno*, the Supreme Court stated that _____ under the Bail Reform Act of 1984 did not violate due process or the Eighth Amendment.
   a. pretrial release
   b. mandatory detention for murderers
   c. requiring house arrest for child molesters
   d. preventive detention
   ANS: D
   REF: 399
   LO: 4

13.19 The _____ helped indigent defendants through release on recognizance (ROR)..
   a. American Civil Liberties Union
   b. Judiciary Act of 1789.
   c. Bail Reform Act of 1966.
   d. Bail Reform Act of 1984.
   ANS: C
   REF: 398
   LO: 4

13.20 The definition of cruel and unusual punishment is:
   a. established by state referendum.
   b. dependent on society.
   c. defined in the Eighth Amendment.
   d. specifically stated by the Supreme Court.
   ANS: B
   REF: 404
   LO: 9

13.21 The Supreme Court has not prohibited execution of:
   a. juveniles
   b. the mentally ill
   c. the handicapped
   d. the mentally retarded
   ANS: C
   REF: 414-416
   LO: 13, 14

13.22 The landmark case in which the Supreme Court called for a ban on the death penalty in Georgia, ruling its law was capricious, and hence, cruel and unusual punishment is:
   a. *Furman v. Georgia*
   b. *Coker v. Department of Corrections*
   c. *Gregg v. Georgia*
   d. *Ford v. Georgia*
   ANS: A
   REF: 412
   LO: 11

13.23 Which of the following has been held to be a violation of a prisoner's right against cruel and unusual punishment?
a. Suspending visiting privileges for an inmate who failed more than one drug test.
b. Exposure to second-hand smoke posing an unreasonable risk of damage to health.
c. A prisoner shot in the leg during a riot to maintain discipline.
d. The use of chain gangs.
ANS: B
REF: 419-420
LO: 15

13.24 In *United States v. Ursery*, the Supreme Court ruled that since forfeiture is a civil action, not an additional criminal action, it is not:
a. double jeopardy
b. an excessive fine
c. cruel and unusual punishment
d. applicable to the states through the Fourteenth Amendment
ANS: A
REF: 403
LO: 7

13.25 The Supreme Court upheld corporal punishment as necessary for the proper education of a child and maintenance of group discipline and not an Eighth Amendment issue in:
a. *United States v. Ursery*
b. *Trop v. Dulles*
c. *Solem v. Helm*
d. *Ingraham v. Wright*
ANS: D
REF: 406
LO: 10

13.26 In *Trop v. Dulles*, the Supreme Court held that the standard for determining whether a punishment is cruel and unusual is:
a. "socially acceptable practices"
b. "evolving standards of decency "
c. "evolving social norms"
d. "retribution v. rehabilitation"
ANS: B
REF: 404
LO: 9

13.27 The Supreme Court ruled that capital punishment can only be imposed by a jury or by a judge following a jury's recommendation in:
a. *Powell v. Alabama*
b. *Trop v. Dulles*
c. *Brown v. Mississippi*
d. *Ring v. Arizona*
ANS: D
REF: 412
LO: 12

13.28 Defendants cannot be sentenced to life without parole for a non-homicide crime if, when they committed the crime, they were below the age of:
a. 15
b. 16
c. 17
d. 18
ANS: D
REF: 405
LO: 10

13.29 Which state does not allow hanging as a method of execution?
a. Washington
b. Delaware
c. Texas
d. New Hampshire
ANS: C
REF: 410-411
LO: 11

13.30 Asset forfeiture is unconstitutional if:
a. the owner of a residence or vehicle is unaware of its illegal use.
b. the forfeiture is "grossly disproportionate" to the offense .
c. forfeiture is accompanied by a loss of liberty in violation of double jeopardy.
d. the government converts the assets for public use.
ANS: B
REF: 403
LO: 8

True/False

13.31 The Massachusetts Body of Liberties (1641) provided a right to bail and prohibited cruel and inhumane punishment.
ANS: T
REF: 397
LO: 1

13.32 The amount of bail must be an amount the accused can afford to pay.
ANS: F
REF: 398
LO: 3, 5

13.33 State courts are free to forbid preventive detention of state and local prisoners.
ANS: T
REF: 401
LO: 4, 6

13.34 The Supreme Court has held that the Eighth Amendment prohibits execution of anyone who was under age 21 at the time they committed the capital offense.
ANS: F
REF: 414
LO: 13

13.35 The government may detain dangerous defendants who become incompetent to stand trial.
ANS: T
REF: 399
LO: 3

13.36 A person who becomes mentally ill while in prison cannot be executed.
ANS: T
REF: 416
LO: 11, 15

13.37 The Eighth Amendment guarantees the right to bail.
ANS: F
REF: 398
LO: 1, 3, 5

13.38 Asset forfeiture may constitute double jeopardy.
ANS: F
REF: 403
LO: 7

13.39 The Supreme Court has held that California's "three-strikes" law did not violate the Eighth Amendment.
ANS: T
REF: 405
LO: 10

13.40 The Supreme Court has upheld the execution of mentally retarded offenders.
ANS: F
REF: 415
LO: 14

Fill-In

13.41 *Estelle v. Gamble* held that _____ to prisoners' serious medical needs constituted unnecessary and wanton infliction of pain.
ANS: deliberate indifference
REF: 419
LO: 15

13.42 In _____, the Supreme Court reinstated the Georgia death penalty by sustaining its revised death penalty law.
ANS: *Gregg v. Georgia*
REF: 412
LO: 11, 12

13.43 Denying bail on the basis of danger to the community or of risk to not appear at trial is known as _____.
ANS: preventive detention
REF: 399
LO: 2

13.44 The seizure of property connected with illegal activity is known as _____.
ANS: asset forfeiture
REF: 402
LO: 7

13.45 The Supreme Court has held that forfeiture is not double jeopardy because it is a _____ action.
ANS: civil
REF: 403
LO: 7

13.46 A capital case in which the death penalty might be involved requires two proceedings, one to determine guilt, and one to determine _____.
ANS: the sentence
REF: 412
LO: 12

13.47 According to the Eighth Amendment, punishment shall not be _____.
ANS: cruel and unusual
REF: 404
LO: 10

13.48 A _____ trial is required for death penalty cases.
ANS: bifurcated
REF: 412
LO: 12

13.49 The percentage of _____ who have been executed far exceeds their proportion of the general population.
ANS: blacks
REF: 415
LO: 11

13.50 According to the Eighth Amendment, bail shall not be _____.
ANS: excessive
REF: 398
LO: 3

Essay

13.51 Discuss the Eighth Amendment rights often claimed by prisoners, citing examples.

ANS: Eighth Amendment rights violations commonly claimed by prisoners include cruel and unusual punishment (overcrowding, solitary confinement, corporal punishment, physical abuse, use of force), treatment and rehabilitation, the right not to be treated and the death penalty.

In *Helling v. McKinney*, a case involving second-hand smoke, the Court ruled in favor of the inmate. The Supreme Court stated that the Nevada Department of Prisons showed deliberate indifference by allowing the inmate to be exposed to second-hand smoke, posing an unreasonable risk to his health. On the other hand, the Supreme Court ruled in *Whitney v. Albers* that a prisoner shot in the leg during a riot didn't suffer cruel and unusual punishment if the action was taken in good faith to maintain discipline and not for the purpose of causing harm.
REF: 418-420
LO: 15

13.52   Discuss capital punishment in the United States—its history, how the Supreme Court has viewed it, and how and on whom it may be carried out.

ANS: Capital punishment has existed for centuries, the methods fluctuating with the "sensibilities" of society. Although capital punishment may appear cruel and unusual to some, the Supreme Court has not held this to be the case. *Furman* v. *Georgia* (1972) was the landmark case in which the Supreme Court called for a ban on the death penalty in Georgia, ruling its law *as it stood* was capricious and, hence, cruel and unusual. In *Gregg* v. *Georgia* (1976) the Supreme Court reinstated the Georgia death penalty by sustaining its revised death penalty law.

The United States currently uses several methods of execution, including hanging, firing squad, electrocution, the gas chamber and lethal injection, which is the most commonly used method.

Issues surrounding who can be executed involve the age and mental capacity of the offender. The Supreme Court has prohibited the execution of the mentally retarded, the mentally ill, and those who committed their capital offense when they were less than 18 years of age.
REF: 409-416
LO: 11

13.53   Describe the rights protected by the Eighth Amendment and which, if any, have been incorporated to apply to the states.

ANS: The three rights protected by the Eighth Amendment are that excessive bail shall not be required, that excessive fines shall not be imposed, and that cruel and unusual punishment shall not be inflicted. Only the third provision, the prohibition against cruel and unusual punishment, has been incorporated to apply to the states.
REF: 398-410
LO: 1

13.54   Explain asset forfeiture. Why is it considered in a discussion of the Eighth Amendment?

ANS: Asset forfeiture is seizure by the government of money or property connected with illegal activity. Such seizure is intended to take the gain or profit out of crime. While it is considered a civil action initiated by the government and not a criminal action *per se,* the high court has recognized it as an area subject to the Eighth Amendment because forfeiture "constitutes payment to a sovereign as punishment for some offenses. . . and, as such, is subject to the limitations of the Eighth Amendment's Excessive Fines Clause" *(Austin v. United States,* 1993). Thus, the Court has held that the amount seized through asset forfeiture must bear some relationship to the value of the illegal enterprise.]
REF: 402-403
LO: 7, 8

13.55 Explain the purpose of bail, who is eligible for it, and the criteria considered when calculating the appropriate amount of bail.

ANS: The purpose of bail is to help assure the appearance of the accused at future court proceedings, and to maintain the presumption of innocence, avoiding the continued incarceration of people not yet convicted of crime.

Not everyone is eligible for bail, however. In fact, the Constitution does not guarantee the right to bail, only that bail not be excessive. Bail may be denied those facing charges of capital crimes, those who have threatened trial witnesses, those who pose a threat to public safety and those who may "jump bail" and flee.

In *Stack v. Boyle* (1951), the Supreme Court held that judicial calculation of the appropriate amount would consider such matters as the seriousness of the offense, the government's evidence, the defendant's connection with the community and family, finances, mental condition, criminal record, and any history of failing to appear when released on bail.
REF: 398-401
LO: 2, 3

Chapter 14
The Remaining Amendments and a Return to the Constitution

LEARNING OBJECTIVES

Upon completing this chapter, the student will know:

1. What the Third Amendment established.
2. What the Seventh Amendment established.
3. What determines whether a person is entitled to a federal jury trial in a civil case.
4. What the Ninth Amendment established.
5. Whether the Ninth Amendment guarantees the right of privacy.
6. What the Tenth Amendment established.
7. The amendment that allows the Supreme Court to make other amendments applicable to the states.

KEY TERMS

- **delegated powers**—Powers of the national government, both enumerated and implied by legal authority, delegated or entrusted to the national government by the states and the people. [p. 431]

- **federalism**—A principle whereby power is shared by the national government and the states; the Tenth Amendment provision reserving for the states those powers not granted to the federal government or withheld from the states. [p. 430]

- **penumbra**—A type of shadow in astronomy with the principle extending to the idea that certain constitutional rights are implied within other constitutional rights. [p. 429]

- **reserve powers**—Powers retained by the states. [p. 431]

- **selective incorporation**—Holds that only the provisions of the Bill of Rights that are fundamental to the American legal system are applied to the states through the due-process clause of the Fourteenth Amendment. Also known as the incorporation doctrine. [p. 434]

- **suits at common law**—Legal controversies arising out of civil law as opposed to criminal law. [p. 426]

- **unenumerated rights**—Rights not specifically listed in the Bill of Rights. [p. 428]

- **zones of privacy**—Areas into which the government may not intrude. [p. 429]

LECTURE OUTLINE

I.   Introduction

II. The Remaining Amendments of the Bill of Rights
     A. The Third Amendment
     B. The Seventh Amendment
        1. Suits at common law defined
     C. The Ninth Amendment
        1. Unenumerated rights
           a. Right to privacy
           b. *Griswold v. Connecticut* (1965)
           c. Penumbra
           d. Zones of privacy
           e. *Roe v. Wade* (1973)
     D. The Tenth Amendment
        1. Federalism
        2. Delegated powers
        3. Reserve powers
        4. *McCulloch v. Maryland* (1819)
        5. *United States v. Lopez* (1995)
           a. Gun Free School Zones Act of 1990
        6. *Printz v. United States* (1997)
           a. Brady Bill

III. Amendments beyond the Bill of Rights
     A. The Eleventh Amendment (1795)
     B. The Thirteenth Amendment (1865)
     C. The Fourteenth Amendment (1868)
        1. Selective incorporation
     D. Amendments Related to Elections and Structure of Congress
     E. Voting Rights
     F. Taxes
     G Prohibition

IV. Attempts at Other Amendments

V.   Summary

CHAPTER SUMMARY

Four additional important amendments of the Bill of Rights are the Third, Seventh, Ninth and Tenth Amendments. The Third Amendment prohibits housing soldiers in private homes during peacetime without the owner's consent and during wartime without legal process. The Seventh Amendment establishes the right to a federal jury trial for all "suits at common law" if the value is more than $20. Cases that involve issues that justify a Seventh Amendment right to a federal jury trial are determined by examining the types of cases heard previously or by a common law analysis. The Ninth Amendment established that the rights of U.S. citizens extend beyond those listed in the Constitution. The right of privacy has been referred to by the Supreme Court and has been used to infer such a right, but the Ninth Amendment does not guarantee this right. The Tenth Amendment embodies the principle of federalism, reserving for the states those powers not granted to the federal government or withheld from the states.

The Supreme Court has chosen, through case law and common law, to selectively apply certain amendments to both federal and state governments through selective incorporation, as stipulated in the Fourteenth Amendment.

SUGGESTED ANSWERS TO THE DISCUSSION QUESTIONS

1. Discuss why the framers of the Constitution probably thought it necessary to include the Ninth and Tenth Amendments.

   Remember these words: *limitations of government control.* This is what the Bill of Rights is all about. Of course the brevity of these two amendments has resulted in significant debate, but the final issue of how much power the government will or won't have is always at the basis of the discussion. In a way, these two amendments provide a broad assertion that even the Constitution will not limit the rights of the people, nor will the federal government have free reign over the states-federal power remains limited once again.

2. With reference to Question 1, would only one or the other have been sufficient? If you were to eliminate the Ninth or Tenth Amendment, which would it be and why?

   Perhaps, but constitutional history shows how carefully wording was selected, and amendments included to satisfy everyone's concerns and the combination of the two amendments makes a stronger assertion as to who is really in charge: the people! Students' answers to the second part of the question will vary.

3. Could the United States not have a federal government? What about a much less powerful federal government, and if so, what would this government do?

   To answer this question the student must return to the initial needs the Constitution addressed and ask whether the passing of time has resulted in a change in these basic needs and whether society has evolved (or digressed?) to a point where change would be beneficial.

4. Having come this far in your study of constitutional law, do you think the United States could ever get along without a written constitution?

   The very nature of Americans must be considered here. Americans have never been content with not being able to demand a response to the questions "Why?" or "Who says?" Our history took us away from accepting a form of government based solely on tradition without formal limitations established through a document such as the Constitution, it had become evident that government could too easily assert power that was not acceptable to us.

5. Does the Constitution works as well as it was meant to? Why or why not?

Considering the size of the United States, both geographically and in terms of population, it appears to work spectacularly well for such a tremendously large and diverse country.

6. Is there any way an internal military dictatorship could take over the present government in America and be successful?

The history of the United States has shown that, occasionally, an individual or domestic group strikes out at what they dislike here. However, any sort of military takeover has not been a serious threat. Consider the various levels of government, the various military branches and the strength of the states, separately and combined. Can students think of additional reasons a takeover would be unlikely?

7. Is there a present-day concern that the national government is too powerful?

This would make a good class debate topic. Whether splinter groups that advocate violent overthrow of the government (militia groups, fringe groups who think government is spying on everyone, controlling us, etc.) or organized lawful protests against government power, there are people who unquestionably believe government has too much power. For example, a major theme in objections to government at all levels is the amount people are taxed and whether there is a need for government that takes this much money from it's citizens.

8. If you were to eliminate any portions of the Constitution, which would they be? Why?

More than likely, any section to be excised would relate to personal and/or political beliefs that one might not agree with.

9. If you were to propose any new amendments, what would they be?

Additions would likely assert personal and/or political beliefs. Whether it would deal with flag desecration, abortion, taxes or other issues, what amendment could withstand the rigorous debate demanded of any addition to the Constitution?

10. Imagine that a time machine would permit those who conceived the Constitution to be present today. What would they think about how their prescription for freedom has endured the challenges of time? What might they not be pleased with, constitutionally?

They would likely be overwhelmed with the scientific, educational and technological developments, the population growth, and our interaction with other world powers. Regardless of the amazement they would have at what exists now, one would guess they

251

would be even more amazed that the document they drafted more than two centuries ago for a fraction of today's population continues to work as well, if not better, than ever before.

STUDENT ACTIVITIES

- The United States Supreme Court overturned *Bowers v. Hardwick* (1986) in *Lawrence v. Texas* (2003), upholding the right to sexual privacy. Have students compare the cases.

- Go to Streetlaw.org's "Landmark Cases of the U.S. Supreme Court" case file on *Roe v. Wade* (1973) to access learning materials and for discussion or assignments at http://www.streetlaw.org/en/case.aspx?id=11.

- Go to "How Stuff Works" for a comprehensive overview of Prohibition at http://history.howstuffworks.com/american-history/prohibition.htm.

- Go to the National Endowment for the Humanities Edcitement webpage to access information and lessons on voting rights for women at http://edsitement.neh.gov/lesson-plan/voting-rights-women-pro-and-anti-suffrage#sect-introduction.

INTERNET CONNECTIONS

- The **Tenth Amendment Center** web site at http://www.tenthamendmentcenter.com/ is a comprehensive information source for issues related to the preservation and protection of states' rights and federalism.

- The **vlex group** provides an outstanding examination of how the Seventh Amendment protects individual rights in civil trials. Access this superb resource at http://www.vlex.us/constitution/Constitution-of-the-United-States-Annotated/Seventh-Amendment-Civil-Trials/2100-295135,01.html.

CHAPTER 14 TEST BANK

Multiple Choice

14.1   The Third Amendment:
a. addresses suits at common law.
b. deals with lawsuits exceeding $20.
c. prohibits the quartering of soldiers in homes during times of peace.
d. has been challenged numerous times throughout the history of America.
ANS: C
REF: 426
LO: 1

14.2   The Constitution gives Congress the power to make laws to carry out its enumerated powers through the:
a. supremacy clause
b. federal powers doctrine
c. necessary and proper clause
d. due diligence doctrine
ANS: C
REF: 431
LO: 6

14.3   The Ninth Amendment deals with the concept(s) of:
a. due process.
b. suits at common law.
c. enumeration of certain rights.
d. federalism.
ANS: C
REF: 428
LO: 4

14.4   Rights not specifically listed in the Bill of Rights:
a. are considered not to exist.
b. are called unenumerated rights.
c. cannot be the basis of a Supreme Court appeal..
d. can only be asserted when no other rights are similar.
ANS: B
REF: 428
LO: 4

14.5   The _____ Amendment has been used by the Supreme Court to infer the right to
        privacy.
        a. Third
        b. Seventh
        c. Ninth
        d. Tenth
        ANS: C
        REF: 428
        LO: 4

14.6   The concept of balanced government being so important to the states, the only
        amendment agreed upon by all the states *recommending* a Bill of Rights was the:
        a. Third Amendment
        b. Seventh Amendment
        c. Ninth Amendment
        d. Tenth Amendment
        ANS: D
        REF: 432
        LO: 6

14.7   In *Griswold v. Connecticut*, Justice Douglas stated that the various Bill of Rights
        guarantees--such as those contained in the Third, Fourth, and Fifth Amendments--created
        areas of life safe from government intrusion known as:
        a. emanating liberties
        b. specific rights
        c. zones of privacy
        d. havens of liberty
        ANS: C
        REF: 429
        LO: 5

14.8   The powers kept by the states under the Tenth Amendment are known as:
        a. delegated powers
        b. reserve powers
        c. primary powers
        d. secondary powers
        ANS: B
        REF: 431
        LO: 6

14.9   Which of the following is *not* an "unenumerated" right?
        a. privacy
        b. interstate and international travel
        c. freedom of association
        d. freedom of assembly
        ANS: D
        REF: 428
        LO: 4

14.10   The powers of the national government, both enumerated and implied, are known as the:
        a. delegated powers
        b. reserve powers
        c. primary powers
        d. federalist powers
        ANS: A
        REF: 431
        LO: 6

14.11   Selective incorporation is:
        a. incapable of precise constitutional definition.
        b. the concept used to apply certain amendments to state government.
        c. outlined in the Fourteenth Amendment.
        d. the means by which the Constitution applies to the states.
        ANS: B
        REF: 434
        LO: 7

14.12   The _____ Amendment has never been subjected to Supreme Court review.
        a. Third
        b. Seventh
        c. Ninth
        d. Tenth
        ANS: A
        REF: 426
        LO: 1

14.13   The Thirteenth Amendment:
        a. overturned the *Dred Scott* decision and prohibits slavery.
        b. outlines the structure of the federal judiciary.
        c. established how representatives are apportioned and what their qualifications are..
        d. prohibited the sale and purchase of intoxicating liquors.
        ANS: A
        REF: 434
        LO: 7

14.14 The Fourteenth Amendment:
a. guarantees equal protection of the laws.
b. abolished slavery.
c. allows free travel throughout the nation.
d. granted the right to vote to freed male slaves.
ANS: A
REF: 434
LO: 7

14.15 The _____ was designed in response to fear of a national government with too much power which was, at the time, considered to be the greatest threat to liberty.
a. Eleventh Amendment
b. Fourteenth Amendment
c. Tenth Amendment
d. Twelfth Amendment
ANS: C
REF: 431
LO: 6

14.16 In _____, the Supreme Court upheld the Fair Labor Standards Act of 1938.
a. *United States v. Darby*
b. *Bowers v. Hardwick*
c. *Olmstead v. United States*
d. *McCulloch v. Maryland*
ANS: A
REF: 432
LO: 6

14.17 The Supreme Court failed to uphold the right to sexual privacy in:
a. *United States v. Darby*
b. *Bowers v. Hardwick*
c. *Colgrove v. Batten*
d. *McCulloch v. Maryland*
ANS: B
REF: 430
LO: 5

14.18 The United States Supreme Court struck down the portion of the Brady Bill which compelled local law enforcement to perform background checks on handgun applicants, holding the requirement violated:
a. the right to privacy.
b. separate state sovereignty
c. the commerce clause.
d. the Fourth Amendment.
ANS: B
REF: 433
LO: 6

14.19 The federal income tax was established in the:
a. Fifteenth Amendment
b. Sixteenth Amendment
c. Seventeenth Amendment
d. Eighteenth Amendment
ANS: B
REF: 437
LO: n/a

14.20 The _____ Amendment lowered the voting age to 18.
a. Twenty-Sixth (1971)
b. Nineteenth (1920)
c. Twenty-Seventh (1992)
d. Twenty-Second (1951)
ANS: A
REF: 437
LO: n/a

14.21 The _____ Amendment gave the vote to black males.
a. Fifteenth
b. Nineteenth
c. Twenty-First
d. Twenty-Third
ANS: A
REF: 437
LO: n/a

14.22 The Supreme Court held that Congress had the authority to establish a national bank in:
a. *United States v. Darby*
b. *Bowers v. Hardwick*
c. *Olmstead v. United States*
d. *McCulloch v. Maryland*
ANS: D
REF: 432
LO: 6

14.23 Women were given the right to vote by the:
a. Fifteenth Amendment
b. Seventeenth Amendment
c. Nineteenth Amendment
d. Twentieth Amendment
ANS: C
REF: 437
LO: n/a

14.24 *Griswold v. Connecticut* is considered the first case in which the Supreme Court addressed the Ninth Amendment, and dealt with the legality of :
a. pornography
b. abortion
c. interracial marriage
d. contraception
ANS: D
REF: 429
LO: 4, 5

14.25 The first state to pass a victims' rights constitutional amendment was:
a. Texas.
b. Florida.
c. Massachusetts.
d. California.
ANS: D
REF: 437
LO: n/a

14.26 The Supreme Court held there is no right to a federal jury trial when Congress had created other administrative remedies in:
a. *Thomas v. Union Carbide*
b. *Curtis v. Loether*
c. *Colgrove v. Battin*
d. *Griswold v. Connecticut*
ANS: A
REF: 427
LO: 2

14.27　In *Colgrove v. Battin*, the Supreme Court upheld juries comprised of _____ members in federal civil trials.
a. 6
b. 8
c. 10
d. 12
ANS: A
REF: 427
LO: 2

14.28　Whether there is a right to a federal jury trial is based largely on:
a. previous cases heard and common law analysis.
b. the geographical jurisdiction of the offense.
c. whether or not the issue is of local or national importance.
d. whether or not federal civil remedies are sought.
ANS: A
REF: 427
LO: 3

14.29　Congress has <u>not</u> considered an Amendment regarding:
a. establishing victims' rights.
b. prohibiting burning the American flag.
c. banning gay marriage.
d. equal rights for same-sex couples.
ANS: D
REF: 437-438
LO: n/a

14.30　Under federalism:
a. the federal government has the most power.
b. state governments have more power than the federal government.
c. power is shared by the national government and the states.
d. the Constitution is declared the supreme law of the land.
ANS: C
REF: 430
LO: 6

True/False

14.31　*Olmstead* v. *United States* stated that "the most comprehensive of rights and the right most valued by civilized men" is the right to pursue happiness.
ANS: F
REF: 430
LO: 5

14.32 The Tenth Amendment embodies the principle of federalism.
ANS: T
REF: 430
LO: 6

14.33 One of the primary reserve powers kept by the states is police power.
ANS: T
REF: 431
LO: 6

14.34 Suits at common law are legal controversies arising out of criminal law rather than civil law.
ANS: F
REF: 426
LO: 2

14.35 The Ninth Amendment establishes that the rights of U.S. citizens extend beyond those listed in the Constitution.
ANS: T
REF: 428
LO: 4

14.36 The right to a federal jury trial is determined mainly by historical analysis of common law.
ANS: T
REF: 427
LO: 2

14.37 Rights not specifically listed in the Bill of Rights are known as delegated rights.
ANS: F
REF: 428
LO: 4

14.38 The Ninth Amendment specifically guarantees the right to privacy.
ANS: F
REF: 429
LO: 5

14.39 The Supreme Court supported a woman's right to abortion in *Roe* v. *Wade*.
ANS: T
REF: 429
LO: 5

14.40 Selective incorporation has been used to incorporate the entire Bill of Rights to the states through the Fourteenth Amendment.
ANS: F
REF: 434
LO: 7

Fill-In

14.41 The _____ Amendment embodies the principle of federalism.
ANS: Tenth
REF: 430
LO: 6

14.42 The _____ Amendment is sometimes referred to as the forgotten amendment because it is seldom used as a basis for Supreme Court decisions.
ANS: Ninth
REF: 428
LO: 4

14.43 The _____ Amendment prohibited housing soldiers in private homes during peacetime.
ANS: Third
REF: 426
LO: 1

14.44 The _____ Amendment established the right to a federal jury trial for all "suits at common law" if the value was over $20.
ANS: Seventh
REF: 426
LO: 2

14.45 The _____ Amendment has never been subjected to Supreme Court review.
ANS: Third
REF: 426
LO: 1

14.46 Rights not specifically listed in the Bill of Rights are known as _____ rights.
ANS: unenumerated
REF: 428
LO: 5

14.47 Powers of the federal government are known as _____ powers.
ANS: delegated
REF: 431
LO: 6

14.48 Powers retained by the states are known as _____ powers.
       ANS: reserve
       REF: 431
       LO: 6

14.49 *Olmstead v. United States* stated that the most comprehensive and most valued right by
       civilized men was the right _____.
       ANS: to be left alone
       REF: 430
       LO: 5

14.50 Reserving for the states those powers not granted to the federal government or withheld
       from the states is _____.
       ANS: federalism
       REF: 430
       LO: 6

Essay

14.51 Discuss the concept of federalism and how it is embodied in the Tenth Amendment

       ANS: Federalism is the principle of the federal and state governments sharing power.
       The Constitution was written to apply to the federal government; the Tenth Amendment
       states: "The powers not delegated to the United States by the Constitution, nor prohibited
       by it to the states, are reserved to the states respectively, or to the people." Thus, any
       powers not specifically delegated to the federal government belonged to the states. States
       maintain sovereignty over issues not covered in the Constitution, and can make their own
       laws to address such issues. Thus, when Congress tries to pass laws requiring states to
       regulate something, the Supreme Court quashes the effort (i.e., *United States v. Lopez,*
       1995).
       REF: 430-433
       LO: 6

14.52 Discuss the progression and impact of amendments relating to voting.

       ANS: The Fifteenth Amendment gave black males the vote; the Nineteenth Amendment
       gave women the vote; the Twenty-Fourth Amendment required the right to vote not be
       denied by reason of failure to pay taxes; and the Twenty-Sixth Amendment lowered the
       voting age to 18. Though women were given the right to vote fifty years after black
       males, the Twenty-Fourth Amendment was passed to forbid states from disenfranchising
       those who were too poor to pay poll taxes (most often affecting black voters—both male
       and female). Lowering the voting age to 18 allowed all American adults to participate in
       the political process.
       REF: 437
       LO: n/a

14.53   Discuss Prohibition, including its origin and demise and what occurred in between. Relate this to the Harrison Act making certain drugs illegal to sell or possess.

ANS: Prohibition began in 1919 with the passage of the Eighteenth Amendment, which prohibited the sale and purchase of "intoxicating liquors." A hugely unpopular law, a large segment of society ignored this amendment and continued imbibing, thus fueling the black market profit from such illegal activity. As lawmakers began realizing such a ban on alcohol was not only futile but was also making mobsters rich, the law was repealed with passage of the Twenty-First Amendment in 1933. The effects of the Harrison Act have been similar. Passage of the Act has not stopped use of the proscribed drugs. It has also created a black market where drug dealers profit and the government misses out on the tax benefits of legalization.
REF: 437
LO: n/a

14.54   Explain the significance of the Ninth Amendment relative to federal power.

ANS: The Ninth Amendment specifies that the rights of U.S. citizens extend beyond those listed in the Constitution, and supports the Bill of Rights by asserting that even rights that are not specifically listed in the Bill—known as unenumerated rights—are no less important than those that are listed. Among such rights are the rights to privacy, freedom of association, interstate and international travel, and others.
REF: 428-430
LO: 4, 5

14.55   Discuss the significance of the Seventh Amendment.

ANS: Whereas the Sixth Amendment guarantees a jury trial for all criminal proceedings, the Seventh Amendment extends this right to federal civil proceedings—"suits at common law"-- involving more than $20 (which was a large sum when the Bill of Rights was passed in 1791).
REF: 426-427
LO: 2

Teaching Using Learning Objectives

Section One:

Introduction and Overview of Supplements that Contain Learning Objectives

Cengage Learning recognizes the challenges of teaching and seeks to support faculty in their efforts to educate students. In pursuit of this goal, this supplement has been provided to aid faculty in using the Learning Objectives included in the textbooks and supplementary materials adopted for your class. Learning Objectives can make teaching and learning an easier and more profitable exercise. This supplement is intended to assist you in incorporating the Learning Objectives into your classroom.

How do Learning Objectives make teaching easier? Learning Objectives can be the organizing framework for all of the information taught in class. This supplement will show you how the ancillary materials tie all of the textbook information together for you using the Learning Objectives for each chapter in our instructor and student resources. These resources are available in print and electronically via various products, downloads, and companion websites provided by Cengage Learning.

How do Learning Objectives make learning easier? Students who know what is expected of them are more likely to succeed. Learning Objectives let the student know exactly what you expect them to learn, while the Study Guide and various tutorials available in our products and on our companion websites show them how to achieve the Learning Objectives. Making students aware of these materials provides them with a roadmap to successful completion of the class.

Learning Objectives make it a simple process to communicate what students are expected to know by the end of the class, thus making your job easier. Additionally, the Learning Objectives are used repeatedly in the textbook and study materials, and on the companion website available to each student. Repetition of this information promotes student success.

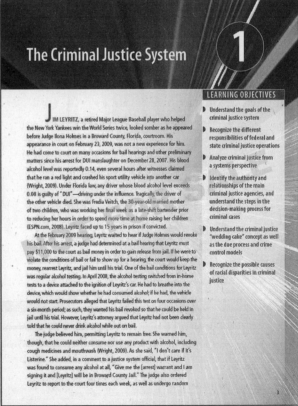

The Criminal Justice System — 1

JIM LEYRITZ, a retired Major League Baseball player who helped the New York Yankees win the World Series twice, looked somber as he appeared before Judge Ilona Holmes in a Broward County, Florida, courtroom. His appearance in court on February 23, 2009, was not a new experience for him. He had come to court on many occasions for bail hearings and other preliminary matters since his arrest for DUI manslaughter on December 28, 2007. His blood alcohol level was reportedly 0.14, even several hours after witnesses claimed that he ran a red light and crashed his sport utility vehicle into another car (Wright, 2009). Under Florida law, any driver whose blood alcohol level exceeds 0.08 is guilty of "DUI"—driving under the influence. Tragically, the driver of the other vehicle died. She was Fredia Veitch, the 30-year-old married mother of two children, who was working her final week as a late-shift bartender prior to reducing her hours in order to spend more time at home raising her children (ESPN.com, 2008). Leyritz faced up to 15 years in prison if convicted.

At the February 2009 hearing, Leyritz waited to hear if Judge Holmes would revoke his bail. After his arrest, a judge had determined at a bail hearing that Leyritz must pay $11,000 to the court as bail money in order to gain release from jail. If he were to violate the conditions of bail or fail to show up for a hearing, the court would keep the money, rearrest Leyritz, and jail him until his trial. One of the bail conditions for Leyritz was regular alcohol testing. In April 2008, the alcohol testing switched from in-home tests to a device attached to the ignition of Leyritz's car. He had to breathe into the device, which would show whether he had consumed alcohol; if he had, the vehicle would not start. Prosecutors alleged that Leyritz failed this test on four occasions over a six-month period; as such, they wanted his bail revoked so that he could be held in jail until his trial. However, Leyritz's attorney argued that Leyritz had not been clearly told that he could never drink alcohol while out on bail.

The judge believed him, permitting Leyritz to remain free. She warned him, though, that he could neither consume nor use any product with alcohol, including cough medicines and mouthwash (Wright, 2009). As she said, "I don't care if it's Listerine." She added, in a comment to a justice system official, that if Leyritz was found to consume any alcohol at all, "Give me the [arrest] warrant and I am signing it and [Leyritz] will be in Broward County Jail." The judge also ordered Leyritz to report to the court four times each week, as well as undergo random

LEARNING OBJECTIVES

▶ Understand the goals of the criminal justice system

▶ Recognize the different responsibilities of federal and state criminal justice operations

▶ Analyze criminal justice from a systems perspective

▶ Identify the authority and relationships of the main criminal justice agencies, and understand the steps in the decision-making process for criminal cases

▶ Understand the criminal justice "wedding cake" concept as well as the due process and crime control models

▶ Recognize the possible causes of racial disparities in criminal justice

Instructor Resources

Learning Objectives are available in a variety of materials for you and your students. An Annotated Instructor's Edition is available for some titles, and includes a list of all of the tools we offer for instructors and students. Some of the key features of the **Annotated Instructor's Edition** include Teaching Tips, Discussion Tips, Web Tips, and Media Tips for each chapter. These tips are specifically designed to assist you in incorporating the Learning Objectives into the classroom through assignments, discussion, and use of the internet. Additionally, these tips are highlighted in blue in the margins of the textbook to help you spot them easily when preparing for classes.

The **Instructor's Manual with Test Bank** includes Learning Objectives, a Chapter Outline, Key Terms, and a Test Bank. Each question in the Test Bank is coded to the appropriate Learning Objective for that question. This allows you the opportunity to focus on the Learning Objectives you feel are most important for your students to understand.

▶ The Lesson Plans include two sample syllabi, Learning Objectives, Lecture Notes, Discussion Topics, Class Activities, tips for classroom presentation of the chapter material, and Assignments.

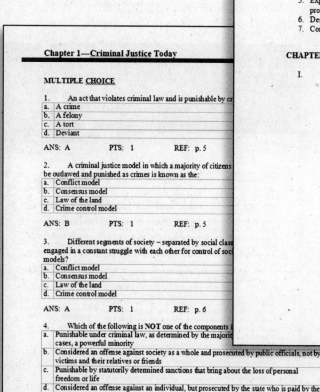

CHAPTER 1
CRIMINAL JUSTICE TODAY

LEARNING OBJECTIVES

After reading this chapter, students should be able to:
1. Describe the two most common models of how society determines which acts are criminal.
2. Define crime and identify the different types of crime.
3. Outline the three levels of law enforcement.
4. List the essential elements of the corrections system.
5. Explain the difference between the formal and informal criminal justice processes.
6. Describe the layers of the "wedding cake" model.
7. Contrast the crime control and due process models.

CHAPTER OUTLINE

I. What Is Crime?
   a. An act proclaimed by law as a wrong against society and, if committed under certain circumstances, punishable by society
   b. Two common models for deciding what acts are criminal
      i. Consensus model
         1. Assumes that as people gather together to form a society, its members will naturally come to a basic agreement with regard to shared norms and values
         2. Assumes, to a certain extent, that a diverse group of people can have similar morals
      ii. Conflict model
         1. Assumes that different segments of society, separated by social class, income, age, and rage, will inevitably have different value systems and shared norms, and are engaged in a constant struggle with one another for control of society
         2. What is deemed criminal activity is determined by whichever group happens to be holding power at any given time
   c. An integrated definition of crime
      i. Takes into consideration both the consensus and conflict models
      ii. Constructs a definition of crime in that it is any action or activity that includes the following:
         1. Is punishable under criminal law, as determined by the majority of society, or in some cases, a powerful minority
         2. Is considered an *offense* against society *as a whole* and prosecuted by public officials

---

Chapter 1—Criminal Justice Today

MULTIPLE CHOICE

1. An act that violates criminal law and is punishable by cr

a.	A crime
b.	A felony
c.	A tort
d.	Deviant

ANS: A   PTS: 1   REF: p. 5

2. A criminal justice model in which a majority of citizens be outlawed and punished as crimes is known as the:

a.	Conflict model
b.	Consensus model
c.	Law of the land
d.	Crime control model

ANS: B   PTS: 1   REF: p. 5

3. Different segments of society – separated by social class engaged in a constant struggle with each other for control of soci models?

a.	Conflict model
b.	Consensus model
c.	Law of the land
d.	Crime control model

ANS: A   PTS: 1   REF: p. 6

4. Which of the following is **NOT** one of the components i

a.	Punishable under criminal law, as determined by the majorit cases, a powerful minority
b.	Considered an offense against society as a whole and prosecuted by public officials, not by victims and their relatives or friends
c.	Punishable by statutorily determined sanctions that bring about the loss of personal freedom or life
d.	Considered an offense against an individual, but prosecuted by the state who is paid by the victim

ANS: D   PTS: 1   REF: p. 7   OBJ: LO 1

5. What is deviance?

a.	An objective concept that all members of society agree upon
b.	Another term used to describe all criminal activity
c.	Behavior that is considered to go against the norms established by society
d.	Behavior that is always considered criminal in nature

ANS: C   PTS: 1   REF: p. 7   OBJ: LO 1

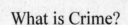

Power**Lecture**™

The **PowerLecture DVD** is a compilation of all of the above tools except the Annotated Instructor's Edition, plus some additional resources. Included on the **PowerLecture DVD** are PowerPoint slides, an Image Library, the Instructor's Manual, the Test Bank, the Lesson Plans, ExamView, JoinIn for Clickers, and videos. ExamView includes all of the Test Bank questions from the Instructor's Manual with Test Bank in customizable electronic format. It creates tests for you and allows you to choose multiple choice, true/false, fill-in-the-blank and essay questions that focus on the Learning Objectives of your choice. Using ExamView, you can view the test results as you create the test, and edit the test as you create it.

▶ Microsoft® PowerPoint® slide presentations are available for each chapter of the textbook and provide a lecture presentation focused on the Learning Objectives.

What is Crime?

Crime:

1. Violates criminal law.

2. Is punishable by criminal sanctions.

Student Resources

The **Study Guide** is the student's version of the Instructor's Manual. It provides the student with the Learning Objectives for each chapter, a Chapter Outline, Key Terms and the pages on which they can be found in the textbook, special projects that can be used as assignments for class, and a Practice Test Bank with answers coded to the Learning Objectives.

CengageNOW is an interactive online learning resource for students. This tool provides students with study tools for each chapter such as essay questions, flashcards, and tutorial quizzes, all of which are centered on the Learning Objectives to ensure that students understand what material to focus on while studying.

Both the Study Guide and CengageNOW allow you to target your students' study time on the Learning Objectives while enabling you to communicate the focus of each chapter in the text to your students, as well as where you want them to be at the end of the term.

Learning Objectives

After reading this chapter, you should be able to:

LO1: Describe the two most common models of how society determines which acts are criminal.
LO2: Define "crime" and list the different types of crime.
LO3: Outline the three levels of law enforcement.
LO4: List the essential elements of the correctional system.
LO5: Explain the difference between the formal and informal criminal justice processes.
LO6: Describe the layers of the "wedding cake" model.
LO7: Contrast the crime control and due process models.
LO8: List the major issues in criminal justice today.

Chapter Outline

Using the Supplements to Integrate Learning Objectives into Your Classroom

One of the first tasks for you in teaching using Learning Objectives is to tie them into the Chapter Outline and lecture materials. This process is made easy through the use of the supplementary materials discussed in Section One. Let's take a look at how each of these supplements can work for you.

The Instructor's Manual with Test Bank is available to instructors in print and electronically. The Instructor's Manual portion can be downloaded from the companion website for the book, and the full version is available electronically as part of the PowerLecture DVD or through a download by contacting your Cengage Learning sales representative. The Lesson Plans and PowerPoint slides are both available electronically as a download by contacting your Cengage Learning sales representative, or as part of the PowerLecture DVD.

The Instructor's Manual with Test Bank includes a Chapter Outline for each chapter of the textbook adopted for your class. A quick look at each of the headings for the Outline provides you with the ability to tie each section of the Outline to the Learning Objectives for that chapter. For example, in *Criminal Justice in Action: The Core*, the Learning Objectives for Chapter One can be linked directly to the sections in the Outline. Table 2.1 demonstrates how each of the Learning Objectives for this chapter connects to the Outline in the Instructor's Manual.

Table 2.1 Connection Between Learning Objectives and Outline Sections

Learning Objective		Outline Section	
1.	Describe the two most common models that show how society determines which acts are criminal.	3.	Values of the Criminal Justice System
2.	Define crime and identify the different types of crime.	1.	What is Crime
3.	Outline the three levels of law enforcement.	2.	The Criminal Justice System
4.	List the essential elements of the corrections system.	2.	The Criminal Justice System
5.	Explain the difference between the formal and informal criminal justice processes.	2.	The Criminal Justice System
6.	Describe the layers of the "wedding cake" model.	2.	The Criminal Justice System
7.	Contrast the crime control and due process models.	3.	Values of the Criminal Justice System

The Annotated Instructor's Edition is another powerful tool to help you teach using Learning Objectives. The marginal callouts mentioned in the first section (Teaching Tips, Discussion Tips, Web Tips, and Media Tips) correlate to the Learning Objectives, and can provide you with ideas as to how to generate discussion on the Learning Objectives and be creative in incorporating them into your classes. For example, regarding Learning Objective One from above, one of the Teaching Tips suggests having students research how violent crimes are classified in your state. It suggests asking students to name the specific circumstances required for each degree of an offense. Such an assignment not only explores the deeper meaning of crime but also investigates the criminal justice system in a way that can be more meaningful to the student as she or he considers the criminal justice system in her or his own local area.

Discussion Tips also help focus the class on Learning Objectives by providing topics for group and class discussion directly related to the Learning Objectives. One such Discussion Tip relates to Learning Objectives One and Three from above. The Discussion Tip suggests having students work in small groups to brainstorm examples of offenses that fit the conflict model of criminal justice, focusing on which groups hold the power and which do not. A discussion such as this not only focuses the students on the Learning Objectives, but also helps them understand how the different concepts in the Learning Objectives are applied in the criminal justice system.

The Annotated Instructor's Edition also provides an End of Chapter Summary with links to the Learning Objectives. This summary offers a synopsis of all of the Learning Objectives, providing a quick reference for review of the Learning Objectives prior to class discussion. Additionally, the End of Chapter Summary can be used as a tool in class to review the topics covered with students at the end of class, and reinforce discussion of any or all of the Learning Objectives covered.

The Study Guide incorporates the Learning Objectives as well as a Chapter Outline, Key Terms, and Practice Test Bank. Students can be assigned to group the Learning Objectives to the Outline, per the example above, prior to each class so they will come prepared. Additionally, just as the Instructor's Manual includes a Test Bank with answers mapped to the Learning Objectives, the Study Guide also provides the appropriate Learning Objectives with each answer to the Practice Test Bank questions, and the questions in the CengageNOW online tutorials test the student's knowledge of the Learning Objectives as well.

Using the PowerPoint slides allows you to lecture based on a PowerPoint presentation created specifically for each of the chapters in the book. The slides are prepared for you by instructors who teach the material, so they reflect what instructors using the book want to see in their classrooms. The Learning Objectives are incorporated into the PowerPoint slides, making it quick and easy for you to lecture in the classroom using the Learning Objectives as your focus.

For those who prefer not to use PowerPoint slides, the Lesson Plans also include the Learning Objectives as the foundation for lectures, as well as discussion questions and possible activities to use in the classroom.

Including the Learning Objectives in your syllabus can also aid students in understanding the focus for each class session and help them to be prepared prior to class. These materials can all work together to allow you to organize classes easily and enable you to have a greater impact. See Figure 2.1 below for an example of a syllabus based on the information from Table 2.1. The materials included in the Instructor's Manual with

Figure 2.1 – Incorporating the Learning Objectives into a Class Syllabus

Professor Bell   Fall Semester – 2009

Syllabus – Criminal Justice in Action

Date	Text Book Chapter	Topics	Learning Objective(s)
9/12/2009	One	What is Crime?	Two
		The Criminal Justice System	Three, Four, Five, Six
		Values of the Criminal Justice System	One, Seven

Test Bank can differ slightly from book to book. They always include Learning Objectives, Key Terms, a Chapter Outline, Discussion Topics, Student Activities, and the Test Bank, but can also include Activity Suggestions for Online Courses, Internet Connections, and Using Media in the Classroom resources.

The Lesson Plans can help you integrate Learning Objectives into your teaching style in the classroom. The Learning Objectives are included in the sample syllabi and can also easily be integrated into the Chapter Outline as shown above.

Now that we have covered some of the materials available to assist you in Teaching Using Learning Objectives, we will discuss some other ways you can use the material included in these resources in your classroom.

Key Terms

Key Terms are a very helpful tool for implementing Learning Objectives while teaching in the classroom, and are provided in almost all of the supplemental materials we've discussed. As you read this supplement, think about the different classes you took as a student in college. In order to acquire an undergraduate degree it is almost always necessary to take classes known as "core" classes. These classes are not directly related to the major you are taking, but are required of many undergraduate programs to ensure that students are well-rounded when they receive their degree.

One of the first things necessary when taking a class in a field you are not familiar with is to learn the language. Medical students must learn medical terminology, psychology students must learn psychological terminology, and criminal justice students must learn criminal justice terminology. Therefore, for a student to be able to gain a firm grasp of the concepts in the Learning Objectives, it is necessary to understand the language of that material. One of the best ways to understand the language is to first learn the Key Terms.

[Inset reproduction of textbook page:]

criminal behavior the social conditions that bear on the individual. Three types of sociological theory are social structure theories, social process theories, and critical theories, including social conflict theories.

▶ Feminist theories call attention to scholars' neglect of women's criminal behavior. Such theories often take a

Analyze crime causation theories and women offenders

▶ The criminality of women has only recently been studied. Some argue that, as society increasingly treats women and men as equals, the number of crimes committed by women will increase.

▶ Theories of criminality are criticized for focusing too exclusively on lower-class and male perpetrators.

Questions for Review

1. What are the six types of crimes?
2. What are the positive and negative attributes of the two major sources of crime data?
3. Who is most likely to be victimized by crime?
4. What are the costs of crime?
5. How does the criminal justice system treat victims?
6. What are the major theories of criminality?
7. What have scholars learned about the criminal behavior of women?

Key Terms and Cases

anomie (p. 00)
biological explanations (p. 00)
classical criminology (p. 00)
control theories (p. 00)
crimes without victims (p. 00)
criminogenic (p. 00)
critical criminology (p. 00)
cyber crimes (p. 00)
dark figure of crime (p. 00)
feminist theories (p. 00)
integrated theories (p. 00)
labeling theories (p. 00)

learning theories (p. 00)
life course theories (p. 00)
mala in se (p. 00)
mala prohibita (p. 00)
money laundering (p. 00)
National Crime Victimization Surveys (NCVS) (p. 00)
National Incident-Based Reporting System (NIBRS) (p. 00)
occupational crimes (p. 00)
organized crime (p. 00)
political crime (p. 00)

positivist criminology (p. 00)
psychological explanations (p. 00)
social conflict theories (p. 00)
social process theories (p. 00)
social structure theories (p. 00)
sociological explanations (p. 00)
theory of differential association (p. 00)
Uniform Crime Reports (UCR) (p. 00)
victimology (p. 00)
visible crime (p. 00)

Each of the Key Terms can be directly categorized under a Learning Objective. Although each of the Key Terms are directly related to one particular Learning Objective, some of them may apply to more than one. Table 3.1 shows an example of how the Key Terms connect to the Learning Objectives in Chapter One of *Criminal Justice in Action: The Core*.

Table 3.1 Connection between Learning Objectives and Key Terms

Learning Objective	Key Terms
1. Describe the two most common models that show how society determines which acts are criminal.	Consensus model, conflict model
2. Define crime and identify the different types of crime.	Crime, deviance, murder, sexual assault, assault, larceny, battery, public order crime, white-collar crime, organized crime, terrorism
3. Outline the three levels of law enforcement.	Homeland Security
4. List the essential elements of the criminal justice system.	Federalism, criminal justice system
5. Explain the difference between the formal and informal criminal justice processes.	Federalism, criminal justice system, discretion, Civil Rights
6. Describe the layers of the "wedding cake" model.	"Wedding Cake" Model
7. Contrast the crime control and due process models.	Crime Control Model, Due Process Model

A good example of an ongoing homework assignment is to have the students list each Learning Objective with the Key Terms that are related to it and explain how they are related. The assignment should be due on the day of class that each topic is to be covered. This provides an opportunity for class discussion as well as opening students up to interject a fresh perspective on the material. Although the Key Terms do apply to some Learning Objectives more than others, it is important to remember that such an assignment is primarily about getting the student to think about the Key Terms and the Learning Objectives, and how they apply to the subject of that particular chapter. Thus, it is possible that more than one answer is correct in such an assignment.

The Key Terms can also be used in class or as a homework assignment using some of the study tools available to the student through CengageNOW.

Flashcards of Key Terms are available for students and instructors, and can be used as an activity in class to keep students involved.

Students can be asked to define a Key Term and then relate it to the appropriate Learning Objective. One way to increase participation with this kind of exercise is to offer extra credit points for correlating the definitions with the correct Learning Objectives. The amount of extra credit does not have to be large, and an activity such as this accomplishes several goals at the same time. First, students quickly learn that the way to gain extra credit is to come to class. Second, the students will relate the Key Terms to the Learning Objectives and develop an understanding of the language necessary to understand the information. Finally, students are encouraged to participate in class. It's a good idea to limit the number of times each student can answer, so as to allow all students the opportunity to participate.

Section Four:

Online Study Tools

CengageNOW provides online study tools that allow students to take Pre- and Post-tests with questions that correlate directly to the Learning Objectives. As you can see in the figure below, the student can take a Pre-test on material related to the Learning Objectives, and the program offers them a personalized study plan based on the results of the Pre-test. After the student has completed the personalized study plan, a Post-test evaluates her or his improved comprehension of the chapter content. The student has electronic access to all of the information from the chapter as he or she is studying, and can access video information as well.

Use of tools such as these can not only help you incorporate Learning Objectives into your teaching in the classroom, but can also help make the material more compelling for the student. Reviewing material in more than one format can help students gain a better grasp of the material by reinforcing the same information in various contexts.

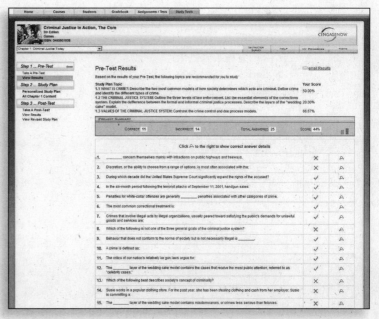

Additionally, making the material available to students in more than one format helps ensure that all students are presented the material in a format which is most conducive to their learning style.

Section Five:
Conclusion

Although we have covered a number of ways that Learning Objectives can be used as part of teaching in the classroom, there are many more possibilities. The goal of this supplement is to provide you with a few examples of how you can incorporate Learning Objectives into your teaching style to make teaching easier and more productive.

All of the tools provided to instructors by Cengage Learning can aid you in teaching using Learning Objectives. These tools are available in a number of different platforms to enable you to choose the version you're most comfortable with, that best suits your teaching style and the various learning styles of your students. Whether you prefer using print supplements such as the Instructor's Manual with Test Bank or Annotated Instructor's Edition, the electronic option of the PowerLecture that includes everything on a single DVD, or the CengageNOW convenience of interactive online tools, Cengage Learning has a resource for you and your students. Incorporating the tools created specifically for use with the textbook you use in your class can make teaching more rewarding for you and more effective for your students.

Teaching using Learning Objectives has the potential to make your classroom, whether traditional or online, a learning-friendly environment in which students can get the most out of the academic experience. Providing students with alternatives to traditional lecture formats can make for a more dynamic and successful learning experience. Teaching a class that is enjoyable for students makes the teaching experience enjoyable as well. We hope that this supplement has provided you with some ideas on how to incorporate Learning Objectives into your classroom and how to make better use of the tools available to you to help your students learn the material you present in class.